The Ideology of the Text

Christopher Hampton

Open University Press
Milton Keynes · Philadelphia

Open University Press
Celtic Court
22 Ballmoor
Buckingham
MK18 1XW

and

1900 Frost Road, Suite 101
Bristol, PA 19007, USA

First Published 1990

British Library Cataloguing in Publication Data

Hampton, Christopher, *1929–*
   The ideology of the text.
   1. Literature. Marxist criticism
   I. Title
   801.95

   ISBN 0–335–09416–3
   ISBN 0–335–09415–5 pbk

Library of Congress Cataloging in Publication Number Available

Typeset by Scarborough Typesetting Services
Printed in Great Britain by Biddles Ltd
Guildford and Kings Lynn

The Ideology of the Text

WITHDRAWN

To my daughter Rebecca

Contents

Preface

Parts One and Three of this book form a theoretical framework to the eight chapters of Part Two. Part One, grounded on a Marxist refutation of certain forms of post-structuralist, post-modernist critical discourse which reflect the crisis of capitalist culture, provides a theoretical position from which to reappraise, in context, the work of specific writers, from Shakespeare to Eliot. This reappraisal is undertaken in Part Two. Part Three then examines certain theoretical issues emerging from the historical context – first by studying the work of Raymond Williams in its development towards his concept of cultural materialism, and finally by redefining the argument for historical materialism in terms of E. P. Thompson's polemical attack on the structuralist Marxism of Louis Althusser.

Part One

1

Signs of the times

To be in any position to consider the problems of literary theory and practice, it is necessary first of all to consider the problems of context – the underlying conditions which define the functions and limits of cultural activity, including language and literature as forms of creative social practice. And since language itself is a changing product of the interactive process of material reality in the long perspectives of the history of social struggle, it is necessary to consider this, too, and to consider it in the light of the fact that language is centrally an instrument of ideological contention between the opposing forces that compete for domination and control of the social process.

In these terms, it may be said that *all* cultural manifestations in society are to be defined on the basis of the economic forces and relations of production, as determined by their particular place in history and by the stage of material development of the operative social system and the structures (institutions, laws, politics, beliefs, etc.) it gives rise to, which in turn have their own influence on the underlying conditions of production.

Assuming this is so – and I make no apology for accepting the dialectic analysis of history on which such an assumption is based – the ideology of the operative system, as generated by the class interests that control it, throws up idealized reflections of these underlying conditions, transformed into 'eternal laws of nature and of reason' (Marx 1973a: 83), including the mystifying dislocation of theory and practice embodied in the forms of literary discourse, as a justifying veil for the repressive process by which the system enforces the submission of majorities into acquiescence and conformity with minority will. Thus ideas, values, beliefs – represented as 'natural' and 'permanent', though in reality 'historical and transitory products' of the changing social process that shapes people's lives – are an indirect and often distorted reflection of that struggle for 'rights', 'needs' and 'living conditions', which Marx has historically identified as the *class* struggle, 'the collective struggle to wrest a Realm of Freedom from the Realm of Necessity' – a struggle determined, that is, not by individual will but by the 'contradictions of material life' (Marx 1977: 820).

If this is familiar ground, it is ground that needs to be constantly reaffirmed and clarified, since it is always being attacked, undermined, eroded. Indeed, it was Marx's immediate task, in applying his rigorous materialist dialectic to the complex ways in which capitalism functioned as a system of production, not

simply to define that system but to unmask its contradictory conditions in order
to provide grounds, material *pre*conditions, from which to build a revolutionary
theory of social transformation for the liberation of men and women from the
oppressive, alienating conditions of a class-divided society. For it is only when
people have become fully conscious of the nature of the conditions they are
controlled by that 'the development of human energy' as 'an end in itself, the
true Realm of Freedom', can begin – because it is an unreal freedom that does
not have 'the Realm of Necessity as its basis'. Hence, though it can be said, as
Engels declared, that 'we make our history ourselves', we make it 'in the first
place under very definite assumptions and conditions' and 'in the second place
. . . in such a way that the final result always arises from conflicts between many
individual wills, . . . and what emerges is something that no one person willed',
though 'each of us contributes to the result' (Marx and Engels 1968: 683). Which
defines not only the *problems* of necessity as imposed upon us by the process of
historical change but also their tantalizing *challenge*.

So what are we to make of the so-called New Times of the 1980s, confronted by
the bewildering variety of conflicting voices generated by the antagonistic
ideologies of advanced capitalism in what has been persistently described as the
crisis of contemporary culture? For clearly they are contesting the very
conditions and grounds for any possible left-wing concept of freedom and
necessity, and are in the process of enacting new forms of ideological and
economic pressure aimed at undermining and neutralizing all opposition. In
such a context, intellectuals on the Left are presented with problems of daunting
complexity, and responsibilities at once challenging and inescapable. For if it is
possible to argue, as many have done, perhaps to justify their own acceptance of
the operative system, that the world is now more firmly controlled and more
rationally organized against disaster than it was in the first half of the twentieth
century, no one can pretend that this is any more than an illusion. These New
Times, after all, have their roots still in the irrational histories of that pre-1945
past; and the barriers that divide, the rifts and dislocations that characterize
social and cultural existence in Britain – now being exposed to forms of material
practice ruthlessly intent upon the wholesale privatization of social life – were
determined afresh after the devastation of war by the deliberate engineering of
cold war enmity. The last 45 years have in fact been increasingly dominated by
the lethal forces of militarist competition, an economic war based upon the
production of weapons of mass destruction, creating a 'balance of terror'
(described as Mutual Assured Destruction or MAD) which has dragged the
world to the edge of breakdown and impoverishment. And though the
ideologists of the 'free' world never tire of telling us that the insane build-up of
nuclear weapons (not to mention the production and sale of conventional
armaments to all who can buy them) has kept the peace for more than four
decades, what they conveniently ignore is the 130 wars their armaments policies
have fomented everywhere, with 12 million dead, and countless others in the
Third World decimated by the starvation and poverty imposed upon them as a
consequence of the economic-military exploitation of neo-colonialist expansion.

Faced by the appalling proofs of such a record, there can be little cause for
confidence that the foundations of this new world are any the more secure, or
that they hold out any greater promise for emancipatory change in the future. If
anything, the great advances achieved since 1945 in science and technology have

created a situation potentially more dangerous than ever, because more abstract, more sophisticated, more insidious, and as such less easy to combat or even to recognize as dangerous. Having so deeply extended, transformed and invaded the environments of people's lives, they are being accepted and utilized (at least in the advanced world) exactly as if they were the indispensable instruments of social progress. Indeed, however stultifying in effect, what they *appear* to be capable of offering in terms of the easing of conditions and the raising of living standards for the underprivileged and the dispossessed has already to a great extent conditioned people into believing that they are at last being provided with the means and the power to fulfil their intrinsic human needs. And it is at precisely this level, in the sheer pervasiveness, the ubiquitous presence of these technological resources and the ways in which they are being exploited, that the dangers and the threats to human freedoms are to be identified. Because whatever their potentiality as instruments of human advancement and as a rational means of answering the problems of the world, such resources are peculiarly suited to the hidden aims of those who control the institutions of society, and thus to being utilized as weapons of totalitarian power to deceive and to subjugate.

In this sense, the intellectual has a particularly important part to play, not only in defining and clarifying the issues involved but also in resisting and exposing the ruthless forces of ideological manipulation that are at work upon us all. For the trivializing and divisive welter of signs and signifiers these forces are continually generating as the agents of the commodity system they function in terms of is threatening to reduce everything indiscriminately to the level of the consumerist demands the system itself has set up. As Marcuse (1972a: 58) puts it trenchantly: 'The music of the soul is also the music of salesmanship'. And because the texts produced by intellectuals – whether as philosophers, political thinkers, theorists of literature, psychologists or creative writers – are themselves involved in the ideological process that dominates our lives, they are as vulnerable as any other manifestation of the prevailing material process to manipulation in the service of the commodity system. Thus all arguments for social and cultural advance have been persistently challenged and undermined in the post-war period by new forms of restrictive control based upon the revolutionary technologies developed out of war and sharpened by the monopoly techniques of war, whose destabilizing effect has been to substitute spuriously factual, quantitative concepts of reality for the qualitative historical complexities of the human struggle. Indeed, the pervasive intrusion of these forms of control into the privacy of the home has disrupted the practical initiatives people are capable of, undermining their sense of themselves as active makers, as participants in the history of their time, their power to influence the course of history or to change it. As Marcuse (1972a: 88) has pointed out, referring directly to the manner in which technology is being deployed to maintain the passive servitude of men and women:

> The suppression of the dimension of thought and of action [in society] is a suppression of history, and this is not an academic but a political affair. It is a suppression of society's own past – and of its future, insofar as the future invokes qualitative change, the negation of the present. A universe of discourse in which the categories of freedom have become interchangeable and even identical with their opposites is not only putting into practice Orwellian or Aesopian language but is also

repulsing and ignoring historical reality – the horror of fascism; the idea of socialism; the pre-conditions of democracy; the content of freedom. If it is possible for a bureaucratic dictatorship to define communist society, for Fascist regimes to function as partners of the Free World, for the welfare programme of enlightened capitalism to be successfully defeated by labelling it 'socialism', and the foundations of democracy to be harmoniously abrogated in democracy, then the old historical concepts have been invalidated by . . . re-definitions . . . which, imposed by the powers that be and the powers of fact, serve to transform truth into falsehood.

In this respect 'the established universe of discourse bears throughout the marks of the specific modes of domination, organization and manipulation to which the members of society are subjected'; and such restrictions are difficult to evade.

People depend for their living on bosses and politicians and jobs and neighbours, who make them speak and behave as they do; they are compelled, by societal necessity, to identify their own personal lives with the things they function in terms of. How do we know? Because we watch television, listen to the radio, read the magazines and newspapers, talk to people (Marcuse 1972a: 156).

What this suggests is that, in terms of the technological developments and triumphs of the post-atomic world, history is being radically falsified and people's historical struggle for awareness and emancipation and co-operative social interchange neutralized, suppressed. Thus we are faced with difficult questions. As Marcuse (1972a: 195) has put it:

How can the administered individuals – who have made their mutilation into their own liberties and satisfactions, and thus reproduced it on an enlarged scale – liberate themselves from themselves as well as from their masters? How is it even thinkable for the vicious circle to be broken?

It would perhaps be useful to keep such questions in mind in making one's way through the intellectual landscapes of the 1980s as they have been defined and mapped out by the theorists of what is now being habitually described as a 'post-industrial', 'post-modernist', 'pluralist' world. For what is striking about these new formulations of the cultural and social process is the extent to which they appear to have transformed the topography and structure of the material world their makers are at work upon. It is as if the fundamental oppositional terms of Marcuse's argument, his grasp of 'the dimension of thought and of action', the determining material conditions (the 'latent content') of historical struggle that lie behind the redefinitions of the cultural-social process, had been eliminated; or as if these redefinitions (as interchangeable signs detached from their referents) had now become the accepted norms, the starting points for debate: a reality transposed and absorbed into its signifiers.

Faced with such terms, it would seem advisable to step back, to withdraw from the insulated circle, to take bearings, to check this labyrinth of signs and intercrossing paths and structures against the material, physical characteristics of the world one has entered it from. For indeed one risks losing contact with the sources and breeding grounds of all that is now being redefined if one does not keep one's eyes on the geographical and historically-determined landmarks which define one's place in the world of material social practice.

What is at any rate clear is that we cannot expect to make much sense of the phenomena these new forms of investigative theory are attempting to demonstrate in the various ways in which they have chosen to resume the long-fought saga of metaphysical battles concerning the nature of meaning and reality except in the contexts they derive their significance from, the material-social conditions they are the product of. If, that is to say, the principles and terms of discourse characteristic of so much of the work of the new philosophers and critical theorists of Western culture in the post-modernist era are to be accepted as specific manifestations of the infrastructures of material practice in the world of advanced capitalism, it is in terms of these conditions that they will need to be assessed rather than their own. For the conflicting variety of signs and signals they describe – the 'floating signifiers' that surround us at every turn – do not exist in a vacuum. They are part of an ideological process which has its roots in the engine-rooms and inner chambers of an internationally organized system of monopolies rooted in the vast profits of the military-industrial complex. As Fischer (1963: 197) pointed out: 'The industrialized, commercialized capitalist world has become an *outside world* of impenetrable material connections and relationships' in which 'illusion displaces contradiction'. And what has to be spelt out in the clearest possible terms is the extent to which this destructive system – now capable of reducing the earth to a radioactive wasteland – is at the same time psychotically involved in producing commodities and mechanisms that are perverting and destabilizing our environment and the ecology of the planet itself.

That this is no illusion conjured up by some malign theorist of disaster the facts of twentieth-century physics have conclusively demonstrated. The destructive consequences may seem to have been made invisible. None the less, they exist as history and in the secretive militarist systems that dominate our world – there to terrorize 'twenty centuries of stony sleep', an absent presence in the atmosphere, built into the very forms and structures of social order. And the transnational companies that are the instruments of this process have set up their networks of interest all over the world, imposing their conditions indiscriminately and no doubt with the intention of remaking everything in their own image, or of eliminating or suppressing whatever they cannot remake – all that arises from direct transaction with the earth as the products of hand and eye and brain, the long-evolved, slow-developing rhythms of human life and its histories. So that the externalizing illusions of the surface in this technologically activated Las Vegas-like world of signs that is our environment brings into being the characteristic conditions and life-styles and synthetic cultural artefacts of the so-called post-industrial, post-modernist universe.

This is to suggest that the forms of material practice that govern our world are being further and further distanced from us by its abstracts, and that in the world of floating signifiers created by the forces of market exploitation, the individual is reduced to an alienated unit, whose only refuge is his privacy. As Jameson (1974: xvii) puts it:

> Our experience is no longer whole: we are no longer able to make any felt connection between the concerns of private life, as it follows its own course within the walls and confines of the affluent society, and the structural projections of the systems in the outside world . . . In psychological terms, we may say that as a service-economy we are henceforth so far removed from the realities of production and

work in the world that we inhabit a dream world of artificial stimuli and televised experience.

The disabling consequence, as Jameson (1974: xviii) emphasizes, is that 'never in any previous civilization have the great metaphysical preoccupations, the fundamental questions of being and the meaning of life, seemed so utterly remote and pointless'.

This process of occultation, brought about by the systematic development of the forces of monopoly capitalism, has affected everyone – and not least those among the new intellectual elite who occupy the intellectual marketplace of academic discourse. Indeed, of these sophisticated theorists of cultural activity it could even be said, with Edward Said (1984: 25), that 'we have reached the stage at which specialization and professionalism, allied with cultural dogma, barely sublimated ethnocentrism and nationalism, as well as a surprisingly insistent quasi-religious quietism, have transported the professional and academic critic of literature – the most focussed and intensely trained interpreter of texts produced by the culture – into another world altogether'. And

in that relatively untroubled, secluded world there seems to be no contact with the world of events and societies, which modern history, intellectuals, and critics have in fact built. Instead, contemporary criticism is an institution for publicly affirming the values of our, that is, European, dominant elite culture, and for privately setting loose the unrestrained interpretation of a universe defined in advance as the endless misreading of a misinterpretation. The result has been the regulated, not to say calculated, irrelevance of criticism, except as an adornment to what the powers of modern industrial society transact: the hegemony of militarism and a new cold war, the depoliticization of the citizenry, the overall compliance of the intellectual class to which critics belong.

In this view, any direct apprehension of external reality is marginalized, and literary discourse becomes 'a babel of arguments for the limitlessness of all interpretation, of ideologies that proclaim the eternal yet determined value of literature or the "humanities" ' or of systems 'that in asserting their capacity to perform essentially self-confirming tasks allow for no counterfactual evidence' (Said 1984: 230).

For Said (1984: 230), on the contrary, 'the relationship of theory and criticism, on the one hand, and society and culture on the other' is not one which is answerable in terms of theoretical closure – which, 'like social convention or cultural dogma, is anathema to critical consciousness'. In fact, critical consciousness 'loses its profession when it loses its active sense of an open world in which its faculties must be exercised' (Said 1984: 242), and becomes part of that process which is currently paralysing intellectual debate on the Left, and forcing it continually to yield ground to the individualistic, privatizing dogmas of the Right, backed up by successful economic practice.

There is no substitute, in other words, for those direct oppositional forms of critical response which demand that the critic treat literature as a manifestation of the historical and social conditions out of which its contextual and formal concerns are produced. Criticism has to be conceived, that is, as sceptical, probing, 'trained in a discipline of attentive disbelief' (Thompson 1978: 221), and 'constitutively opposed to every form of tyranny, domination and abuse; its social goals are noncoercive knowledge produced in the interests of human freedom' (Said 1984: 29) – a discipline acting 'on behalf of those alternative acts and alternative institutions whose advancement is a fundamental human and intellectual obligation' (Said 1984: 30).

This is a concept of criticism that appears to have suffered some kind of eclipse over the last two decades. For in the changed circumstances of the 1980s, it is the self-appointed theorists of the New Times of market competition who dominate the intellectual climate. And they have adopted a strategy of a very different kind. By advocating the closest attention to issues arising out of 'the labyrinth of textuality', they make it apparent that their 'peculiar mode of appropriating [their] subject matter . . . is [specifically] not to appropriate anything that is worldly, circumstantial, or socially contaminated' (Said 1984: 3).

And in so far as they persist in maintaining such a programme of critical inquiry, whose most characteristic feature is its assertion of a self-contained and self-confirming detachment, even in commenting on the confusions and distortions of the world that surrounds it, they reflect the ideological pressures of a world in which specific activities and disciplines have grown increasingly abstract and insulated from each other – to confirm, in effect, a new division of intellectual labour. As Rickword (1978: 100) observed, writing (in 1937) of the destructive consequences of nineteenth-century capitalism:

> With the rush to power of machine-industry, the specialisation of intellectual work, like the minute subdivision of factory processes, is carried to its extremes. Each branch of activity is carried on in isolation from the other, the philosopher from the laboratory, the scientist from the studio, the writer from the financier, and all in general from the tremendous creation and re-creation of life going on in factory, mine and farm, which alone provides the leisure in which these various activities can be pursued. In this way the habit of thinking of culture as an independent activity becomes ingrained, and the freedom of the artist, the independence of the scientist, and the disinterestedness of the philosopher become dogmas.

Today, in the fashionable terms of the post-modernist critique, things have been taken much further. It is now no longer merely a question of the 'ingrained independence' of cultural activity, as formulated by the liberal humanists. According to Jean Baudrillard, for instance, the semiological patterns produced by Western capitalism have become so completely 'detached from their supposed referents' as to make it possible for him to argue that now, in the late twentieth century, the links have altogether vanished. In other words, there *are* no referents. 'Like the forms of money it has engendered, the signs and images of contemporary capitalism float detached and forever separate from what used to be called the real world' (Rotman 1988: 27).

But this is not unique to the late twentieth century. It characterizes the mystifying ways in which, by 'the unseen hand', the manipulators of the money-markets, the so-called 'makers of wealth', have habitually proceeded. In the nineteenth century they often worked out their plans behind the closed doors of exclusive clubs and in cabals, where monetary, business and territorial transactions affecting the living conditions of millions were decided on. Momentous things, the takeover of whole industries and institutions and foreign countries, happened behind the backs of almost everyone, and their legitimacy was confirmed by nothing more substantial than a note or a signature, according to the mysterious rituals of the initiated few, the controllers of wealth, the engineers of power. And sometimes even a nod or a wink or a raised finger, such as one sees at work these days during the auction of some prestigious masterpiece by Renoir or Van Gogh, would suffice.

In other words, what Baudrillard and others fashionably define as a late twentieth century demolition of meaning simply confirms the impact of the capitalist ideology of 'seduction'. In the wake, that is, of technological advances which have transformed the industrial process and the conditions of material production, a new and 'sweeping re-definition of thought itself, of its function and content' (Marcuse 1972a: 92), is being imposed upon us. And in this context the arguments of post-structuralist, post-modernist critics are clearly also 'post-Marxist' in that their intellectual positions amount to a denial of those materialist forms of thinking, based upon specific conditions of historical change, which might have had the strength to resist fashionable dogmas. Indeed, they seem often to reassert the ahistorical concerns of idealist metaphysics. What Lacan (1977: 154) has called the 'incessant sliding of the signified *under* the signifier', and Derrida (1981: 20) a process in which 'every signified is also in the position of a signifier', detaches the forms and meanings of language from their sources, the determining social contexts they are the product of. It is then no longer possible to think of language, in Raymond Williams's words, as 'the living evidence of a continuing social process, into which individuals are born and within which they are shaped, but to which they also actively contribute' (1977: 37). For it becomes part of an abstract ahistorical process in which forms and meanings appear to be interchangeable and fluid, an indiscriminate flood of images and signs, much like those imposed upon us by the quantitative terms of the mass media. The problem is how to register for ourselves a sense of place, of position, of historical continuity, of active presence, at once assenting and resisting, so that we can harness and anchor and make sense of what we are faced with and not be swept along by it all to the point at which 'all contradiction is . . . made to seem irrational and all counteraction impossible' (Marcuse 1972a: 22). For where even counteraction is merely an extension of the circularity of an ideological trap defined by language – language loosed from its referents, the pre-existent material conditions that determine its function as an *instrument* of social articulation – then all opposition is neutralized. We are back, it seems, to 'the philosophical legacy of the late Nietzsche, in its relentless denunciation of the illusion of truth and the fixity of meaning' (Anderson 1983: 46), and to a metaphysics of the mythical and interchangeable; which brings us to the semiological jugglings of Baudrillard, in terms of which 'the image bears no relation to any reality' (Rotman 1988: 27), but is what it simulates.

We have moved a long way, that is, from the kind of argument put forward by theorists such as Raymond Williams, which defines the writer's work as an interaction between language and actuality, language as a material product, as creative social practice, as a consequence of the historical struggle men and women are engaged in at all levels in their attempt to make sense of the material contradictions of their world. Yet the literary act has its roots in this struggle, emerging out of it – out of the signifying conditions that make it a voice that speaks to others, concerned with the particular, the actual, the intricate human contexts (physical, spatial, temporal, psychological, sensate) that involve us all. And in celebrating the immediacies, the fluctuating fortunes, the struggles, doubts and longings of people in the subtlety of their response to circumstance, to history, time and change, it reasserts the sanity of connectedness, continuity and interaction that determines the pattern of the lives of real people and the conditions which give them reality, which are not to be reduced to a mere simulation of what language and its images signify. The point is that the literary act as work of art – the significant work of art, that is – seeks not reduction but intensification, the kind of illumination that transforms and penetrates the surfaces of things to enrich and deepen our experience of reality.

Of course, it has to be said that all cultural texts are ambiguously involved, at one level or another, in the ideological privatizing process that is at work upon contemporary society. Thus any attempt to understand, to unmask, what is really going on and to find ways of making sense of the historical struggle we are involved in at this particular stage of advanced capitalism means grappling with and registering the underlying conditions the cultural text functions in terms of. Accepting ideology in the Marxist sense as 'the operation of false consciousness', it is necessary to distinguish texts which conform to its demands from those which might be defined as 'progressive'. For in this sense ideology (as reactionary thought) encourages and reinforces, in Jameson's words,

> that structural, experiential and conceptual gap between the public and the private, between the social and the psychological, or the political and the poetic, between history or society and the 'individual', which – the tendential law of social life under capitalism – maims our existence as individual subjects and paralyses our thinking about time and change just as surely as it alienates us from our speech itself (1981a: 20).

And for us

> to imagine that, sheltered from the omnipresence of history and the implacable influence of the social, there already exists a realm of freedom – whether it be that of the microscopic experience of words in a text or the ecstasies and intensities of the various private religions – is only to strengthen the grip of Necessity over all such blind zones in which the individual seeks refuge . . . The only effective liberation from such constraint begins with the recognition that there is nothing that is not social and historical – indeed, that everything is 'in the last analysis' political (Jameson 1981a: 20).

Bertolt Brecht, for one, did not doubt this. Using language, the teasing play of words, to combat or to expose illusion, he made his work an exploration of the contradictory grounds of material reality. For it was the artist's duty, as he believed,

> to be intelligible to the broad masses of the people, taking up their forms of expression and enriching them – adopting and strengthening their point of view – representing the most progressive section of the people in such a way that it can take over the leadership (Brecht 1975: 423).

For him the central issue was the manner in which language could be made an instrument in the articulation of the struggle for material transformation, a revolutionary change in the structure of society. It was not a matter of language as an insulated process endlessly circling round its own ambiguities, but of breaking that seductive spell. And since his dialectic grasp of the social process made it clear to him that 'there is no more difficult advance than back to reason', he knew that the writer could only make himself an instrument in the cause of that advance by facing up to the contradictory conditions of the struggle for progress. The task, as he saw it, was 'to uncover the causal complex in society – to

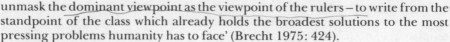

unmask the dominant viewpoint as the viewpoint of the rulers – to write from the standpoint of the class which already holds the broadest solutions to the most pressing problems humanity has to face' (Brecht 1975: 424).

And today that task remains. It is the fundamentally critical task that refuses to permit one manifestation of material reality to thrive at the expense of another, and therefore insists on treating literature as an ideological product of the contending forces of reaction and progress in society. In which sense, the seemingly interchangeable sliding terms of post-modernist discourse are to be seen as a peculiarly characteristic product of capitalist ideology and its mystification of the underlying conditions of the social mechanism at work. And here the problem is to maintain a level of critical awareness alert enough to the hidden traps of the system to be able to think beyond its repressive satisfactions, and begin to create the grounds for a social alternative that will encourage the fulfilment of those basic needs – 'aesthetic, intellectual, the need to love, create, protect and enjoy' – without which, in Edward Bond's view, people cannot realize their potentialities. It may be that Western society as we know it pays lip service to such needs, but it 'has no real interest in them, for they are of course incompatible with the strident competitiveness of a commercial culture' (Bond 1978: 10–11). But to the critic and the writer for whom language is an act of creative social practice involved in the dialectic process of the struggle for any sort of progressive human order worth having these needs are indispensable, and therefore have to be defended against the forces in society that would deny them.

And it is only by thinking our way beyond the alienating conditions by which the capitalist system maintains its dislocating class order that we can do this. Asserting the independence of art will not do it. Writing 'a book about nothing', as Flaubert wanted to, will not do it. Poems that demonstrate solipsistic withdrawal from involvement or that see the world as emptied of meaning will not do it. Taking the path of disillusioned worldliness or of apolitical detachment will not do it. Nor will any argument, however sophisticated, that the material content of social existence has been absorbed into the manifest appearances of things, the 'hyperreality' of the media. If it has to be accepted that knowledge is painful, as Arthur Clough once put it in the anguish of knowing it is not enough, still we have to make the connections, so that we can go on thinking forward against the ugliness of the system, the disillusionment, the denial of potentiality, the visionless mediocrity imposed upon us by the material forces that control our lives. Literature, and the language it uses, have to be more than instruments of the privileged, the substitutive satisfactions and servants of escape. They need to be integrated into the body of society so that they can function as witnesses to the complex interactions of social reality, as an aesthetic of renewal, a force for change, for reorientation and awareness; as part of a tougher and deeper humanism whose concern, in a divided world, is to create grounds from which to build for the future.

2

Unmasking the new idealism

It is a paradoxical fact of the historical development of advanced capitalist society over the last 15 years – a period dominated by the brutalist material practice of a reactionary 'New Realism' which threatens to reduce all forms of communal social practice to the level of the consumerist demands of the market – that there should have emerged in the field of critical theory certain ahistorical, apolitical forms of thinking about literature which are intent on applying the methods of abstract philosophical inquiry to the study of the literary text. Here, it would seem, the question of language as an essentially social product, a dialogic process rooted in the material conditions of people's lives and the dialectic interactions of history, is irrelevant. Indeed, it is suggested that literary discourse is first and last a linguistic phenomenon; that language itself is 'an autonomous process . . . unhinged from reality' (Callinicos 1982: 169); and that all texts originate from, and are determined by, acts of language.

Thus, even as the forces of reactionary materialism are making use of the newest and most seductive forms of post-modernist information technology with the undisguised intention of bringing about the wholesale privatization of social life, these forms of theoretical discourse – structuralist and post-structuralist in tendency – are contending that 'all knowledge is knowledge by description, mediated, organized *in* discourse, connecting with "things" only through "words"' (Callinicos 1982: 168), and that there is therefore no direct 'connection between texts and the existential actualities of human life, politics, societies, and events' (Said 1984: 5). Arguing that all reality is textual, and that the discourse of the literary text can only be answered by a parallel system of discourse, they appear to deny that

> the realities of power and authority – as well as the resistances offered by men, women, and social movements to institutions, authorities and orthodoxies – are the realities that make texts possible, that deliver them to their readers, that solicit the attention of critics (Said 1984: 5).

In these terms, language is a self-contained system which defines everything we are. As Derrida (1976: 158–9) puts it, 'there is nothing outside the text'. The linguistic process, contained *within* the text, is determined *by* the text, by the order of language – or, to put it in Louis Althusser's theoretical concept of that process, by the order of thought, which is insulated from the order of reality even as the theory of history is from the practice of history. So that theory becomes 'the theory of theory and practice and their relationship' (Althusser 1979: 129), a hermetic pursuit with its own self-validating verbal criteria, and the process of historical materialism itself ('real' history, the material changing process of history in action) is reduced to 'a process without a subject' (Althusser 1976: 51), a contentless abstraction, a theoretical concept proof against the intrusion of the temporal. In short, 'the order of thought' and 'the order of the real' are incompatible.

This is as much as to say that, since we can conceive nothing without words, we cannot even concede the priority of the subject or of man ('human sensuous activity' (Marx and Engels 1968: 28)), let alone a pre-existent material world which determines our activities. Thus, such forms of theoretical disquisition, even in their questioning of conventions and of the assumptions most of us naively construct our lives on, postulate an essentially substanceless world, a world entirely dependent on the metaphysics of the word. And in demonstrating the unknowability of the material process which determines the production of literary texts, together with the 'historical moments in which they are located and interpreted' and the material determinants of the historical process itself, what emerges is a 'philosophy of pure textuality and critical noninterference' (Said 1984: 4), and in effect a new kind of idealism.

It may sometimes seem, as West (1975: 26) puts it, that 'words and their arguments correspond to those who speak, not to that which is spoken about'; and (citing Coleridge) that 'it is a fundamental mistake . . . to suppose that words and their syntax are the immediate representatives of *things*'. But this does not settle the issue. For language is undeniably an activity regulated by social relations, and those who speak actually do so in terms of that which is spoken about, of which the word (if not an immediate representative) is all the same a token, a sign. Indeed, as Voloshinov (1986: 41) observes, 'a word in the mouth of a particular individual person is a *product* of the living interaction of social forces', which themselves are defined and given meaning by 'verbal interaction'. That is, the word is essentially an 'ideological product' which 'reflects and refracts another reality outside it'. And as with everything ideological, it 'possesses *meaning*: it represents, depicts, or stands for something lying outside itself. In other words, it is a sign.' And 'without signs there is no ideology' (Voloshinov 1986: 9) – for 'the domain of ideology coincides with the domain of signs' (1986: 10) – and every sign is 'a reflection, a shadow' of the reality it stands for, but 'also itself a material segment of that very reality' (1986: 11) by which the individual consciousness ('ideological through and through' (1986: 22)) is conditioned, nurtured, determined.

For Voloshinov (or Mikhail Bakhtin, who is even thought to have written *Marxism and the Philosophy of Language* under his friend's name), 'language . . . was a field of ideological contention, not a monolithic system' (Eagleton 1983: 117). And in these terms theory should be directed towards clarifying and clearing away the obstacles which mask the interactions between language and reality and emphasizing the dialogic nature of language as a social activity. But when linguistic theory conceives of language as an abstract self-contained system which separates it from the social process that generates it, such theory then begins to operate as a bewildering and mystifying form of evasion. When, that is, on the Saussurian principle, it is argued that pre-existent material conditions can only be assumed through the medium of the verbal concepts (the signified) of these conditions and their signifiers; that whatever exists 'out there' beyond the constructs of language exists as an unformulated 'other' phenomenon which can only be made comprehensible in so far as it can be made sense of as language; and that everything is therefore determined by the linguistic structures it is given – then we are in danger of breaking the threads that hold us down to the contexts of material reality out of which language emerges and of floating off into an illusory transcendent world of theory in which the problems of material social reality become increasingly irrelevant.

The problem here, as defined by Sebastiano Timpanaro (1980: 154) in his discussion of structuralism, is that if language

> does not refer back to any sensory-conceptual experience which is distinguishable from language itself (even though incapable of developing without the aid of language as a tool) or represent a common point of reference for those who speak different languages, then one arrives at two possible conclusions, both equally unacceptable: either language becomes a *système pour la système* which has no meaning and serves no purpose, or else it is asserted that there are as many conceptions of the world as there are languages.

In Timpanaro's view, Saussure himself

> is very far from attempting a reduction of all reality to language, or to a 'system' in a formalistic sense. Rather, he has a strong sense of the non-conventionality . . . of everything in life and human society which is not language. In his general vision of reality, to the degree that it appears in the interstices of his reflections on linguistics, he is even more of a realist than in his conception of language (1980: 158).

But it is a different matter when we come to the theories that have developed out of his system. 'We have to distinguish', according to Timpanaro (1980: 170), 'the authentic Saussure from a later schematized and idealized Saussurianism', and particularly 'when we move from linguistic structuralism to that mélange of linguistics, ethnology and psychoanalysis which began to take shape in French culture during the nineteen fifties and sixties, and which has increasingly shown, in the works of Lévi-Strauss, Foucault and Lacan, an ambition to elevate itself to the status of philosophy, of a 'science of man in general' (Timpanaro 1980: 171). For

> the altogether disproportionate fame enjoyed by these authors . . . is not a consequence of the scientific side of their work, but rather, for the most part, . . . of its charlatanesque features: that mixture of abstract scientism and aestheticist spiritualism which, however patently contradictory it may be, nonetheless represents a perfect solution for the needs of the bourgeoisie, which at one and the same time worships science and attempts to strip it of its demystificatory and liberating force (Timpanaro 1980: 176).

Such theories are in essence a refutation of the Marxist position, which takes its stand on the assumption that there are pre-existent material conditions which we can identify and relate to, and which determine the ways in which we act and think and feel. A reality which can only be registered by reflection, by substitution, explodes all certainties of this sort, and denies that there are any rooted material conditions we can measure ourselves by or use as referents to build our concepts of social, political and psychological meaning upon. There is only a plurality of 'meanings', a relativist cluster of ambiguous abstracts built upon the mystifying and equivocal structures of language; and it is only within the structures of language that any sort of equilibrium can be found – by constructing verbal forms and patterns which will be internally consistent. Thus, these forms of critical theory are continually attacking and undermining grounds we have for accepting that material conditions precede the language in terms of which we conceive them.

Against this textualist position, it could, of course, be argued that the thinking mind would be incapable of producing anything, let alone language, without the body that contains it, the complex biological-psychological system in which the brain is implanted and on which it is entirely dependent for its activity. But that is to put the stress upon a pre-existent biological process, what Antonio Labriola called the 'natural terrain'. And it is a fact that 'philosophy, science and art do not draw stimulus and nourishment solely from the "artificial terrain" of society, but also from the "natural terrain"' (Timpanaro 1980: 48). As Labriola (1966: 220–1) defines the process:

> Men, living socially, do not cease to live also naturally. They are certainly not bound to nature like animals . . . But nature is always the immediate subsoil of the artificial terrain of society, and is the ambience which envelops us all. Technique has interposed modifications, diversions and attenuations of natural influences between ourselves as social animals and nature; but it has not thereby destroyed their efficacy, which on the contrary we experience continuously. Just as we are born naturally male and female, die nearly always in spite of ourselves, are dominated by a reproductive instinct, so we also bear within our temperament specific conditions, which education in the broad sense of the word, or accommodation to society, may certainly modify within limits, but can never eliminate. These conditions of temperament, repeated in many individuals and developed through many individuals through the centuries, constitute what is called ethnic character. For all these reasons, our dependence on nature, however diminished since pre-historic times, persists amidst our social life . . .

It may be that the ambiguity of this dependence remains a problem, but such arguments offer convincing grounds for accepting that the world we live in is material and rooted in the time-space conditions of the earth itself and its life-forms, as identified by the biological sciences; that this material structure preceded the existence of human beings in the process of evolution; and that this pre-existent environment provides the basic conditions by which our lives are determined. I do not have any difficulty therefore in confirming that essentially this material structure, as perceived by the senses, has objective reality, and that the evidence of the senses can be objectively verified by scientific observation, thus demonstrating the existence of an independent material world. And since it is this world outside me that determines my identity and the particular conditions of my existence, the ways in which I think and feel and act and react, it is *this* world I have to try to make sense of by acting upon it and thinking about it and questioning its distinguishable elements, the forms it takes, its observable phenomena, theoretically and practically. But above all, it is my activity which defines and signifies by creating out of what is involved in a social product, which will include 'the language in which the thinker is active'. So that in essence 'what I create for myself I create for society, conscious of myself as a social being' (Marx 1975: 350). My (abstract) consciousness is in *this* sense 'only the *theoretical* form of that whose living form is the real community, society' (Marx 1975: 350). Or, to put it another way, as Marx (1975: 354) emphasizes:

> The resolution of theoretical antitheses . . . is possible only in a practical way, only through the practical energy of people, and . . . their resolution is for that reason by no means only a problem of knowledge. It is also a *real* problem, which philosophy was unable to solve because it treated it as a *purely* theoretical problem.

Such a statement, an early formulation of Marx's denunciatory onslaught upon the divisive conditions of the capitalist system, does not solve the problem of the interaction of theory and practice. But it puts it into focus, identifies the tasks that face all intellectuals, and critical theorists of literature no less than others. What is important here is to recognize the necessity of 'the transformation of passive, contemplative consciousness into active, critical consciousness' (Said 1984: 232), for otherwise there is the danger that theory will become 'an ideological trap'. Indeed, it may be a crucial part of the critic's job

> to provide resistances to theory, to open it up toward historical reality, toward society, toward human needs and interests, to point up those concrete instances drawn from everyday reality that lie outside or just beyond the interpretative area necessarily designated in advance and thereafter circumscribed by every theory (Said 1984: 242).

For Marx, in this sense, theoretical closure, theory as an ideological trap, was anathema. He refused to separate thinking from acting, to permit himself to fall into the traps laid by philosophical dogma, and to treat problems as purely theoretical. The mind and the body – the non-material products of the mind and the material conditions they are nourished on – are not dualistic but dialectical in their relation to each other. It might even be said that the mind's products, its systems of thought, its ideas, its propositions, are *themselves* material products. In terms of the dialectical materialism of Marx and Engels, language is of necessity a product of a pre-existent objective reality – the world itself as a physical, material structure which in its complex interrelationships is to be registered by the senses as the matter out of which language constructs its meanings, and which is therefore part of the structure of 'meaning'. And if, as the Saussurians then declare, meaning may appear to be inconceivable without language since the concept of reality can only be formulated by *means* of language, this does not give anyone the right to assume that the forms of reality that precede language are not our concern – for they are clearly the grounds on which language builds. As Marx and Engels (1970: 51) point out: 'Language is as old as consciousness, language *is* practical consciousness'; and 'like consciousness, [it] only arises from the need, the necessity, of intercourse with other men. Where there exists a relationship, it exists for me'; and so language like 'consciousness . . . is, therefore, from the very beginning a social product'.

In this sense, language is part of the struggle that has to be joined if there is to be any hope of challenging the operative powers and their maintenance of an oppressive superstructure which holds millions in restrictive servitude. And this struggle is going to have to be recognized as a struggle against materially organized and systematically constructed (produced) *orders* of power. But this is no mere intellectual game *confined* to language. It is going on 'out there' at every level of social life, visible and invisible – in the organization of work, the manipulation of the worker, the technological process which cheats him of his rights; the ways people eat and drive; the impact of the visual image on their lives; the manner in which money is transferred and juggled with and accumulated and lost on world markets; in the wordless nod that confers authority, and the silence that condemns. And where language has its part to play is in identifying, defining, making visible, spelling out precisely *what* is going on and being done behind the screens of falsification and pretence in the name of 'justice ', 'peace', 'freedom', 'democracy', the 'free world', 'decency', 'human-ity', 'moral values', and so on. For there is in fact a whole array of words and phrases and structures which have become suspect and debased by the uses to which they have been put by propagandists and ideologists assuming control over people's minds; and these clearly need to be deconstructed, broken up, denounced, exposed. Perhaps many of them have even now become so polluted that they can never be used again without irony. But this does not mean that *everything* has to be swept aside, however rigorously subjected to critical examination. If reality is difficult to define as a concept, few of us doubt that beyond such semantic problems we live in a materially substantial and definable world which can be made accountable to our social needs. And complex though it is, it is there as our environment – earth, stone, grass, air, the space we walk in, the sky, the roads, the buildings we live and work in, the cars and ships and weapons and factories and computers we have built, the books we read; and irreducibly the people, who are *not* words; who are more and other than the languages they speak or the books they appear in.

This raises the question of what one is to make of the intellectual position of a writer like Roland Barthes, who, in Susan Sontag's admiring comment,

> understood (as Sartre did not) that literature is first of all, last of all, language. It is language that is everything. Which is to say that all reality is presented in the form of language . . . And Barthes takes for granted (as Sartre, with his notion of writing as communication did not) what he calls 'the radical exploration of writing' undertaken by Mallarmé, Joyce, Proust, and their successors. That no venture is valuable unless it can be conceived as a species of radicalism, *radicalism thereby unhinged from any distinctive content*, is perhaps the essence of what we call modernism (1982: xx).

The symptomatic clause here is that which stresses the 'unhinging of content' – that is, detachment from what Lukács calls 'the objective driving forces of society', the contexts which give writing its place in its world, the interests and social interactions determined by the historical contradictions of the writer's world, which *are* its content, and define its specific concerns, its texture and form, its recurrent obsessions, the issues that dominate. For the peculiar characteristic of modernism is its sacrifice of content for linguistic play, of social and political context for the patterns of subjective observation, the aesthetic process – which of course 'make language everything' and become at their expense the obscure forms of word-play we get in *Finnegan's Wake*, where writing as communication has been reduced almost to zero. (As Joyce himself comments, on *Finnegan's Wake*: 'I know it is only a game, but children might as well play as not. The ogre will come in any case.' Which seems to suggest that from such a position there is no way forward.)

The contention of Roland Barthes is that writing at this level opens up the potentialities of language beyond the restrictive conditions imposed upon us by the limitations and demands of material and social reality, because it is then free to range across all frontiers unhindered and does not need to 'account for its actions'. The responsibility is not to the logic of any form of systematic moral argument or to the social needs of people, but only to the sensate powers of language itself, to register the subtlest shift and flicker of the individual sensibility. Its aim is to subvert the structures of reality. And so, in Sontag's words, 'liberty is a state that consists in remaining plural, fluid, vibrating with doctrine; whose price is being indecisive, apprehensive, fearful of being taken for an impostor' (1982: xxxii).

And so it is one notes that Barthes' own definitions tend continually to glance off and to veer away from the problems of 'meaning' – which he himself in certain of his earlier (structuralist) writings has so meticulously explored. For example, he sees 'language as a natural phenomenon' – though it could be convincingly argued that it is, on the contrary, highly artificial. He describes it as 'a kind of natural ambience wholly pervading the writer's expression'; as enfolding 'the whole of literary creation much as the earth, the sky, and the line where they meet, outlining a familiar habitat for mankind'; as 'a horizon', a 'frontier'. Apparently, it is not 'the locus of a social commitment but merely a reflex response' (Barthes 1982: 31). And yet, as elsewhere defined, 'it is a social object by definition'; which would seem to contradict that it is 'a kind of natural ambience'. Furthermore (and vaguely), it seems that behind the medium of language 'the whole of history stands unified and complete in the manner of a Natural Order' (Barthes 1982: 32).

The problem with definitions of this kind is that they are so imprecise as to be virtually meaningless, which cannot be Barthes' intention, even if he *is* concerned to avoid any fixities of meaning. What purpose is served, one has to ask, by stating that language enfolds 'the whole of literary creation', other than that literary creation is indubitably a matter of language? And if it also enfolds 'the whole of history' as something 'unified and complete', what is one supposed to make of this? It is little more than a rhetorical gesture, symptomatic of the abstract universalizing metaphysics of idealism – a gesture that sweepingly bypasses (and therefore dismisses) all distinction in claiming to confirm the potentialities of language, and therefore leaves us more or less where we were. History as a Natural Order? What can this be said to mean? That history develops and changes like trees or animals? That the social and economic structures in terms of which people's lives are organized and which generate historical events are natural? That the differences between what is natural and what is artificial do not matter? That it is not the material relations organized by men and women in their social intercourse that generate historical events, but something akin to the organic cyclic process of the natural world, that functions by chemical and vegetable action to produce and reproduce its 'life-forms'?

The truth is that history is no more a Natural Order than art is. Nor can 'the whole of history' ever stand unified and complete behind the medium of language. For history is *not* unified; it is diverse, confusing, contradictory, generated by many complex energies and conditions – or, in Sontag's (1982) words, 'plural, fluid, vibrating with doctrine', as with dissonance, with conflict, with unlike and uncomplete and un-unifiable issues. And since so much of history is made by the wordless actions of people responding to events in which words are only one element, it can never stand complete behind the medium of language. How can we therefore talk in any *meaningful* sense of literary creation enfolding the whole of history? This is to venture into the realm of myth, which leads, in Auerbach's words, 'to a smoothing down and harmonising of events, to a simplification of motives, to a static definition of characters which avoids conflict, vacillation, and development' (1953: 20); or into that realm of the transcendent which has enabled the liberal humanists, with their superior idealist aims, to talk of literature as 'an organic order' and of culture as an abstract 'pursuit of harmonious perfection' insulated from the economic conditions which give its apologists their privileged status. For it blurs over those very terms and conditions which *give* meaning substance, and which actually determine the strengths of writing – its particularity, its power to reveal, to disclose, to probe below the surface, behind the façades that conceal, and thus to demystify. Not that I am suggesting that it is the purpose of literary creation to demystify. But I *do* believe that writing has to be anchored, and I do not think it is to be disputed that the critic's duty is to create for the reader as for himself a precise awareness of the conditions that make for meaning and which determine what it is that writing (or any piece of writing) functions in the context or the shadow of.

Barthes (1982: 43) hazards the view that 'it is because writing derives from a meaningful gesture of the writer that it reaches the deeper layers of History'; and this may be so. But for the writer's gesture to be meaningful, it must have the power to be more than a mere gesture. Writing is unlikely to reach the deeper layers of history unless it is grounded upon the concrete material *conditions* of history, its content, its contemporaneity, what goes into the making of it. Barthes cannot expect to get very far by providing generalizations as unspecific and as inconsistent as this. But then he is continually leaving one suspended in such an amorphous mist of language, which swings first one way and then another through generality after generality. For example, he seems convinced that 'all modes of writing have in common the fact of being "closed" and thus different from spoken language', and follows this with the assertion that 'writing is in no way an instrument for communication' (Barthes 1982: 43). Both contentions, being at once abstract and doctrinal, are highly questionable. In the first place, it is at least conceivable that some modes of writing are less closed than others, and could even be described as open, though they may not be as open as some modes of speech. Secondly, if writing is not an instrument for communication, an attempt to reach across the frontiers between the self and the other, the other *in* the self, the self *beyond* the self, one would want to know why Barthes seeks to cast his work in the form of the book, which is itself a vessel containing verbal structures intended to be read by others. And if Barthes is making an attempt to produce propositions intended to serve as definitions of what writing is supposed to be, then he is making at least an attempt to communicate. Indeed, one has to ask what else writing *can* be if it is not *also* and in the essential sense an instrument for communication.

I have to say that when I write I write to clarify, to define, to distinguish, to try to disentangle *one* skein of thought or of feeling from another, to resolve or to reveal contradictions and confusions, to attempt an argument, to open the text up or to open it out so that it will fairly convey the complexities I am writing in terms of. And if I do this, I do it to communicate what I am thinking to *others*, or to *myself*, by means of the varied resources of the language I have at my command

and in the act of creating structures and patterns of words which will correspond as precisely as I can make them.

What do I do it for otherwise? For the pleasure of writing *nothing*, or of attempting to write something that can exist for its own sake or in its own right? But what can that ever be made to mean? Words either serve a function or they do not. They *are* instruments. They do *not* exist in their own right. And they do not function in a vacuum. They signify a relationship, an interchange, the conditions of an active social practice. In other words, to repeat what Marx and Engels (1970: 51) said in *The German Ideology*, 'language, like consciousness, only arises from the need, the necessity, of intercourse with other men'. It is a mode of 'primary material production' which is 'from the beginning a social relationship' (Williams 1977: 28–9). Nor does this mode act or function merely as a

> 'reflection' or 'expression' of 'material reality.' What we have, rather, is a grasping of this reality through language, which as practical consciousness is saturated by and saturates all social activity. And since this grasping is social and continuous . . . it occurs within an active and changing society. It is of and to this experience – the lost middle term between the abstract entities, 'subject' and 'object', on which the propositions of idealism and orthodox materialism are erected – that language speaks. Or to put it more directly, language is the articulation of this active and changing experience; a dynamic and articulated social presence in the world (Williams 1977: 37–8).

It is articulated as a *process*, emerging out of a context, 'rooted in something beyond language', as Barthes puts it, and 'continually available, in social and material ways, in manifest communication', as a product of a 'complex of communicative systems' (Williams 1977: 41).

In this sense, and in his references to the work of Voloshinov, Williams (1977: 211–12) directly refutes the Barthes contention:

> Writing is always communication, but it cannot always be reduced to simple communication . . . Writing is always in some sense self-composition and social composition, but it cannot always be reduced to its precipitate in personality or ideology, and even where it is so reduced it has still to be seen as active . . . Writing is often a new articulation and in effect a new formulation, extending beyond its own modes. But to separate this as art, which in practice includes, always partly and sometimes wholly, elements elsewhere in the continuum, is to lose contact with the substantive creative process and then to idealize it; to put it above or below the social, when it is in fact the social in one of its most distinctive, durable, and total forms.

Can it therefore *ever* be 'unhinged from any distinctive content'? Since 'all writing carries references, meanings and values', and 'to suppress or displace them is in the end impossible', as Williams (1977: 155) puts it, its content cannot be obliterated or unhinged without making it strictly meaningless, as Flaubert's 'book about nothing' would have been.

As for writing being a 'closed' system, this (as I have said) may be so in the purely abstract sense – in the sense, that is, that its language (as opposed to that of speech) is fixed, made permanent. But since it is a potentiality modified by the activity upon it of the reader (and of the reader at different times differently), it is a closed system that is exposed to a variety of interpretations or responses that loosen or that open up its patterns. It is not just that words, being ambiguous, are never fixed in their meanings. As signs, they indicate and connect with conditions which are brought to them by the reader – his or her own complex and socially conditioned identity. And the reader (like the speaker) reads consequentially from one moment to the next, moving with the words, stopping at them, giving meaning to them or producing meaning *from* them, going back to question or to reread them, being moved by them or annoyed or startled, and injecting into them his/her own psychology and sensibility. In other words, a piece of writing is only seemingly closed. For though it will always have the same order and pattern of signs, the same sequences of structures, moving in a direction which has been articulated by the writer, yet it is the impact and the experience of this process (complex enough in itself but even more so when the variable responsiveness of the reader is added to it) that matter; and these may well be very different at different times.

Barthes postulates the need to escape from the external apparatus of doctrine, the need to be free, to create patterns of language that will break loose from the closures that fix writing within certain congealing or limiting conditions. That is to say, since writing is not open-ended, fluid and unfixed, like speech, it must therefore be given the greatest possible flexibility to compensate for this defect. It must be opened up, 'unhinged from any distinctive content'. But that is to bring us back once more to the fundamental problems the writer is faced with, as and when he/she writes – of making sense, of creating structures that will not be either strait-jackets of doctrine (a closed system) or so open-ended they become emptied of content. The problem is to construct forms and patterns that will avoid restrictive closures without being unhinged from what they are saying to the point of becoming nonsense; that will remain open to the underlying contradictions of reality; that will not fall into either dogma on the one hand or amorphousness and irresponsibility, the indulgence of the aesthete on the other; that will convey what they mean, and mean what they say, rather than conceal what they mean.

Barthes suggests that what he calls 'the power of language' is 'fascist'. But this surely depends on how that power is used rather than upon the power itself – otherwise all great writing would have to be classified as fascist! Clearly there are fascist uses of language, involving an irresponsible, irrational and perverted exploitation of meaning, embodied in the rant of 'monolithic ideologies' like Hitler's; and these, even at their subtlest, have little respect for clarity or for keeping distinctions clear. They generate, that is, a mystifying romanticism, a species of aestheticism, which deliberately obscures all that is distinctive, all that keeps things clear, all that insists upon precise definition; a power bred upon the *un*defined threat, the undisclosed, suggestive meaning, the induced intent, the violation of integrity. To say that language is everything may seem to protect the writer from the dogmas of materialism. But it is a dangerous abstraction, for such an assumption cuts words off from their contexts, and suggests that the work is subject only to its own laws as an independent (autonomous) entity – satisfying in itself and for its own sake, irrespective of substance, content, the social realities that surround it, and everything that is more (and other than) language.

But no piece of writing that is intended to be read by others can ever be an autonomous entity. Though it has to be judged or responded to in terms of the laws of the language it uses, it is at once exposed to the mediating influence of the reader's own identity and the possibly very different assumptions (social, psychological, aesthetic) which he/she brings to the writer's work. Thus, the piece of writing no more exists for *its own* sake (as it is read by the reader) than it exists for the sake of the writer. It is a potentiality, and its language speaks of many things carried by the words – meanings, possibilities implicit with resonances and echoes from the world it was produced in and (however indirectly) refers back to, as well as the new historical contexts it may now exist as a commentary on or a counterpoint to. Nor can its 'style' – the way it runs and is shaped; the texture, the aesthetic balance it assumes from the writer's choice of words and sentences – ever be unhinged from the argument it gives shape to. For this is surely what matters – what this 'style' functions in terms of, what it serves, rather than what it is in itself. Barthes (1982: 32) goes so far as to assert, of style, that 'its frame of reference is biological or biographical, not historical: it is the writer's "thing", his glory and his prison; it is his solitude'. Which is acceptable as far as it cares to go; for it remains peculiarly indistinct, and arbitrary. One would want to know why, if 'its frame of reference is biological and biographical', it is not *also* historical, since the biographical emerges from the historical and is inescapably rooted in the social and the economic, the material conditioning which *determine* the biographical. So what *is* this writer's 'thing'? What is it supposed to signify? Style as 'glory', 'prison', 'solitude', seems little more than a sort of mysterious effluescence of atmosphere that hovers round the work – a sort of insulating mist referring to the 'spiritual', the 'transcendent', the 'numinous'. Can this, or the assumption that 'writing is in no way an instrument for communication', or that it does not need to 'account for its actions', be squared with the assumption that it 'derives from a meaningful gesture of the writer'? Can style have any function at all if it has nothing to communicate? Can gestures 'unhinged from any distinctive content' be meaningful?

Barthes (1982: 35) attempts further definitions:

A language and a style are objects; a mode of writing is a function; it is a relationship between creation and society, the literary language transformed by its social finality, form considered as a human intention and thus linked to the great crisis of history.

But these definitions bristle with questions; for they suggest that the literary language *is* determined by its social contexts, *is* concerned with meanings, and *does* have a content; that if writing is a function it has something to communicate; that style is an attribute of that function; that it is no more a 'prison' than it is a 'solitude', that it speaks of other things beyond itself; and that its frame of reference is as inescapably historical as it is biological and biographical.

There are confusions here which one finds difficult to reconcile, since the terms often cancel each other out. And it seems to me that the writer has a responsibility as much to make his *language* 'account for its actions' as *he* has to account for *his* – and nowhere more crucially than in defining and clarifying the terms in which his writing functions and in recognizing the conditioning influences that motivate what he writes and how and why. To evade such issues or to sidestep them as if the writer had some sort of special rights which the rest of us do not have is an indulgence and an irresponsibility – for the uninitiated are likely to find themselves already bewildered, if not mystified, by the shifts and turns of an ideological apparatus dictated by the elitist concepts that govern their world.

It is hardly surprising that a mode of thinking that can accept such propositions as those I have drawn attention to should be disposed to make the dismissive assertion that, since it is 'linked to action, Marxist writing has rapidly become, in fact, a language expressing value judgements'. What *is* surprising is that a complex dialectical process and a diversity of texts, not to mention the controversies that have raged around them, can be so peremptorily dismissed. Worse, Barthes makes a leap in one sentence from this revelation – as 'already visible in Marx, whose writing however remains in general explanatory' – to 'the era of triumphant Stalinism' (Barthes 1982: 43), exactly as if it were a single step of logic (or of direct transition) from the one to the other, thus sweeping aside the whole entangled history of Marxist thinking, everything of significance in the development of the theory and practice of Marxism.

But then it is clear from the ideological position Barthes has chosen to adopt that he is not prepared to respond to the intellectual challenge involved in the Marxist response to literary discourse. Instead, he puts up the shutters, and offers us a bourgeois equivalent of Stalinism – a literary Stalinism of the Right; an alogical justification of modernist sensibility. And this is no more convincing in its defence of the bourgeois writer's autonomy than the Stakhanovite realism of the Stalinists. For in its rejection of what Barthes considers the intrusion of the political, it sets up such exclusive ideological conditions for the writer as those which had led earlier modernists into positions of regressive retreat from social involvement, thus confirming the divisive logic of the capitalist system. It is his view, for instance, that

> the spreading influence of political and social facts into the literary field of consciousness has produced a new kind of scriptus, halfway between the party member and the writer, deriving from the former an ideal image of committed man, and from the latter the notion that a written work is an act (Barthes 1982: 44).

But this is merely to define the differences between two *kinds* of writer, the political and the non-political, and to presume to register the attitudes that divide them, which at the deepest level reflect the disastrous insulation of culture from politics determined by the economic divisiveness of nineteenth-century industrial capitalism and are still today unreconciled. For it does not do much else. When Barthes talks of 'the literary field of consciousness' he assumes that there *is* a territory set apart from and uncontaminated by 'political and social facts'; that the political and the literary are separate territories which have little or nothing in common. Whereas in reality there are no such arbitrary distinctions to be made; the literary is as inescapably political as it is social, even when it claims to have nothing to do with politics. Of course there are different *kinds* of writer, and some are more political than others; and it may *be* that there is a 'type of scriptus' to be described as 'halfway between the party member and the writer'. But he is not a new type – he goes back at least as far as Aristophanes, and is to be recognized in men like Froissart and Aretino. And even here the distinctions would need to be made between those who are, in fact, party members, and those who (like Milton or Dickens or Tolstoy or Sartre) are primarily writers. For the work they produce is likely to be utterly different. Both are indeed (at least in one sense) 'writers'; but the 'party member' is by definition *not* primarily a writer but a politician, even when he writes well.

Such distinctions are essential, but Barthes does nothing to make them clear. Instead, he talks of the 'scriptus' (the writer who insists on dragging politics into literature) as one who comes 'to adopt a closed system of language', as against those whose aim is what he calls 'an ideally free language', a literary language, the language of the 'writer' (he who keeps politics out of literature) – though he has already declared that '*all* modes of writing have in common the fact of being "closed"' (Barthes 1982: 43).

This, however, seems not to be the point. The point is whether or not a work hinges on the political. If it *is* political, the writer is a mere 'scriptus', not a 'writer' at all – a sort of party hack. And on this Barthes is at once blunt, unequivocal and absolute. For him, it seems, 'any political mode of writing' exists to 'uphold a police world'. And just in case we should doubt the equation, he extends it to cover 'any intellectual mode of writing', as tending to lead us into 'a complete blind alley', to 'complicity and impotence, which means, in either case, to alienation' (Barthes 1982: 44). So much for the attempt of the writer to reach across the barriers that hold him separated, insulated, from the political. It is bound to fail. As a writer, he must resist the political *and* the intellectual modes and be content to remain unattached in his world of 'free associations', 'conscienceless', 'unethical'. And if he cannot – if he insists on utilizing political or intellectual or even ethical modes of writing – then 'one no longer ventures to call him a writer' (Barthes 1982: 44).

Directives of this sort leave the writer where the ideology of 'the dominant interests' in society would have him remain – an inhabitant of the transcendental world of metaphysical interplay, 'that relatively untroubled and secluded world' where, as Edward Said (1984: 25) has it, 'there seems to be no contact with the world of events and societies, which modern history, intellectuals, and critics have in fact built'. In these terms the socially destructive powers of monopoly capitalism cannot be confronted, challenged, analysed or exposed. Instead, the writer becomes 'an adornment to what the powers of modern industrial society transact: the hegemony of militarism and a new cold war, the depoliticisation of the citizenry, the overall compliance of the intellectual class to which critics [and writers] belong' (Said 1984: 25).

For Barthes, in the anti-materialistic drift of the early 1970s characterized by French post-structuralist philosophy in its flirtation with literature, it seems that all structures, and with them 'all theory, ideology, determinate meaning, social commitment' have become suspect, 'inherently terroristic' (Eagleton 1983: 141), and 'writing' is to be reasserted as an end in itself. But if that is what the act of writing is to be envisaged as – a process in which 'language does not have to account for its actions', and the writer believes he occupies a 'Realm of Freedom' owing nothing to the 'Realm of Necessity' – then even when this kind of writer sees himself as 'the watcher who stands at the crossroads of all other discourses' (Sontag 1982: xxi), he is unlikely to be in any position to challenge the dominant interests, let alone to force them to account for *their* actions.

It is 'when we think of language as something we *do*, as indissociably interwoven with our practical forms of life' (Eagleton 1983: 147) and with the material social conditions that generate the power to act, that the work of the writer takes on its urgency and becomes a challenge to the operative powers. For then it becomes a real discourse, a dialogic process, part of the active process of history in action, involved in the struggle with the repressive forces of institutionalized power which keep people subservient and divided from each other and which substitute unreal, mystifying structures for the primary determining conditions which breed the *will* to act. Its greatest strength lies not in any metaphysical contemplation of the forms, but rather in identifying and exposing the grounds on which the forms are built, as in Shakespeare, Dickens, Tolstoy and Brecht. To argue that the writer is a detached creator whose work is objective, autonomous, is to cut him off from the grounds – the historical-social conditions – that his work is rooted in and produced from. Of course art is not *life*; but it is a cultural-material product, and even as illusion it sets up a dialectic to which the writer is answerable, and it is in its interaction with reality that it has its richest contribution to make to the life of its time or to the future that takes it over.

But so long as this mystificatory detachment is confirmed in the spirit in which Barthes confirms it, as a textualization of reality, a textualization of a text, a free play of language, *all* texts are escape routes, bridges thrown across the flowing currents of history – substitutive satisfactions leading from 'unknown shore' to 'unknown shore', the indistinct settings of a mystifying 'other world beyond this world's perplexing wastes', the 'immense panorama of futility and anarchy which is contemporary history' (Eliot 1965: 681) and its 'twittering' concerns. For in these terms, the complex changing conditions of reality and its dialogic interplay, all that precisely identifies, the struggle and clash and collision of ideas and arguments, the difficult logic that demands a dialectic of response, are ignored, subsumed and absorbed into the 'universalizing' forms of the writer's 'literary consciousness', leaving the hidden ideological interests, the 'terroristic' forces of repression that are its surrounding context, in control.

Part Two

3

Shakespeare:
a subversive dialectic

So: our virtues
Lie in the interpretation of the time
Coriolanus IV. vii.

Conclusion

Shakespeare's work has for so long held an assured place at the heart of the
cultural institutions of British society as to make it seem virtually inseparable
from those institutions. At this level of abstraction it takes on monolithic
proportions, and itself becomes an institution, a 'monument to its own
magnificence', existing outside history, transcending time and change, reflecting
some sort of universalizing, essentially mythical and fixed order of things.

This is, of course, nothing but a mystifying absurdity. For the actual work, and
its place in our culture, is neither static nor fixed. Like any other manifestation of
cultural life, it is a product of the complex forces of society in action, and as such
has been continually exposed to the changing pressures and conditions of
historical development – first as a body of writing generated by Shakespeare
himself in the course of his own lifetime, then (in the centuries since his death) by
the ways in which dominant ideological-cultural interests have acted upon,
modified, influenced and used it.

In other words, this work has no abstract existence, except as a collection of
historical documents. It is a historically embodied form of communication that
comes to life only in the present, only when it becomes an active process, an
instrument of exploration. It is what readers, critics, actors, people who see the
plays enacted in the theatre, make of it as a cultural product reflecting and
counterpointing and commenting upon the interests of their own time, the
history they are in the act of making or of being shaped by. What people made of
it in the past belongs to another history, and has another place.

In this sense, the contemporary significance of Shakespeare's work – as
conceived, that is, in the context of late twentieth-century capitalist society – is
likely to depend at least as much on the kinds of question we ask ourselves about
the conventions of the institutional framework within which the plays are taught
or acted or seen as upon questions of strictly textual analysis. But above all, it is a
matter of whether the issues dealt with in the plays or the language they speak
can be shown to have significant bearing on the lives of those who read them in
school or see them in the theatre and on the conditions that shape their lives, in a
world which must often seem (particularly to the young) utterly remote from
that of Shakespeare. To argue, as I shall want to argue, that the age of

Elizabethan and Jacobean England was an age, like our own, of radical transition, of historical upheaval and crisis, involving profound changes in the economic and social order and the impact of an aggressive market capitalism, is to suggest that the plays do have such bearing; that here, if anywhere, it is possible to bring Shakespeare close to what most concerns us; and that there are parallels and interactions to be discovered between our world and Shakespeare's which make his work more relevant to this particular period in the history of Western culture than to any other in the 370-odd years since his death.

But this, of course, is 'to speak about literature ideologically', to 'reintroduce the world' (Abbott White 1972: 441); to make certain claims about the function of literature and literary criticism which admit that our readings of texts get their colour, stress and meaning as much from the pressures and surrounding conditions that are brought to bear upon us (knowingly or unknowingly) as from the texts themselves. Indeed, it would require no more than a cursory look through current reviews and critical commentaries on Shakespeare to recognize just how deeply we are influenced by the ideological forces that surround us; which makes it all the more important for those who have any responsibility for making sense of the plays to confront such issues. And this is bound to involve calling into question many of the assumptions associated with the institution of Shakespeare studies in the schools and universities; for it is here that the process begins and that Shakespeare becomes part of the machinery of cultural production by which ideological conventions are maintained. And since, in Sinfield's words, the plays here 'constitute an influential medium through which certain ways of thinking about the world are promoted and others impeded', it is the teacher's (and the critic's) task to open up this medium to radical questioning and to make the texts 'a site of cultural struggle and change' (1985: 131).

Assuming this, the argument about relevance is inevitably bound up with the question of how we read the plays and what preconceptions we bring to them or become aware of as we read. And this in itself is a problem. It is not just a question of responding to the presence and authority of Shakespeare's work. For the diversity and range, the dialectic energy and ambiguity of that work, have made it a fertile breeding ground for a wide variety of interpretations which it is clearly important for us to be in a position to examine critically. We need to be able, that is, to recognize how open the plays are to manipulation from ideological assumptions of one kind or another. But once we have begun to do that, it will then become increasingly apparent that such interpretations tend to fall into one *group* or another. There are readings, for instance, of a liberal-humanist caste – idealist, romantic, or realist – which include Shakespeare as the poet of national sovereignty; the royalist defending the hierarchic order of society against the forces of evil – 'democracy in strict subservience to the crown' (Knight 1982: 67) – or the individualist struggling for place in a world of intrigue and conspiracy. There are modernist readings, in which Shakespearean tragedy is seen as a prototype of the Theatre of the Absurd, registering the essential futility and meaninglessness of the universe and of man's (if not woman's) place in it. There are psychoanalytic, structuralist, post-structuralist, deconstructionist and feminist readings. And there are those classified as Marxist, clearly my kind, which look at everything that happens in terms of incipient class struggle, with men and women motivated by historical change and acted upon by the conditioning forces of the social structure they are part of.

We can take our pick, it seems. For, as Hawkes (1986: 117) has pointed out, the texts are

> a site, or an area, of conflicting and often contradictory potential interpretations . . .
> no single one or group of which can claim 'intrinsic' primacy or 'inherent' authority,
> and all of which are always ideological in nature and subject to extrinsic political and
> economic determinants.

In other words, since Shakespeare's theatre deals with so many assumptions and is continually moving into disconcertingly uncharted and ambiguous territory, the critic is left with plenty of room to bend the text to fit his ideology.

This immediately raises the problem of how to decide between one reading and another. For the fact is that whatever interpretation we choose will be largely dependent on how we are taught or conditioned to read the plays in the first place. Naturally, the professional critic will want to persuade us that he comes to the work with an open mind. But his argument and the licence he takes with the text will nevertheless be determined by the preconceptions (however concealed) of his cultural background and class allegiance. In this sense we can all of us make a case for our own version of Shakespeare, however far-fetched. And there are risible extremes to which this licence can be taken. The recent example of Knight (1982: 67) using Cranmer's speech at the end of *Henry VIII* to justify his support for the Falklands War should be chastening enough. And another comes to mind of a certain monetarist Chancellor, who proclaimed on the strength of a few resonant lines from *Troilus and Cressida* and the aggressive patrician values of Coriolanus that 'Shakespeare was a Tory, without any doubt' (Lawson 1983: 19) – thus reducing to absurdity the complex ironies and contradictions of the texts. One is tempted to put such people in their place with Thersites' caustic dismissal of Achilles: 'Would the fountain of your mind were clear again, that I might water an ass at it! I had rather be a tick in a sheep than such a valiant ignorance' (*Troilus*, III. iii).

It is easy enough perhaps for us to deal with this kind of thing. But there are other more formidable commentators whose subtler methods nevertheless leave much to be desired in their approach to the text. T. S. Eliot (1953: 53), for instance, rejects the contention that Shakespeare ever 'thought to any purpose; that he had any coherent view of life, or that he recommended any procedure to follow'. To him, it seems, 'none of the plays of Shakespeare has a "meaning"'. Apparently 'great poetry' does not need to concern itself with any such dangerous and possibly subversive issues. The meaning and content of the text can safely be left to their own devices, absorbed into the ways in which the language works. It is enough that a play provides 'the illusion of life', and 'expresses in perfect language some permanent human impulse'. Or, to put it in other words:

> Shakespeare was occupied in the struggle – which alone constitutes life for a poet – to
> transmute his personal and private agonies into something rich and strange,
> something universal and impersonal. The rage of Dante against Florence, or Pistoia,
> or what not, the deep surge of Shakespeare's general cynicism and disillusionment,
> are merely gigantic attempts to metamorphose private failures and disappointments
> (Eliot 1953: 55).

The passage bristles with questions, for it is grounded upon certain dubious assumptions. What, for instance, *are* these private failures and disappointments?

What does this 'something universal and impersonal' actually *mean*? For it is surely the specific conditions of the product, how the text is constructed and worked out, what the language itself signifies, that matter. If this is what is meant by 'universal' and 'impersonal', then Eliot should have taken the trouble to define it in these terms. But this he chooses not to do. Instead, he talks about the plays as '*merely* gigantic attempts to metamorphose' what is private. But we are concerned not with the subjective agonies of Shakespeare but with the publicly exposed conditions, the verbal proofs, of the plays themselves. And it is in the *objective* terms of the metamorphosis and what it brings into being (in other words the text) that Shakespeare's attempts are to be judged.

As for the question of Shakespeare's 'greatness', it is, of course, also rooted in the text, which is the only basis on which any valid judgement can be made. And Eliot (1953: 55) tells us next to nothing about this when he declares, in his most seductive manner, that 'The great poet, in writing himself, writes his time'; and that, in this sense, 'Shakespeare, hardly knowing it, became the representative of the 16th century'. For one finds oneself wanting to know exactly what is meant by 'writing oneself', and whether in fact it is ever possible to write oneself or one's time if one hardly knows what one is doing. How can any poet, however great, write his time without at least a modicum of 'thinking to a purpose' – without, that is, some sort of objective intellectual and imaginative grasp of what is going on around him? But for Eliot there is no problem. As he sees it, Shakespeare's business was 'to express the greatest emotional intensity of his time, based on whatever his time happened to think' (Eliot 1953: 55). Moreover, it seems that because Shakespeare was not a philosopher, and because poetry 'has its own function' (Eliot 1953: 56), it was not Shakespeare's function as a poet to think; or that poets do not (or cannot?) think. If this is so, how was it possible to conceive plays geared to certain complex conditions, certain structural laws, or to sustain any sort of coherence in defining, say, the role played by the money-market in Shylock's Venice, or the rottenness of the state of Denmark, or repressive authority versus sexual gratification in Angelo's Vienna? Is it to be seriously argued that a writer in whose work as a whole, as Eliot (1953: 103) himself claims, 'there is to be read the profoundest, and indeed one of the most sombre studies of humanity that has ever been made in poetry', had no need to be intellectually alert and did 'no thinking on his own' (1953: 54)? But then to Eliot all of the work (all 36 plays) is 'one poem'; and in the light of such mystification, thinking is an inconvenience, not to say a danger, because it insists on questioning and distinguishing and articulating differences. We should not be surprised therefore to find Eliot (1953: 102–3) claiming that 'in Elizabethan and Jacobean drama . . . there is almost no analysis of the particular society of the times'. Apparently the dramatists 'believed in their own age' and, having no *need* to analyse, were thus 'in a position to concentrate their attention . . . upon the common characteristics of humanity in all ages, rather than upon the differences'. That this could be said of writers as anarchic and probing and critical as Marlowe, Marston, Tourneur, Webster and Middleton, is beyond belief. But then for Eliot differences are not the issue. What he is concerned with is universality, an undifferentiated oneness of purpose. And what makes Shakespeare's work one poem is the 'one significant, consistent, and developing personality' that produced it; not 'the poetry of isolated lines and passages . . . or even of whole poems' (Eliot 1953: 103) but the force of personality, the unthinking impulse, the 'greatness', in a word the 'unity', of Shakespeare.

All this leaves us very much in the air, with almost all questions relating to the texts and their significance unanswered. And if we are looking for answers we are going to have to turn to other critics – critics with far more pertinent and penetrating things to say about the plays, who are prepared to take the trouble to face up to the intellectual and imaginative challenge of Shakespeare's art. And among such critics, the most convincing – the most able to hold their own in face of changing fashions and demands – are likely to be those who build their arguments on certain fundamental conditions: conditions rooted in the system of values characteristic of Shakespeare's world, its historical, political, cultural perspectives, and which (transmuted into the work) define and determine the limits of the work's potentialities, as embodied in the practice of the playwright, his insistent and recurring preoccupations. One may put it that the theoretical grasp of Shakespeare's thinking, that sense we have of a mind harnessing and controlling the direction of an argument, is absorbed into the practice of the poet. And that practice, in metaphorical terms, enacts the dialectic interplay of reality, of individual-social struggle, of antagonistic interchange, of ambition and will driven towards alienation or reconciliation, destructiveness or renewal, as determined by the conditioning forces in society.

And if it is, therefore, misleading to describe Shakespeare's work, in Eliot's claim for it, as a unity, a 'single poem', all the same its characteristic preoccupations make it an intellectual and imaginative order which (even beyond the transmutations of time and place, of geographical setting) is always recognizably the work of one writer and a cultural product of the structures of Elizabethan or of Jacobean England. Or rather it is that and it is more than that. The Verona of Romeo, the Illyria of Viola, the Rome of Julius Caesar, the Athens of Timon are historically designated in the sense that they have the specific settings they have. But at the same time these settings (with direct allusions to and characters drawn from contemporary London and provincial life) are fictive embodiments of the social situation of late Elizabethan and Jacobean England. There are even plausible grounds for arguing that after writing *Henry V* Shakespeare was forced to switch to non-English settings because in mid-1599 the authorities had clamped down on the contemporary representation of English history by banning all books on it; and it might well have been dangerous to write in such pointedly critical ways of the *English* monarchy. Whatever the setting, therefore, it is contemporary England that remains the focus for the plays and gives them their urgency – a world undergoing radical and radically disorientating transformation, as the forces of a collapsing feudal system and the forces of competitive individualism met and collided in the struggle for economic and political power.

These are crucial contexts for the understanding of Shakespeare. And I do not believe we can afford to ignore what the plays continually register – that historically this was a period during which the medieval world order and its economic system was giving way to the pressures of capitalism. The phenomenon is clearly definable at different levels in all European countries – a pattern of change and upheaval dictated by economic conditions which gave power and influence to the rising merchant class and to the expanding markets set up to facilitate trade with the Orient and the Middle East, which made the accumulation of 'independent' wealth possible. Indeed, in Elizabeth's England, with private enterprise 'given the benefit of hitherto unheard-of protection, the acquisitive economy rose uninterruptedly and the spirit of profit-making connected with it embraced the whole nation. Everybody who was economically mobile indulged in speculation' (Hauser 1962: 137).

But this age of 'national ascent and economic prosperity' (Hauser 1962: 140), with its ruthless appetite for power, was also an age of deepening political and religious unrest among the oppressed. As Dollimore (1985: 77) observes, there was

> a constant fear among those in charge of Elizabethan and Jacobean England that dissatisfaction might escalate into organized resistance. This anxiety surfaces repeatedly in official discourse: any circumstance, institution or occasion which might unite the vagabonds and masterless men – for example famine, the theatres, congregations of the unemployed – was the object of almost paranoid surveillance.

Thus it is not surprising to find Sir Francis Bacon (1914: 23) reflecting in 1597 on 'the causes and motives of seditions' and listing them as

> innovation in religion, taxes, alteration of laws and customs, breaking of privileges, general oppression, advancement of unworthy persons, strangers, dearths, disbanded soldiers, factions grown desperate; and whatsoever in offending people joineth and knitteth them in a common cause.

And the remedy was to ensure 'that the treasure and money in a state be not gathered into few hands. For otherwise a state may have a great stock, and yet starve. And money is like muck, not good except it be spread.'

But money was not spread. It remained in too few hands, encouraging 'the multiplying of nobility and other degrees of quality', including 'an overgrown clergy' and 'the devouring trades of usury, ingrossing, great pasturages, and the like' (Bacon 1914: 23). And there is much evidence to support the contention of the anonymous writer of *The Mirror of Policy* (1598), that in the Elizabethan age 'to live under monarchy is very dangerous and to be feared, considering the frailty of man, and the great liberty that kings have to do what they like, whether it be good or evil' (Moretti 1983: 47). It comes from many sources, including the archives of London and the records of Philip Stubbes (1583) and John Stow (1605, 1631). And nowhere are the harsh injustices of the age revealed with more trenchancy than in Stow's account of the Pouch rebellion of 1607, a major uprising of the people of Middle England against enclosures, which was only suppressed by armed forces led by the highest officers of the state. According to Stow (1631: 892), the people had risen up 'in this riotous and traitorous manner . . . chiefly because it has been credibly reported unto them by many that of late years there were 340 towns decayed and depopulated'.

Which is to suggest that late Elizabethan and Jacobean England, far from being in a condition of 'comparative settlement' (Cruttwell 1970: 113) and of 'spiritual unity' (1970: 135), was a society in crisis, undergoing fundamental change. And it is evident from any close examination of the major writers of the period, as Dollimore (1984: 5) confirms, that 'the response of the drama to crisis was not a retreat into aesthetic and ideological conceptions of order, integration, equilibrium, and so on; on the contrary, it confronted and articulated that crisis, indeed actually helped to precipitate it'.

This is above all true of Shakespeare's work, which, in its constant probing of the grounds on which the struggle for power is fought out, can be described as an insistent quest for what might constitute, in Edward Bond's words, 'the rational nature of political development and the rational structure of history' (1978: x). And from at least *Henry IV* onward, it is increasingly obsessed with a sense of crisis, focusing again and again, with metaphors of disquieting intensity, on the ways in which the deceits of power and of corrupt authority, of ambition, appetite and will, 'the insane root / That takes the reason prisoner' (*Macbeth*, I. iii), breed unrest, revolt and derangement in the whole body politic.

Of course, it is not possible to link the actual events of the time (such as the 1607 rising referred to above) in any direct way to the imaginative concerns of the dramatist. But the parallels that abound in the plays of this period would appear to demonstrate beyond doubt that Shakespeare was only too acutely aware of what was going on around him. They have an edge of actuality about them. The indignation and the urgency thrust out at us from the text with the immediacy of things personally witnessed. 'What, art mad?' says Lear.

> A man may see how this world goes with no eyes. Look with thine ears: see how yond justice rails upon yond simple thief. Hark, in thine ear: change places, and, handy-dandy, which is the justice, which is the thief? (*King Lear*, IV. vi)

And who can doubt that when, in *Timon of Athens*, Shakespeare represents Timon digging for roots and finding gold, he is making some sort of fundamental comment on the conditions of his own world – that spirit of competitive rivalry which, breaking the bonds of a decaying feudalism, had given licence and incentive to the New Men of Europe – the adventurers, the traders, the merchants, the businessmen, the controllers of the markets; men for whom 'policy sits above conscience' (*Timon*, III. ii), and who, making will 'the scope of justice' (V. iii) in the ruthless acquisition of wealth, were taking over positions of authority and power in the state.

This is, of course, already to offer a particular interpretation of the text – a response, that is, in which certain assumptions and conclusions come to seem inevitable. For Shakespeare himself, writing so perilously and subversively close to the sources of political and social power at a time of crisis and transition, was involved in a similar process, faced with the challenge of responding to the potentialities of a situation, and developing it in one direction or another, in one direction *rather* than another. Which means that in the end it is the terms of this process which give an interpretation its cogency and logic – the evidence embodied in the metaphorical and the dialogic terms in which each play is enacted, as determined by the indisputable conditions which provide it with its own political and social context to define the argument and the action of the play.

Take *Hamlet*, which, like all the works of these years (1597–1608), explores a situation of dangerous instability and unrest brought about by the misuse of power and authority. From the opening lines it is established that Denmark is in a state of warlike preparation, with 'strict and most observant watch' set on the castle and people working round the clock to produce ships and weapons for war. This is not because of the murderous act which brought Claudius to the throne, since as yet no one knows about it; but because Fortinbras of Norway is threatening the country. Indeed, Shakespeare is careful to make the determining political issue clear; for it seems the dead King Hamlet 'was and is the question of these wars'. When in the first scene Horatio answers the questions of Marcellus, he reports how King Hamlet had killed Fortinbras of Norway over a territorial dispute, and that as a consequence Fortinbras's son has mobilized an army (described here as 'a list of lawless resolutes') 'to recover of us, by strong hand / And terms compulsatory, those foresaid lands / So by his father lost'.

One would have supposed that such events, which have their own persistent comment to make on the claustrophobic action of the play and which are the cause of such feverish activity, would have registered even with Hamlet. But, as Shakespeare makes clear from the start, Hamlet has no interest either in the politics of this seemingly tangential dispute or in Fortinbras; and he shows no sign of recognizing the striking parallels that exist between Fortinbras and himself – two men of roughly similar age and position, each with an uncle on the throne, and each seeking (in his own way) to avenge a father's death – which is the more surprising in the light of the fact that it was Hamlet's *own* father who had killed King Fortinbras.

There would be no excuse in any ordinary sense for him not to know what is going on, since he is at least physically present in court when Claudius confirms the presence of Fortinbras on the frontier, 'colleagued with the dream of his advantage'. But that is not the point. In what provides a strangely *ironic* parallel with Fortinbras, Hamlet is also a kind of absent presence, but in this case passive, irresolute, self-preoccupied, psychically disabled, shut away, having 'that within which passeth show'. No doubt he hears the sound of Claudius's voice announcing he has written to Fortinbras's uncle asking him to restrain his nephew and despatching Cornelius and Voltimand to convey this message to old Norway; but if so he is clearly not listening. And though he is not actually present when this embassy returns in Act II, Scene ii with the news that Fortinbras has promised 'never more / To give the assay of arms' against Denmark, it would quickly have become common knowledge in the court, bringing about an immediate lessening of tension; but to Hamlet it means nothing. As for the request of Fortinbras for 'quiet pass' through Denmark in his action ' 'gainst the Polack', this manoeuvre is decisively confirmed when (in Act IV, Scene iv) Fortinbras appears in person for the first time, on 'a plain in Denmark'. And here, significantly, he just misses (perhaps even avoids) meeting Hamlet, who (by sheer chance) turns up on his way to England, and is left to question one of the soldiers, from whom he innocently accepts that this force of armed men is off to contest nothing more than 'a little patch of ground / That hath in it no profit but the name'.

What is extraordinary about all this – the apparently peripheral course of the dispute, the absent presence of Fortinbras, the calculated strategy of his movements on the borders of Denmark, this determined, resolute will to action – is the manner in which it frames and defines Hamlet's distractedness, his political *naïveté*, his metaphysical confusion, his inability to grasp the logic of what is happening. But above all it signifies the tightening and closing of the circle around him, even as the psychic pressures of what Freud has identified as his Oedipal obsession are intensifying within him. Hamlet, in other words, is seen to be unable to break out of the trap of his subjective conditioning. The fact that he should have chosen to act against the hated Claudius by invoking the substitute realities of theatrical charade and followed this diversionary tactic by turning on his mother, and in the process killing (by mischance) someone else's father, demonstrates how little he is in control of anything, let alone himself. So one should not expect him to be in any state to make comparisons or parallels between himself and Fortinbras. And yet it is surprising that he does not, considering the *closeness* of the parallels. And the fact that Shakespeare even makes the point of having Hamlet *himself* attempt a comparison underlines the extent of his failure to make connections; for he talks of the actions of Fortinbras as if they were taking place in another world, on another planet. Straddled between illusion and reality, intent on his own dilemma, driven to 'thinking too precisely on the event', his response to the presence of a Norwegian army in Denmark is merely to ask 'Why yet I live to say this thing's to do', believing he has greater 'cause and will and strength and means / To do't' than Fortinbras – whose own father does not seem to count since Hamlet sees him risking 'fortune, death and danger' for nothing more significant than 'an eggshell'. He then swears to act resolutely, like Fortinbras! But having already submitted to being sent to England, he tamely goes. And returning later (after his hazardous journey) he is discovered philosophizing in the graveyard, where he improvises action by leaping into Ophelia's grave.

The Wittenberg scholar, the psychically disassociated son, the alienated thinker, is clearly not the kind of man to set things right. Not only does he have no aptitude for politics; he is incapable of exploiting the potential strength of his position, however 'loved of the distracted multitude' (IV. iii), either to his own advantage or the state's, for indeed the idea of the state and what it might require of its leaders hardly exists for him. Caught up in a world he does not understand and can only react subjectively to, he continually misreads or acts wrongly on the evidence. As a man of goodwill, that is, he has disaster in the bloodstream. By 'accidental judgements, casual slaughters, . . . purposes mistook', in Horatio's summing up (V. ii), he reduces his world to ruins, to a kind of *grand guignol* scene of carnage, which might almost be described (but for its malign and tragic overtones) as melodrama or black farce.

And into this, with perfect timing, heralded by the 'warlike noise' of his army, steps Fortinbras, already prepared to take over, the political man of action coming to claim his rights in the kingdom. ('The rest is not silence', as Zbigniew Herbert's Fortinbras puts it, 'but belongs to me' (1979: 21–2).) There is no more to be said – except perhaps to note that Fortinbras, though absent for most of the play, has never been very far in his strategic pursuit of justice from where he now stands. Not that it can be said that justice has been seen to be done; for the silence that hangs over the dead is heavy with ambiguities and unanswered questions and thwarted possibilities. A deadly closure has been imposed upon the poisonous atmosphere of the Danish court. The king who killed a king who killed a king is dead, and the surviving son assumes control. So this, it seems, even in face of such melancholy wastage, is not the end. It is, in a sense, a beginning; for the struggle goes on. Now other questions will have to be asked, and new answers attempted. In the objective terms of Shakespeare's art, the material world, the world of history, time and change, of power and the limits of power, have become involved in a demystifying vision of what there is to be fought for in society. Here, ultimately, it is not the ineffectual and deadly actions of individuals that command the narrative, however central a part they play in it, but the forces, the defining conditions, the contradictory dialectical energies that dictate their actions (Heinemann 1985: 206).

This is nowhere more starkly presented than in *Timon of Athens*. For the insistent theme of this play is the manner in which money, 'the visible god . . .

that speak'st with every tongue, / To every purpose', corrupts and perverts human character, and sets men against each other, 'that beasts / May have the world in empire' (*Timon*, IV. iii). In this sense, *Timon* is by far the bleakest of the tragedies – vituperative, polemical, more overtly a tirade, less contained within its characters, with more of the raw and unabsorbed shock of feeling left exposed in the form and the language than in any other play of the period, as if Shakespeare had not fully distanced into art the impact upon him of his appalled sense of the realities of his world. For in parts the play itself seems open, raw, exposed – Timon's disaffection is absolute, his hatred uncompromising, and there is no healing of the wound in him. As Burke (1963: 25–6) has written:

> Timon can round things out by translating any particular situation into its corresponding absolute. If he digs for roots to eat ('Earth, yield me roots'), they become universal roots. If in the course of thus digging in the 'common mother' he finds gold, it is an ironically Midas-like gold, fecal gold, gold as defined by the touch that turns everything into the idea of corruption . . . It is a foul form of gold that this play features, a quality of imagery in keeping with the fact that invective itself is a way of fighting by means of verbal filth, and Timon's absolute brand of it would besmear all mankind.

In its historical-social setting, the play directly reflects the atmosphere of the princely courts of the Renaissance and their lavish patronage. But appetite, greed, the will to possession, seem to have become the dominating impulses, sweeping aside or making subservient to their aims all higher considerations, all principles, all moral values. And the confrontation between this new world and the old is violent and irreconcilable, signifying the break-up of the intricate ceremonial order of the medieval world and the assertion of an aggressive individualism based upon new sources of wealth in the period of primitive accumulation.

The influence of money dominates the play, a corroding, alienating force that transforms everything into its opposite. Timon sets himself not against the wills of other individuals, but against Athenian society as a whole and the naked self-interest that determines its priorities. And he does so not in any spirit of active opposition, like Alcibiades, but by withdrawing in disgust from all contact with his world. Unlike any other major character in Shakespearian tragedy, he stands alone – a man without family and without close relationships of any kind, even without a definable past, 'As if a man were author of himself / And knew no other kin', as Coriolanus says of himself (*Coriolanus*, V. iii). He is there like some natural physical element, not to be explained away, or evaded.

So we are forced to ask ourselves why Shakespeare should have found it necessary to create a character quite so adamant and forbidding. And surely at least part of the answer has to be that he was driven to do so as a consequence of the questions he *himself* had found it necessary to ask about his world and its concerns. Timon veers from one extreme – of lavish Renaissance hospitality, of unstinting generosity and trust – to the other; from 'I could deal kingdoms to my friends, / And ne'er be weary' (*Timon*, I. ii) to 'Destruction fang mankind' (IV. iii). His disillusionment is total because his illusions about the people who surround him and the convictions they profess are so disastrously wrong. He *believes* implicitly (and blindly, since Apemantus warns him bluntly enough) that Athenian society is as free and as magnanimous as he is. Being, as he thinks, wealthy in his friends, he believes 'we are born to do benefits', and asks what 'better or properer can we call our own than the riches of our friends?' Indeed, he is visibly moved by what he calls the 'precious comfort' of having 'so many like brothers commanding one another's fortunes' (*Timon*, I. ii). But this naive utopianism, being the irrational indulgence of a rich man addicted to giving and himself seduced by the bargaining power of money, leaves him totally exposed. For what he fails to appreciate is that his Athens is not the Athens of Pericles or Solon, but a mean city of commerce whose social order is determined by and built upon the ethics of the marketplace. Its citizens are motivated, that is, by thrift and calculation, a commonsense eye to profit; and to them it is simple foolishness to behave like Timon, to give away one's property 'upon bare friendship without security' (*Timon*, III. i). They understand their world for what it is; money and the accumulation of riches are the priorities – money, not men. Men merely reflect their economic position. If they are rich they are powerful. But deprived of the power their property gives them they become worthless, as the Poet puts it at the start of the play. Man as man – simply as a human being – does not count.

It is the shock of the realization of this that turns Timon into a hater of mankind. For him there is no middle ground. His disillusionment is as extreme as his illusions. He is in a sense a kind of innocent, an indulgent idealist caught uncomprehending in a world in which money rules and policy dominates conscience – a world he does not understand because he has misinterpreted it from the start, attributing to it values that are no part of the way it actually functions.

Under such conditions, discovering such disease of fellowship, such 'base metal' (*Timon*, III. iii) among those he had thought of as his friends, it is hardly surprising that a man like Timon should have turned his back upon society and preferred – 'a dedicated beggar to the air, / With his disease of all-shunned poverty' – to walk 'like contempt, alone' (IV. ii). And it is significant that, apart from the praise given by the three strangers to Athens who appear briefly in Act III, and the response of Alcibiades, recognition of his goodness and humanity should come only from the dependent poor. As Timon's loyal steward comments, after sharing out among his fellow servants the little that remains of his master's household money:

Who would not wish to be from wealth exempt,
Since riches point to misery and contempt?
Who would be so mock'd with glory? or to live
But in a dream of friendship?
To have his pomp, and all what state compounds,
But only painted, like his varnish'd friends? (IV. ii).

It is the bitterness of Timon's feeling against these 'mouth-friends', these 'glass-eyed' flatterers, which lets loose the withering force of his invective. He is a man who has lived, and acted, on the mistaken assumption that the riches of friendship and community are the true wealth of society, and that material wealth is there to be shared; because with him 'promise and performance' are indivisible. He is therefore the more shattered to discover what his friends are really like – how these people, finding he has nothing more to offer them, 'slink all away', leaving only 'their false vows with him, / Like empty purses pick'd'

Timon, IV. ii). Disgusted with Athens, he retires to the woods, to live on roots and berries, refusing all inducements to return – choosing instead to die alone, offstage, his last words bleak with negation, hinting that he is planning to bury himself alive in an act of ultimate protest:

> Come not to me again: but say to Athens,
> Timon hath made his everlasting mansion
> Upon the beached verge of the salt flood,
> Who once a day with his embossed froth
> The turbulent surge shall cover: thither come,
> And let my grave-stone be your oracle.
> Lips, let sour words go by and language end:
> What is amiss, plague and infection mend!
> Graves only be men's works, and death their gain!
> Sun, hide thy beams! Timon hath done his reign (*Timon*, V. i).

Such bleakness as this, such unqualified harshness, makes it difficult to come to terms with *Timon of Athens*. Yet come to terms with it we must if we wish to understand Shakespeare, his psychology, the nature of his vision of reality, the pressures and difficulties he was himself having to contend with. And what he makes of *Timon* is a strange, starkly contrasted morality play whose hero stands deluded in 'a dream of friendship', with his court a charade he believes in (or refuses not to believe in) till shocked awake by economic ruin, confronted by the reality – a man stripped bare, a 'naked gull' in a world of self-seekers, hypocrites, 'mouth-friends'; who from then on, in the wreckage of all he had built his life upon, is driven to the opposite extreme, deranged by the baseness. For now he sees how deeply money rules; and his discovery seems to strike at the very roots of human interchange and to contaminate every decency. Gold, as he puts it, 'solder'st close impossibilities, / And mak'st them kiss'. It turns everything into its opposite – makes 'black white, foul fair, / Wrong right, base noble, old young, coward valiant' (*Timon*, IV. iii). Or, as Marx (1975: 378–9) spells it out, commenting on these very words:

> What I as a man cannot do, i.e. what all my individual powers cannot do, I can do with the help of *money*. Money therefore transforms each of these essential powers into something which it is not, into its opposite . . . [It] is the external, universal means and power . . . to turn imagination into reality and reality into mere imagination . . . [It] appears as an inverting power in relation to the individual and to those social and other bonds which claim to be essences in themselves. It transforms loyalty into treason, love into hate, hate into love, virtue into vice, vice into virtue, servant into master, master into servant, nonsense into reason and reason into nonsense . . .

Thus the creative intuition of Shakespeare probes the incipient roots of a new and ruthless order bred from the ruins of the old, and reaches beyond its growing forms to anticipate in the outrage of Timon's vision the social inhumanities of nineteenth-century capitalism and the deep-running force of Marxian indignation. For Timon's language is unremitting in its condemnation of the 'smiling, smooth, detested parasites', these 'vapours and minute-jacks' (*Timon*, III. vi), who have betrayed him. It is a language that registers the death agonies of the medieval order, the break-up of a world in which (as Timon wills it in his impotent curse):

    Piety and fear,
    Religion to the gods, peace, justice, truth,
    Domestic awe, night-rest and neighbourhood,
    Instruction, manners, mysteries and trades,
    Degrees, observances, customs, and laws (IV. i).

seem to be collapsing against the thrust and force of 'confounding contraries'. It is the language of Lear writ large, made absolute, pushed beyond the limit, beyond help or hope, launched against mankind in a general indictment.

But this is only one man's voice – not the end, though it may seem so. It is one man's end, the collapse of a particular world within the larger world of social action. And Shakespeare moves beyond it into the transformed atmospheres of the last plays, generating out of his profound grasp of the dialectic process of reality a new and affirmative sense of the complexities and puzzlements of the human struggle, which (through the interaction of dream and actuality) looks toward the making of a new world.

Of course, it may not be possible quite to claim for Shakespeare, as Rickword (1978: 171) could for Milton 30 years on in the midst of revolutionary upheaval, that 'he ardently embraced the progressive world outlook as against the cosmogony of dying feudalism'. But in probing the underlying contradictions of his age he went a long way towards preparing the ground for the revolutionary changes to come. And the subversive dialectic that is at work in the plays is such as to reduce the institutional structures of the existing order of Jacobean society to an ideological battleground. For if this system can be described by Ulysses as 'the ladder to all high designs', it seems (after Shakespeare's tragedies have done their work) more and more to resemble the kind of place where, in Yeats's desolating view of his own life, one has no choice but to 'lie down where all the ladders start, / In the foul rag-and-bone shop of the heart' (1950: 391–2).

And yet not so. For the differences between the two are fundamental. The Shakespearean dialectic refuses such nihilism and the metaphysics on which it is built – for Yeats 'a mound of refuse or the sweepings of a street', etc. Shakespeare's images, to start with, are not built on 'heart-mysteries' or on 'dream', the subjective longing for a non-existent unity. They are 'masterful' not 'because complete' or because they 'grew in pure mind', the substanceless fictions of idealism; but precisely because they are founded on the incompleteness and impurity of material reality, as determined by the changing laws of causality and of history, in terms of which the subjective energies of human beings are seen to be caught up in cross-currents of action and reaction, the struggle to make sense of their lives. And as such, they contain within them the seeds of the future and its objective conditions.

Thus, what we have to get into focus is how this process works. And as readers, teachers, critics of the late twentieth-century, we have to decide what meanings we can make it yield, faced with questions and ambiguities that are likely to demand from us new and radical ways of reading our world and of probing its mystifying surfaces for conditions which will enable us to come to some sort of understanding of our world so that we can build beyond despair or disillusionment or privacy. That is the telling witness of the plays. They urge upon us, and subvert us into, questions that expose, reveal and transform the conditions on which we construct our concepts of reality.

4

Eliot on Milton:
an ideology masked

It seems to have been T. S. Eliot's intention in writing about Milton, as F. R. Leavis (1984: 27–8) confirms, to 'put a decisive end' to the influence of a poet whose concept of the functions of literature in society he finds himself at almost every level diametrically opposed to. Fortunately, Milton has managed to survive this attack, which can now be seen (in the context of the ideology that lay behind it) to demonstrate the incompatibility of Eliot's position, as a largely undeclared apologist for certain kinds of institutionalized conservatism, with that of Milton the revolutionary, the iconoclast, the heretic. But it remains a fact that, for at least three decades, 'the result of [Eliot's] work as critic and poet was', in Leavis's words, 'Milton's dislodgement' (1984: 12).

Under these conditions, it is, I think, necessary to re-examine the underlying terms of Eliot's argument. Indeed, his commanding place in the literary establishment, and the influence his work is likely to continue to have in the formulation of literary judgement among those who are coming to English literature for the first time, make such a reassessment indispensable, especially since Eliot himself assumed objectivity in attempting to redirect the course of literary history.

He begins his 1936 essay, 'A Note on the Verse of John Milton', with the admission that 'Milton is a very great poet indeed'. But the sentence in which this tribute appears is so qualified as to make it little more than a gesture to the conventions. And it is immediately followed by a series of unsubstantiated assumptions which, purporting to reflect the objective judgement of cultivated opinion at large, amount to a casual (and insidious) attempt to undermine the grounds on which Milton's reputation rests. In these terms, Milton is not only 'antipathetic' as a man. He is also, from almost every other point of view – the moralist's, the theologian's, the psychologist's, the political philosopher's, and even by 'the ordinary standards of likeableness as a human being' – 'unsatisfactory' (Eliot 1953: 123). In other words, as Leavis (1984: 12) has it: 'Mr Eliot, in his well-known pontifical way, says "Milton's no good." '

In a later essay on the same subject, written in 1947, Eliot (1953: 132) confesses to a desire to rectify certain 'errors and prejudices' about Milton that 'have been associated with my own name', in the belief (as he adds with insinuating modesty) 'that my only claim upon your attention, in speaking of Milton or any other great poet, is by appeal to your curiosity, in the hope that you may care to know what a contemporary writer of verse thinks of one of his predecessors'. The confession is disarming and deceptively frank; for Eliot shows little interest in correcting his 'errors'. On the contrary, the drift of his argument very soon confirms the original strictures; and he takes them further still in refuting the very conditions of Milton's 'intellectual mastership' (Eliot 1953: 145). For even his declaration that 'the practitioner should be able, when he is the right poet talking about the right poet, to make an older masterpiece actual, give it contemporary importance, and persuade his audience that it is interesting, exciting, enjoyable, and active' (Eliot 1953: 133), is turned against Milton. After all, Eliot has already made it obvious that in this case he is *not* the right poet talking about the right poet, but that he is the *wrong* poet, talking about a poet he has a profound distaste for; and thus it is clearly his purpose to demonstrate that Milton's work does *not* have contemporary importance. To which end he sets out to isolate the poetry from all it is associated with – the historical, political and social contexts, the arguments and ideas which are essential to an understanding of the work – thus *dislocating* it from all that it *means*, all that might 'persuade his audience that it is interesting', and so on. 'Of no other poet', he says, 'is it so difficult to consider the poetry simply as poetry, without our theological and political dispositions, conscious or unconscious, inherited or acquired, making an unlawful entry' (Eliot 1953: 134).

This, of course, tells us a good deal more about Eliot's antipathies than it does about Milton. It seems to be saying that before you can ever get to the point of considering Milton's poetry 'simply as poetry' (whatever that means), you will have to get through (and finally discard) some rather unpalatable and painful issues which ought never to have been there in the first place because they are extraneous to the poetry. But what it is really saying is that Eliot finds these issues distasteful and embarrassing, because Milton insists on their being considered as inseparable from the poetry and lawfully identified with it. There is only one way of dealing with them, and that is to avoid any sort of declaration which might expose Eliot to inconvenient questions and force him to present a less palatable image of himself than he is willing to permit. How otherwise to explain why he should choose to dismiss as unlawful both his own and Milton's theological and political dispositions (which are obviously crucial to any honest discussion of Milton's work), and to take the safe course of attending to 'the poetry for the poetry's sake' (Eliot 1953: 135) – though this, too, is found to reveal 'a perpetual sequence of original acts of lawlessness' (1953: 141).

Eliot seems virtually to be inviting us to empty out not only the substance of Milton's argument in *Paradise Lost* (the politics and the religion) but also its intent and form – the urgency of the great questions raised throughout the poem and the dramatic energy generated in the language by the intellectual demands of the argument, its interactive and colliding forms of logic and invective. What is to be made of 'poetry for the poetry's sake' in the context of, say, God's scathing judgement of man in Book III, which in its bitterness and disillusionment casts an acid shadow of dispute across the events of the poem and at the same time profoundly echoes Milton's own feelings about 'the general defection of a misguided and abused multitude' (1958: 244) in the aftermath of the defeat of the English Commonwealth. This tells us, we recall, that it was (in God's words)

> they themselves decreed
> Their own revolt, not I: if I foreknew,
> Foreknowledge had no influence on their fault,

Which had no less proved certain unforeknown.
So without least impulse or shadow of fate,
Or aught by me immutably foreseen,
They trespass, authors to themselves in all,
Both what they judge and what they choose; for so
I formed them free, and free they must remain
Till they entrall themselves; I else must change
Their nature, and revoke the high decree
Unchangeable, eternal, which ordained
Their freedom; they themselves ordained their fall (Bk III. 116–28).

What gives this passage its harshness and resonance is the precise controlled placing of the words, the ways in which they interact (foreknew on 'fault', 'unforeknown' on 'fate', 'foreseen' on 'free', the double action of 'decree' and 'ordain'), and the tone of gloom and anger that informs them. Or, to put it the other way round, it is the meaning, the political-religious implications of the argument, that generate the energy of the language; the form and the content working upon each other that create the impact.

But Eliot, refusing to countenance such issues, refuses what Fredric Jameson (1981b: 315–16) identifies as 'the historically actual and indispensable task of understanding the relations between religion and politics', and 'of proposing a political reading of *Paradise Lost*, or better still, of de-concealing the political content of *Paradise Lost*' – the ways in which it records and enacts 'the moment of the failure of revolution, the dissipation of the revolutionary ethos, the re-appearance of the old institutions and business as usual (or, in other words, in the language of the time, of sin)'. For Eliot (1953: 134), all such considerations are illegitimate because they involve subjective, party views about a Civil War which has apparently 'never been concluded' and must therefore be classified as harbouring dangerous emotions and dismissed from the agenda. For instance, he claims (in veiled reference to his own disposition) that 'it is now considered grotesque, on political grounds, to be of the party of King Charles'; (why?), even as 'it is now, I believe, considered equally grotesque, on moral grounds, to be of the party of the Puritans; and to most persons today the religious views of both parties may seem equally remote' (Eliot 1953: 134–5). But this is no argument at all. It offers a sequence of preconceived opinions which make arbitrary (and quite irrational) distinctions between the political and the moral, and suggest that the religious conflicts involved are almost completely irrelevant. One finds oneself wanting to know precisely why the grounds are political in the one case and moral in the other; for in fact both parties took up political, moral *and* religious positions which it is possible to recognize (even today) as interactive. As for their grotesqueness, this merely confuses and distorts the issues that are at stake, and serves as an excuse for not facing up to them. And it is surely difficult to argue, on the one hand, that 'the religious views' of seventeenth-century parties are 'equally remote' from most of us today while, on the other, asserting that 'the Civil War of the 17th century . . . has never been concluded', and that 'English society was [then] so convulsed and divided that its effects are still felt' (Eliot 1953: 134).

What we in the twentieth century have to do is to confront the disturbing contradictions that Eliot seems so intent upon suppressing and try to answer them. The reader of Milton should openly concern himself, that is, with 'the historically actual and indispensable task of understanding the relations between religion and politics' (Jameson 1981b: 315–16), both as they appear in Milton's work and as they affect us, in terms of the conflicts and contradictions they enact and embody; since these are what *Milton* is concerned with. But this is not the way Eliot *wishes* to read Milton. For him, politics, morality and religion must first of all be carefully neutralized, defused, separated from the poetry, made safe. For indeed, as he points out in defence of his ideological intent, the passions aroused by such issues remain 'unquenched' – that is to say, dangerous, explosive, open to question, controversial; and 'if we are not very wide awake their smoke will obscure the glass through which we examine Milton's poetry' (Eliot 1953: 135), thus preventing us from seeing the poetry as it is, simply as poetry.

Having (as he thinks) dismissed all that is extraneous to the 'purity' of the 'poetry', to all that clouds it ('So much for our prejudices', he concludes, on the subject of 'taking sides' (Eliot 1953: 135)), Eliot (1953: 137) now considers himself free to deal with 'that view which attends to the language, the syntax, the versification, the imagery', and by this means to be in a better position to demonstrate to his readers 'the unwholesomeness of Milton's influence' (1953: 135) as a poet. Though the questions of context – of the momentous events and the momentous issues Milton's work is inseparably involved in – cannot be so easily detached from any study of the language, it is enough for Eliot that he believes he has conjured them away. And here again unsubstantiated assumptions and preconceptions (both his own and those of Johnson and of Middleton Murry, who are cited to prove his case) are permitted to serve as substitutes for serious consideration of the issues that the poetry so challengingly embodies. The argument proceeds, that is, on the same terms as he had used in 1936, by separation. For it seems that 'when we try to understand the rules of [Milton's] own point of view' – that is, make an attempt to understand what he is actually saying – 'we isolate him'; and it is apparently only 'when we measure him by outside standards' (by which Eliot means not the conditions and values of his own time but 'the standards of language and of something called poetry' (Eliot 1953: 131) that he can assume his place in the proper context of history. This line of argument has the queerest kind of inverted logic, for it suggests that to dislocate the poet from the conditions that dictate 'the rules of his own game' and to measure him by the abstract ahistorical standards of language alone is to locate him. But it serves its purpose – to ensure that all discussion of the substance and content of Milton's work shall be effectively dissociated from the poetry and reduced to irrelevance.

In this light, one is startled to recall that it was Eliot (1953: 117) himself who proclaimed in his 1921 essay on Dryden that 'in the seventeenth century a dissociation of sensibility set in, from which we have never recovered; and [that] this dissociation, as is natural, was due to the influence of the two most powerful poets of the century, Milton and Dryden'. So striking is this pronouncement, especially when set in the context of Eliot's own treatment of Milton, that one is driven to question whether it does not apply with more cogency to Eliot than ever it might have done to Milton; for there are whole areas of debate (involving politics and history and socio-economic change) which Eliot refuses to countenance as valid to literature and which he throws a mystifying veil of silence over or simply dismisses. Nevertheless, for the Eliot of 1947, 26 years later, the phrase 'retains some validity' (Eliot 1953: 139). Not that there is any attempt to explain what he means by either the first or the second assertion. He simply makes the comment that 'if such a dissociation did take place' – and it is significant that he does not refute the assumption – 'the causes are too complex and too profound to justify our accounting for the change in terms of literary criticism. All we can say is, that something like this did happen;' – ah! so it did! – 'that it had something to do with the Civil War; that it would even be unwise to say it was caused by the Civil War, but that it is a consequence of the same causes which brought about the Civil War;' and that, finally, 'for what these causes were, we may dig and dig until we get to a depth at which words and concepts fail us' (Eliot 1953: 139–40).

This is as much as to say that, since it would be fruitless to try to identify these causes, it would be equally fruitless to concern ourselves with the controversies and conflicts they gave rise to. The implication is simply that the dissociation took place and set in; that it had something to do with the Civil War, and that it did great damage to English literature – on which grounds, as far as the literary critic is concerned, 'words and concepts fail us'. But the uncomfortable fact of the matter is that words and concepts are the substance out of which poetry is made, and that John Milton dared to use them as instruments (in prose as in verse) to locate and to confront what was happening in the England of the Civil War and afterwards. It is no answer to the problem of understanding such issues to admit that you are at a loss for words! (Perhaps this is where dissociation of sensibility sets in!) Milton himself *demands* that we make at least as great an effort as he did in his work to respond to the ferment of ideas and of contradictory passions that was unleashed by the Civil War.

But Eliot has no intention of responding. Indeed, in his attempt to isolate the poetry and to get us to accept that any other course 'will obscure the glass through which we examine' it, he successfully avoids the embarrassment of having to deal with the John Milton who set out in pamphlet after pamphlet to argue for the rights and liberties of a free commonwealth against its enemies; who 'found himself defending his country in the face of Europe' (Hill 1979: 170) and writing 'with incomparable energy and eloquence', as Macaulay (1862: 27) puts it, on most of the great issues that came to a head during this period; who took his stand on the side of the people 'in one general and brotherly search after Truth' (Milton 1958: 177). All this, it seems, is not only distasteful to one who does not share such views, but irrelevant; for here, anyway, words and concepts fail us. It is only the poetry that matters – the poetry abstracted from its content; the *language* of the poetry. For this leaves Eliot free to use words and concepts and to take up his case against Milton – to argue the impact upon his work of that vitiating dissociation of sensibility which he professes to be incapable of defining, and to discover for himself 'what permanent strictures of reproof may be drawn' (Eliot 1953: 140) from a study of the poetry.

The fact that he chooses to call Dr Johnson in as witness to 'the essence of the permanent censure of Milton'(!) (Eliot 1953: 140) is no accident; for here is 'the right critic talking to the right critic'. As Hill (1979: 468) observes, Dr Johnson was only too well aware of the relevance of Milton to 'the revival of political activity among the lower and middle classes' of his time. Johnson 'smelt danger and roundly denounced Milton's ideas', in much the same tone and with much the same diversionary tactics as Eliot (1953: 140–1) himself employs, attacking as unarguable the 'perverse and pedantic principle' on which 'he had formed his style', which 'in all his prose is discovered and condemned' and in the poetry comes out as 'a Babylonish dialect, in itself harsh and barbarous'.

It is characteristic of the intellectual dishonesty of both Johnson and Eliot that they should treat the language as an abstract phenomenon, an instrument voided of content, entirely divorced from the issues and arguments it deals with. Not only does such an approach reduce Milton to nonsense; it enables Eliot and Johnson to avoid the necessity of dealing with ideas which they find profoundly unacceptable. So for Eliot (1953: 145) 'the emphasis is on the sound, not the vision, upon the word, not the idea'. It is the *music* that is 'the most conclusive evidence of Milton's supreme mastery', rather than 'his grasp of any *ideas* that he borrowed or invented'. Ideas are to be relegated to the margins, to be kept out of the debate at all costs. For Milton's ideas were a direct challenge to the universalizing renunciatory spirit of Eliot's conservative philosophy, which emphasizes the autonomy of sensation and of feeling and the suppression of all that might bring into question this autonomy.

It may *be* that Milton 'never resolved his tensions – between liberty and discipline, passion and reason, human love and God's providence, the necessity of individualism and the necessity of society, radicalism and elitism'. (Hill 1979: 464). But he did not flinch from them or turn away, withdraw from the field. He went on fighting for interchange and interaction, for 'the liberty to know, to utter, and to argue freely according to conscience'. Nor did he prevaricate, or use his powers of intellectual discourse to misrepresent. He stood his ground as a 'middling' voice for revolutionary change and for those 'conscious and conscientious men who in this world are counted weakest' but without whose unwavering courage 'the force of this world' cannot be defeated. And he stood firm behind the 'glorious rising commonwealth' he had helped to lay the foundations of 'against the abjured and detested thraldom of kingship' (Milton 1958: 223).

For Milton it is fundamental that 'if we look but on the nature of elemental and mixed things, we know they cannot suffer any change of one kind or quality into another, without the struggle of contrarieties' (Hill 1979: 253), and that 'that which purifies us is trial, and trial is by what is contrary' (Milton 1958: 158). In other words, there can be no separation between the ideas as they emerge from the contexts that generate them and the poetry, since the poetry is the vessel for the ideas; and ideas are embodied, engaged and fought out through the *movement* of the language, both in the prose and in the verse.

Take the vitriolic disgust with which God, in Book X of *Paradise Lost*, answers Satan's exultant proclamation of triumph over Adam and Eve. Clearly this cannot be made sense of as pure aesthetics. For if the disgust is there in the words, in the monosyllabic thrust of verb and noun – 'See with what heat these dogs of Hell advance / To waste and havoc yonder World . . . to lick up the draff and filth / Which Man's polluting sin with taint hath shed / On what was pure; till, crammed and gorged', etc. (Bk X. 616–17, 630–2) – these words do not function in a vacuum. They are part of the *action* of the poem, its dramatic content, its intellectual structure. And they are the product of what Milton had forged out of his own experience of social conflict, the ferment of incompatible ideologies he had engaged with, and the bitter defeat he himself had suffered at the hands of his enemies after 20 years spent 'musing, searching, revolving new notions and ideas wherewith to present . . . the approaching Reformation' (Milton 1958: 174) against tyranny and superstition.

But for Eliot (1953: 122) it is this very sense of 'contest' that 'does great damage to the poetry of Milton'. In his view, clearly, Milton's work doesn't 'point in the right direction' (1953: 129). It points in all the wrong directions. Or rather, as he confesses with casual irritation, he cannot feel that his 'appreciation of Milton leads anywhere outside of the mazes of sound' – though a line or two later these content-less mazes appear to give him 'a glimpse of a theology that I find in large part repellent, expressed through a mythology which would have better been left in the Book of Genesis, upon which' – in Eliot's peremptory view at least – 'Milton has not improved' (1953: 130).

The incompatibility is, it seems, complete, though Eliot nowhere substantiates the grounds for that incompatibility. Instead, he adopts a tone of superior detachment which suggests that his view is the view of all normative, reasonable discourse. But this, of course, is a mere stance, for the mildness and the appeal to common sense are a mask that conceals the destructive intent of the prose. Milton may be described as 'a very great poet indeed', but the lamentable defects with which Eliot burdens him persistently argue the contrary, and as Leavis (1984: 12) puts it, 'proclaim Milton's annihilation to the world'. Of this there can be no doubt. This very great poet is antipathetic as a man. He is unsatisfactory as moralist, theologian, psychologist and political philosopher. He is 'a man whose sensuousness, such as it was, had been withered early by book-learning' (Eliot 1953: 124); whose 'language is artificial and conventional' (1953: 125); who fails to 'infuse new life into the word'; and whose writing as a whole has the effect of a 'dead language' (1953: 126). Furthermore, 'a Miltonic sentence is an active complication' of 'what was previously simplified and abstract thought' (1953: 127); and, most damaging of all, it is suggested, in a tone characteristic of its author, that 'Milton may be said never to have seen anything' (1953: 129); and that 'he had little interest in, or understanding of, individual human beings', because it seems that 'in *Paradise Lost* he was not called upon for any of that understanding which comes from an affectionate observation of men and women' (1953: 143).

There can be no mistaking the intent of such barbed language. It is directed towards neutralizing Milton; and Eliot goes about his task with insidious effect by emptying Milton's work of its meaning and its content. There can be no way forward from such a stance. If it is your purpose to set up 'permanent strictures of reproof' which you have already assumed 'to be made by enduring laws of taste' (Eliot 1953: 140), you cannot expect to persuade anyone that you are serious about discovering 'conclusive evidence of Milton's supreme mastery' (1953: 145) – especially when the terms on which you are prepared to discuss the *validity* of Milton's verse are slanted in such a way as to deprive it of all those qualities considered essential to 'greatness'.

Eliot (1953: 142) declares, of the poets he admires, that they 'teach us what to avoid, by showing us what great poetry can do without – how bare it can be'. But for Eliot (1953: 128) Milton is not bare: he is 'rhetorical'. Apparently, whatever 'inner meaning' there is (and Eliot will have nothing to do with *any* sort of meaning in Milton) 'is separated from the surface, and tends to become something occult, or at least without effect upon the reader until fully understood' (Eliot 1953: 129). But that is the way Eliot chooses to read it, occlusively; and since all he chooses to 'glimpse of the meaning' he finds 'in large part repellent' and unrewarding (that is, politically and theologically unacceptable), it is hardly surprising that he should conclude that Milton (for all his 'intellectual mastership') doesn't lead 'anywhere outside the mazes of sound' (Eliot 1953: 130).

Admittedly, he appears to be aware in the last two pages of his 1947 essay of the need to repair the damage he had done to Milton's reputation with his fits of 'irresponsible peevishness' (Eliot 1953: 148). But though he has the grace to concede that poets might after all have something to learn from 'poetry which has a definite meaning', and that they might even find it useful to 'devote some study to Milton' now that they can approach his work 'without danger' (1953: 148), such praise as this is offered so grudgingly and with such superior aloofness as virtually to cancel itself out, leaving the chill shadow of Eliot's condemnatory judgement hanging over the words.

That judgement is, in a sense – even in the very perversity of its intent – a tribute to the defiant conviction and the generosity of Milton's contribution to the struggle for revolutionary change in seventeenth-century England, and to his resilience in coping with the consequent defeat of all he had worked for, which made him 'the greatest English revolutionary who is also a poet, the greatest English poet who is also a revolutionary' (Hill 1979: 4).

Happily, such strength as this is not diminished by the innuendoes and 'slanderous darts' of its detractors. What it does is to bring out the worst in them; and this is as true of F. R. Leavis as it is of Eliot. For Leavis (1984: 11) deplores what he calls 'the almost complete triumph of the "social" (or the "associational") values over those which are the business of the critic', and finds himself in substantial agreement with Eliot. Indeed, in his pursuit of the critic's business, it is Eliot's cue he takes, carefully steering clear of any sort of reference to the contexts in which Milton's work has its urgency and significance. *His* associations are to abstract standards of poetic practice that everywhere exclude the 'social' and the historical, and that, in the absence of any discussion of what Milton was writing in terms of, confirm Eliot's ideological stance. According to the bent of Leavis's argument in 'Mr Eliot and Milton' (and it is a bent which displays preconceptions similar to those of Eliot), *Paradise Lost* was quite simply 'an undertaking . . . for which Milton had no qualifications', and which exhibited him as 'ludicrously unqualified to make even a plausible show of metaphysical capacity' (1984: 23). It seems that what the poem 'illustrates is that lack of self-knowledge which gives us such obvious grounds for saying that in Milton we have to salute character rather than intelligence'. In other words, he had 'no "grasp of ideas", and, whatever he may suppose, is not really interested in the achievement of precise thought of any kind'; which suggests to Leavis that he lacked above all 'the kind of energy of mind needed for sustained analytic and discursive thinking' and that therefore 'the peculiarities of the Miltonic genius'(!) (1984: 26) are such as to defy 'clarity and outline' (1984: 27) and to make for 'inconsistency, muddle and vagueness . . . a great capacity for unawareness' (1984: 27).

In face of such crippling deficiencies as these, it is no more than a step to adduce the pernicious influence of 'the Miltonic inheritance' as it 'appears in varied forms in the great poets of the Romantic period . . . and emerges from

that period to a subtle predominance in the Victorian age' (1984: 29). History, it
seems, can be dispensed with; for though Leavis (1984: 29) agrees that it 'would
take a long separate essay to provide the historical backing' for his assertions, he
nowhere attempts such a task. Even when the opportunity presents itself in the
essay 'Literature and Society' – an attempt to refute the Marxist approach to
literature – he chooses instead to argue against the Romantic critical tradition
('an atmosphere of the unformulated and vague' (1984: 183)) in terms of T. S.
Eliot's 'idea of Tradition', of Literature as 'an organic form', 'an organic order';
stressing 'not economic and material determinants, but intellectual and spiritual', as the expression of 'an inherent human nature' (Leavis 1984: 184). And in
these terms history vanishes; and with it the influence of the changing conditions
of material existence which determine not only the ways in which people's lives
arc shaped but also the cultural products of their thinking, including literature.
In its place stands the undifferentiated ahistorical order of Literature in the
upper case, an order dependent on 'the mind of Europe' (Leavis 1984: 184); an
Upper Case Tradition which in Eliot's work conveniently embodies 'the social
aspect of creative achievement as the Romantic attitude didn't' (Leavis
1984: 185), and is apparently to be discovered at its purest in the archaic
folk-world culture of the Southern Appalachians, which is described as 'a
civilization or "way of life" (in our democratic parlance) that was truly an art of
social living' (1984: 190).

The drift of this argument, which assumes a standpoint of undisputed
authority, and thrives on the suppression of other arguments inconvenient to it,
is surely specious. Not only does it settle for a safe and dematerialized aesthetic as
against the unsafe, suspect, socialized aesthetic of Milton, Blake, Wordsworth
and Shelley; it harks back to a depoliticized and ahistorical past, into which
Leavis injects the values and standards he considers relevant to the business of
the critic, at the same time relegating all historical definition, all controversy and
all sense of struggle, all causes and interests outside 'the individually experiencing mind' (1984: 186) to the sidelines, as injurious to cultural health.

Areopagitica might almost have been written to answer the thinly disguised
antipathy and animosity that lies behind the arguments of critics like Eliot and
Leavis. Not only does its controlled polemic demonstrate a precisely targeted
'grasp of ideas', and 'an energy of mind' capable of sustaining 'analytic and
discursive thinking'; its discourse is directed specifically against those among the
initiated who – concerned at all costs to protect their secretive and mystifying
assumptions from being got at – would set themselves up as men of sober and
impartial judgement, as custodians of value. And in its plea for 'the trial and
exercise of truth', for 'the liberty to know, to utter and to argue freely according
to conscience, above all liberties' (Milton 1958: 180), it is part of that revolutionary process by which, as Milton (1958: 220) later puts it, 'the Parliament of
England, . . . judging kingship by long experience a government unnecessary,
burdensome, and dangerous, justly and magnanimously abolished it, turning
regal bondage into a free commonwealth'.

· In other words, like all Milton's work, including *Paradise Lost* and *Samson
Agonistes, Areopagitica* stands as an open challenge and a reproach to the ideology
of exclusion and of contempt for the common people which defines the social
thinking of such detractors as Eliot and Leavis. Hence their condemnation, the
'cautelous enterprise' (Milton 1958: 160) of these 'inquisiturient bishops'

(1958: 154) of the literary establishment. ' 'Tis their own pride and ignorance', Milton might have answered them, even as he answered the authorities of his own time, 'which causes the disturbing, who neither hear with meekness, nor can convince; yet all must be suppressed which is not found in their syntagma'. For 'they are the troublers, . . . the dividers of unity, who neglect and permit not others to unite these dissevered pieces which are yet wanting to the body of Truth' (Milton 1958: 176). And in Milton's view, we can never come 'to discover onward things remote from our knowledge' (1958: 175) by 'forced and outward union' (1958: 176), but only by 'disputing, reasoning, reading, inventing, discoursing, even to a rarity and admiration, things not before discoursed or written of' (1958: 179).

Milton was, of course, directly responding to the Ordinance for the Regulation of Printing passed by the Puritan majority in Parliament in June 1643, which seemed to him, after the earlier Act abolishing the machinery of state censorship, not only a piece of reactionary legislation but also an insult to adult human beings, and as such unacceptable. Today – in the context of repressive laws enforced in countries throughout the world against freedom of the press, and government attempts in Britain itself to restrict the right of access to information regarded arbitrarily as affecting 'national security' – his argument has lost little of its urgency and relevance. The 'excremental whiteness' (Milton 1958: 158) of officialdom – as registered in the bland hypocrisies of Whitehall, the evasiveness of lobbyists for nuclear power, the downright lies of the Ministry of Defence, or the government's manipulation of public opinion to maintain one set of values for display and another for use – is still with us, debasing and besmearing society. So Milton's anger and scorn, his mockery and derision against those who would 'starch us all into . . . an obedient unanimity' (1958: 173), continues to strike home, whether he is arguing in favour of unlicensed books and the temptations they expose us to, or against Plato, who with 'many edicts to his airy burgomasters . . . seems to tolerate no kind of learning but by unilateral decree' (1958: 161). For Milton has important things to defend and the confidence to know what it is he is speaking for. In *his* concept of the quest for truth 'good and evil . . . grow up together almost inseparably; and the knowledge of good is so involved and interwoven with the knowledge of evil' (1958: 157) that we need to keep ourselves open to all kinds of influence in order to be able to make distinctions and to keep them clear. But you would never get any sense of that from the responses of Eliot and Leavis, perhaps because they know he comes too close to showing them up. As Milton (1958: 168) says: 'Truth and understanding are not such wares as to be monopolised and traded in by tickets and statutes and standards'. They are to be tested in open debate, risked against the contradictions of reality:

> I cannot praise a fugitive and cloistered virtue, unexercised and unbreathed, that never sallies out and sees her adversary, but slinks out of the race, where that immortal garland is to be run for, not without dust and heat. Assuredly we bring not innocence into the world, we bring impurity much rather; that which purifies us is trial, and trial is by what is contrary (1958: 158).

Milton insists, in other words, on the dialectic process which connects the aesthetic concerns of literature with intellectual activity – the rigorous demands of 'universal learning' – and the imperatives of social practice – 'the promotion', that is, 'of real and substantial liberty'. Indeed, it could be said, with Rickword (1978: 176), that 'his repudiation of the authority of any tradition not tested by experience, his assertion of the adequacy of human reason, are essential steps in the process of intellectual emancipation'. And it is precisely the liberating challenge of this process which critics like Eliot and Leavis find so unpalatable, because it calls into question the underlying assumptions on which they take their stand. For their methods are very different. Whenever they encounter ideas and forms of argument inconvenient to their views, they simply sidestep them, invoking the forces of arbitrary custom and tradition to justify their action, thus reinforcing the separation of principle and practice, the mystification of the social process.

It was to combat mystification and to liberate the intellectual energies of the English people from the shackles reimposed upon them by the authorities that Milton launched his attack upon censorship, which to him seemed 'the greatest discouragement and affront that can be offered to learning, and to learned men' (Milton 1958: 166). Because for him this 'wardship of an overseeing fist' (1958: 167) is an insult, not only 'to the written labours and monuments of the dead', the achievements of learning, but also to 'the whole Nation' (1958: 168), and to the 'common people' no less than to the learned. For

> if . . . we dare not trust them with an English pamphlet, what do we but censure them for a giddy, vicious, and ungrounded people; in such a sick and weak state of faith and discretion, as to be able to take nothing down but through the pipe of a licenser? (1958: 169).

The issue is crucial. This 'tonnaging and poundaging of all free-spoken Truth' (Milton 1958: 173) can only hinder and retard the nation. What is needed is 'a little generous prudence, a little forebearance of one another, and [then] some grain of charity might win all these diligences to join and unite in one general and brotherly search after Truth' (1958: 177). Whereas if, on the contrary, 'we think to regulate printing, thereby to rectify manners, we must regulate all recreations and pastimes, all that is delightful to man'. And how shall we do that, Milton (1958: 174) asks, without laying ourselves open to 'incredible loss and detriment', and threatening the liberty even of the poet and the artist. 'No music must be heard, no song be set or sung, but what is grave and Doric. There must be licensing dancers', and 'all the lutes, the violins and the guitars in every house' must be examined. 'And who', he asks, 'shall silence all the airs and madrigals that whisper softness in chambers?' What kind of 'sober workmasters' will there have to be to make sure our garments are 'cut into a less wanton garb'? And 'who shall regulate all the mixed conversation of our youth, male and female together, as is the fashion of this country?' (1958: 162).

Milton's answer is characteristic. He invokes Adam, to whom God gave reason, or 'freedom to choose, for reason is but choosing' (1958: 163). And in the England of 1644, a kingdom shaken 'with strong and healthful commotions to a general reforming' (1958: 183), the right to freedom of choice had become a necessary precondition for the defence of liberty, which the English people were ready to accept, as 'a Nation not slow and dull, but of a quick, ingenious and piercing spirit, acute to invent, subtle and sinewy to discourse, not beneath the reach of any point, the highest that human capacity can soar to' (1958: 176).

The generosity of this tribute may seem, in the light of subsequent events, to have been misplaced; but there is no doubting it. Milton was giving voice to the exhilaration of a people on the move, a people who were to take their revolution much further than this before it would begin to founder and congeal and go sour and turn back upon the 'noxious humour' (1958: 220) of kingship it had freed itself from. And *Areopagitica* communicates the heady promise of that exhilaration. 'We reckon more than five months yet to harvest', Milton (1958: 177) writes; 'there need not be five weeks; had we but eyes to lift up, the fields are white already'. And though it was to take another five *years* before that prophecy could be borne out, the energy and commitment that lay behind the vision was in the end to prove irresistible, and in 1649 – with the abolition of the monarchy and the House of Lords – to bring the revolutionary struggle for the Commonwealth to its moment of fruition.

This high point of achievement, this laying of the foundations for a new kind of society, was not (as we know) to last more than three or at the most four years. There were too many unresolved contradictions, and it was not in the interests of the new masters of England, the propertied gentry who now dominated Parliament and the Council of State, to permit the revolution to be extended any further than it had gone. Nor were there enough people with sufficient stamina, courage and conviction to keep the momentum going and lay the proper grounds for the 'ready and easy way' forward. There were too many of those whose 'cold and neutral and inwardly divided minds' (Milton 1958: 176) remained closed to such prospects and the liberating energies they encouraged. Their aim, on the contrary, as Milton puts it in *The Ready and Easy Way*, writing 'the last words of our expiring liberty' (1958: 244), was to keep 'the People . . . well fleec'd for their shearing' and 'easiest to be kept under. And not only in Fleece but in Mind also sheepishest' (1958: 242).

Of course, it is no accident that *Paradise Lost* should have been conceived and written during the period of gloom and despondency immediately before and after the Restoration. Not only had Milton's choice of theme long been a central preoccupation of seventeenth century religious thinking. It so closely parallels what was happening in the England of that time that we cannot doubt it was a conscious choice on Milton's part – his response to crisis, his way of coping with 'the magnitude of the disaster that had overwhelmed the poet' (Hill 1979: 356) and of finding his way forward beyond the collapse of his hopes and ambitions. To this end, the calm and distanced tone he adopts as narrator are an essential counterbalance. For it is clearly a central purpose of the poem to face up to fundamental questions Milton could no longer hope to find answers for in the external world. The intensity and resonance of the arguments about time, history, freedom, revolt, betrayal, guilt, responsibility, obedience, power, etc., are sufficient proof of that. And if the poem is cast in the form of religious dispute – religious ideology being 'the master-code in which issues are conceived and debated' (Jameson 1981a: 317) – this master-code also operates as a politics: the politics of the War in Heaven, of the disputes between God and Satan, of the Fall itself, which reflect and embody the politics of revolutionary England and its defeat, even as Heaven resembles earth. True, as Fredric Jameson (1981a: 320) observes, 'religion is not a cognitive but a figural mode', and that 'figuration . . . is thus the source of the limits and distortions which the religious or theological master-code imposes on its political content. Yet we must add that the political strength of religion is also intimately related to this very ambiguity'. And if religion 'is the master-code of pre-capitalist society', then we in the twentieth century should 'be able to read its major themes as mystified or distorted anticipations of secular and even scientific preoccupations which are ours today' (1981a: 319).

But Milton's God and Milton's Satan, as represented in the polemic splendours of the language and the thrust of the action, are also great dramatic figures, with ideological ambitions and obsessions. In fact the arguments of the two arch-protagonists are so deeply implicated in the creative ambiguities of Milton's own struggle to resolve the problems of tyranny and revolt, of authoritarianism and liberty, as sometimes to make it seem that Milton *was*, in Blake's words, 'of the Devil's party without knowing it' (1974: 150). And then there is the almost pagan pre-lapsarian beauty of the Garden, on which Milton lavishes all his powers of sensuous description; and the poet's loving treatment of the sexuality of Adam and Eve, which makes 'a carnal heaven on earth' not only imaginable but palpable, close, immediate – a place 'to be sought for here and now by means which in Milton's time have become irredeemably political' (Jameson 1981b: 330); though such is the poignancy and anguish of the actual context in which it is being written about that Milton's embodiment of the lapse itself and its aftermath put it (like the England of his hopes) impossibly out of reach, leaving Adam and Eve (in the ideological trap of their condition) only 'the fallen privatised world of individual belief and individual salvation' (1981b: 333).

Meanwhile, Milton himself was left to the tender mercies of those who triumphed in 1660. Their campaign (like that of their cultural inheritors) had sought to neutralize and to silence the blind poet for daring to hold to his convictions and to go on – 'though fallen on evil days' (*Paradise Lost*, Bk VII. 25), surrounded physically and figuratively by darkness – to write his vision of Adam emparadized and of the courage of Adam and Eve turning to face the future beyond loss in a world of history, time and death.

But Milton has survived. And he puts his enemies to shame, precisely *because* of the generosity and significance of his vision of human freedom, and the tenacity with which he held to it not only through the decades of revolutionary ferment and the years of the Republic, but also beyond the fall of the Commonwealth, in the bitterness of defeat, 'Blind among enemies, O worse than chains, / Dungeon, or beggery, or decrepit age!' (*Samson Agonistes*, 68–9); but knowing 'that suffering for Truth's sake / Is fortitude to highest victory' (*Paradise Lost*, Bk XII. 569–70), and attempting through his work to prove it.

5

Blake's witness: keeping the divine vision in time of trouble

What is now proved was once only imagin'd
The Marriage of Heaven and Hell

To ask ourselves what kind of contribution the millenarian writings of William Blake might have to make to the fundamental issues that confront us in the late twentieth century, at this particular crisis point in the history of the British people and of the dispossessed everywhere, we need first of all to get into focus the scope and range of Blake's imaginative response to a revolutionary age, and then to decide how closely the challenging questions he asked of his world can be applied to ours. This is a task that demands not only an intimate knowledge and understanding of Blake's work as a whole – its Utopian urgency, its Christian antinomianism, its anger and energy, its generosity of spirit, its multiple perspectives, its dialectic – but also an awareness of the historical and cultural perspectives which give his work its place in the context of the struggle between the antithetical forces of progress and reaction which have so fatefully determined the course of human history and are today as threatening as ever.

Indeed, if we are to make any attempt to register the significance for us of Blake's dialectic grasp of the issues of his age, we shall need to set the revolutionary conditions of that age into focus with at least two other great climax points of revolutionary change which have brought these forces into open confrontation – the one fought out in England in the 1640s and 1650s for the establishment of a republican commonwealth, the other in Russia in 1917 in the midst of a devastating capitalist war, with all that has followed. For each is linked by the logic of history and the conditions of economic and political change with the French Revolution; and each represents (in its own terms) a funda-mental challenge to the operative system of ruling-class power and an attempt to bring about an irreversible Utopian shift in the *balance* of power towards the embodiment of what may be called a just society.

Of course, there are those who see in Blake little more than an obscure Christian mystic. Or there are those who would argue that the bulk of his work (and the Prophetic Books in particular) is at once too difficult, too eccentric and too puzzlingly obscure to be of much relevance to the kinds of problems we are faced with today. What are we to make, it might be said, of this naive Utopianism, this attempt 'to restore what the Ancients called the Golden Age' (Blake

1974: 605), made at the very start of the Industrial Revolution by a poet who, in T. S. Eliot's words, 'lacked . . . a framework of accepted and traditional ideas' and was afflicted with 'a certain meanness of culture' (1953: 171); or who, as Leavis (1984: 187) condescendingly puts it, 'had ceased to be capable of taking enough trouble' to know what he was doing? Blake (1974: 621) himself may have claimed that 'every word and every letter is studied and put into its fit place'; that 'all are necessary to each other'; that 'Poetry fetter'd fetters the Human Race'. But Leavis sees nothing of this, or of the astonishing scale and richness of Blake's quest. For him, the work 'failed to develop' (Leavis 1984: 187). And 'again and again one comes on the thing that seems to be neither wholly private nor wholly a poem. It seems not to know what it is or where it belongs, and one suspects that Blake didn't know' (Leavis 1984: 188).

Then there are those who would claim that today we are living in a world that demands the harshest realism – nuclear, post-industrial, dominated by an abstract machinery of technology which has enabled the institutionalized forces of reactionary power to organize the economic resources of the world towards a militarization of earth and space, a balance of terror grounded on weapons of mass destruction and of monopoly interests pursued at immense cost to the social needs and interests of the majority. And though it could be pointed out that this process of exploitation was already actively at work in Blake's time, and that Blake himself clearly understood what was going on, those who consider themselves realists would no doubt answer that too much has happened since his time, that things have gone too far for us to share much common ground with the kind of Utopian positives Blake proposed. For them, in the wake of 1914, the 1919 blockade of socialist Europe, the rise of Fascism, of Hitler and Stalin, the horrors of Auschwitz, Hiroshima and Vietnam, it seems 'Mere anarchy is loosed upon the world, / The blood-dimmed tide is loosed, and everywhere / The ceremony of innocence is drowned' (Yeats 1950: 211); and in Yeats's post-1914 pessimism the very idea of the New Jerusalem becomes a terrifying nightmare that derides all aspiration. No. In the pessimism and despair of the modernist ideology that dominates our literature ('I can connect / Nothing with nothing. / The broken fingernails of dirty hands' (Eliot 1969: 70)), the world is as it is – a place to be lamented, squabbled over, exploited and profited from, or bitterly endured, if that is possible, as a place for the fallen; a place in which there can be no hope that things will change for the better; where there is no Jerusalem, and we are condemned to endless waiting for an absent god, surrounded by 'the immense panorama of futility and anarchy which is contemporary history' (Eliot 1965: 681).

Inevitably for such realists as these, Utopia is always and literally a Nowhere-World, whether spelt backwards or forwards, and whatever News may be filtered through to us (in the Morris sense) from a transformed future. The world as it is is more likely to become what the disillusioned liberal-humanists, inventors of a *Brave New World* or a *1984* or a *Darkness at Noon*, see it becoming as they surrender to the pressures of the operative system and its all-pervading ideologies – the power of the monolithic Party, or the power that money has to speak all tongues, to 'turn imagination into reality and reality into mere imagination' (Marx 1975: 368) – under the domination of which people are reduced to mere instruments, bits of machinery, commodities, things. In the context, that is, of a world that appears to be firmly in the hands of the manipulators and executives of the absolutist state (with its nightmare de-basements) or of an economic and social order based upon the laws of monopoly and finance capitalism – in which (as it seemed to Orwell in 1940, sunk in the depths of a wartime pessimism from which he never recovered) 'progress and reaction have both turned out to be swindles' (Orwell 1961: 158) – the gloom of the modernist sensibility is hardly to be wondered at. The devastating impact of the Second World War was, after all, a consequence of the destructive logic of capitalist competition and its unremitting antagonism to all forms of socialist transformation – which it pursued with a ruthlessness that brought into being the deadly perversions of Fascism and Nazism, and which in the end the people of Europe (and large parts of the rest of the world) had no choice but to fight. And this in turn was to create a post-war balance of cold war power dominated by the immense potential forces of American capitalism and a socialist state order pushed to totalitarian extremes by the long struggles from 1917 onwards of a siege economy and the unimaginable sacrifices imposed upon people and resources first by Stalin and then by a war not of its making. Now, 45 years on, almost any concept which looks beyond the actual to register the possibility of 'that which does not yet exist' is likely to be either derided as impossibly naive or mad, or attacked as a dangerous perversion of reality. Socialism, as its enemies are always saying, is all very well in theory; but it has not worked in practice, and never can.

Such pessimism is now so endemic in Europe as to define the very conditions of the crisis of contemporary culture. Generated by the divisive interests of the capitalist order, it pervades and colours the work of many of our most distinguished writers. Pound, Yeats, Eliot and Joyce all in one way or another reacted against the challenge of the struggle for progressive change, driven by political and economic pressures into positions of regressive retreat. Instead of siding with the revolutionary movements in European society, they remained equivocal voices for, even when they did not actively confirm, a political order which from 1917 onwards proceeded (wherever it could) to isolate what it called 'the creeping disease of socialism'. Indeed, Yeats, Eliot and Pound even saw the Right (including the Fascists) as guardians of the civilizing institutions of Europe, while Joyce chose to distance himself from involvement by withdrawing into aesthetic subjectivity.

This cultural crisis has its roots in the transformation of Europe after the Congress of Vienna, and the triumph of industrial capitalism after 1848, which led to the mid-nineteenth-century insulation of culture from politics and the economic imperialism that set so many artists apart from the people and from the material conditions that determined their place in society. It is a crisis which has still not been resolved because too few of those who have influence in our contemporary culture have made any thoroughgoing attempt (in spite of the efforts of writers like Brecht, MacDiarmid, Grassic Gibbon, Rickword, Edward Thompson, Raymond Williams and Edward Bond) to reach across the barriers set up between the classes by the divisive logic of the capitalist system.

Of course, it could be said that the artist does not choose pessimism or acquiescence or aesthetic neutrality, the path that leads to despair, the 'end of the word'; that he has no choice but to portray the world as it is; that the path he moves down – Joyce's internalizing aesthetic or Beckett's 'self-consuming play' – is chosen for him by the world he lives in. But fortunately we have enough witnesses to demonstrate that there are other paths, and that the artist does have the power to choose to use his or her voice to speak alternatives and fight for the potentialities of 'the other' in the self, to 'keep the winter count' against the odds.

This is the kind of choice that was made by Blake. Though his world did its best, callously and indifferently, to break him, it failed. He was not a pessimist. He saw the world as it was, but he was not content to accept it as it was; for he saw it also as it *could* be. 'Look up! look up!' he cries out in his call for freedom at the end of *The Marriage of Heaven and Hell*. 'O citizen of London, enlarge thy countenance! O Jew, leave counting gold! return to thy oil and wine. O African! black African! (go, winged thought, widen his forehead.)' (Blake 1974: 159). And that is his significance. He refused to be seduced or defeated by the operative powers that ruled his world. In an age of violence and perverted idealism very like our own, he saw things deeply but clearly; and nothing – not neglect or failure or his increasing sense of isolation – could diminish that insight or destroy his happy confidence in himself or his assurance that he was fundamentally right in his commitment to and his vision of humanity. He was a fighter; and his concept of the New Jerusalem – grounded as it was on a dialectic of the contrary states, the 'severe contentions of friendship and the burning fire of thought' (1974: 738) – enabled him to stand firm against surrender, and to generate a language of expectation, defiance and struggle on which to build for a creative alternative to the bankrupt imperatives of the existing order. For him the choice was clear: 'To labour in Knowledge is to Build up Jerusalem, & to Despise Knowledge is to Despise Jerusalem & her builders' (1974: 717).

But he did not delude himself that this struggle could be won without the fullest awareness of what was involved or without the deepest commitment. This he had learned from his earliest experience of the conflicts of his world and its injustices. And one has to remember that the England he lived in was at war for almost half of the 70 years of his life, while its people suffered greatly from the repressive policies of Pitt and Liverpool. The Seven Years War (1756–63) gave way to the American War of Independence, which led almost directly into the French Wars, in a deepening scale of conflict which – more and more international, ideological, ruthless – were to become the economic wars of Napoleon's Decrees and the British Orders in Council, which affected everyone, and especially the poor. 'This is the sequence', as Jacob Bronowski (1972: 14) writes, 'step by step more inhuman and more mechanical, which made Blake identify his two hatreds – hatred of the dehumanised machine (the "dark Satanic Mills"), and hatred of war'.

Such understanding of the forces that were at work in his world generated and released in Blake the antagonistic energies which gave him his sense of urgency. But he knew he had to set himself to master and to harness them; that anger was not enough. And so, confronted by the divisiveness and cruelty of the system under which he lived, he took the trouble to equip himself with the kind of knowledge that would give him the power to build and to think forward. Yes, 'the tygers of wrath are wiser than the horses of instruction' (Blake 1974: 152); but both were necessary.

And books were indispensable. The Annotations he made to those in his possession clearly demonstrate the attentiveness and vigour of his reading, his intellectual curiosity, the depth and perceptiveness of his response to other writers and thinkers – Homer, Virgil, Dante, Chaucer, Bacon, Newton, Milton,

Voltaire, Gibbon, Rousseau, Lavater, Swedenborg, Reynolds, Wordsworth, to name only the most obvious. For him, words and ideas were always actively a source of inspiration, sharpening and clarifying what he felt and thought, and providing him with the instruments he needed for his lifelong tasks as a writer. 'I must create a system', he says in *Jerusalem*, 'or be enslaved by another Man's. / I will not Reason & Compare: my business is to Create' (Blake 1974: 629). In other words, he knew what he was after. In a characteristically illuminating note to a Reynolds Discourse, he observes:

> I read Burke's Treatise [on the Sublime and Beautiful] when very young; at the same time I read Locke on Human Understanding and Bacon's Advancement of Learning; on Every one of these Books I wrote my Opinions, and on looking them over find my Notes on Reynolds in this Book are exactly Similar. I felt the Same Contempt and Abhorrence then that I do now. They mock Inspiration and Vision. Inspiration and Vision was then, and now is, and I hope will always Remain, my Element, my Eternal Dwelling place; how can I then hear it Contemned without returning Scorn for Scorn? (1974: 476–7).

As for his response to Milton, clearly Blake recognized a profound affinity, and no doubt read everything he could lay his hands on. Not only does Milton become a central figure in the Prophetic Book named after him; the mythological system of that book includes an account, as Geoffrey Keynes points out, 'of Milton's descent to earth and his entry into Blake, so that their minds could commune intimately together' (Blake 1974: 909); and Milton himself, coming down into Blake's garden at Felpham, is given the great climactic speech at the end of the Book on 'Self-annihilation and the grandeur of Inspiration' and the casting off of 'all that is not Inspiration' (Blake 1974: 533).

It was no accident that Blake should have felt such affinity. For like Blake, as Hill (1979: 467) puts it, 'Milton's radicalism was still rooted in the Bible, in Christian heresy, in the dialectical thinking of the pre-Newtonian age'. And like Blake, Milton was a man of political commitment, who started out with great hopes for the future and refused to surrender them even in defeat. But above all, Milton takes his place in Blake's register of heroic prophets and fighters for change because of what he stood for during that other great age of revolutionary upheaval and Utopian hope. For he was, after all, 'the greatest English revolutionary who is also a poet, the greatest English poet who is also a revolutionary' (Hill 1979: 4). Not only does he speak as a man who had dedicated all his imaginative powers to ensuring 'the certain hopes of a speedy and immediate settlement for ever' of 'a firm and free commonwealth' (Milton 1958: 223). Having defended regicide 'in the face of all Europe' for the sake of this great concept, in 1659–60 he defiantly 'proclaimed his republicanism from the house-tops' (Hill 1979: 207); and then went on to register through the myth and metaphor of the Fall of Man his visionary sense of fortitude in confronting the anger and bitterness of defeat, as Adam and Eve turn their faces towards the world, 'Where'er our day's work lies' (*Paradise Lost*, Bk XI. 177), carrying with them their sensate knowledge of their pre-lapsarian world, 'a Paradise within' (*Paradise Lost*, Bk XII. 587), to be remade out of the struggle between truth and falsehood and the memory of freedom.

Blake does not fail to respond to the implications of this aborted but continuing challenge. 'Rouse up, O Young Men of the New Age!' he writes in the

Preface to *Milton*. 'Set your foreheads against the ignorant Hirelings! For we have Hirelings in the Camp, the Court, and the University, who would, if they could, for ever depress Mental and prolong Corporeal War' (Blake 1974: 480).

He does not, that is, forget Milton's vision of the 'glorious rising commonwealth' (1958: 223), fought so hard for over 20 years, nor the spirit in which it was envisaged. For he follows this revolutionary injunction with his great (if greatly misused) poem on the Mental Fight for the building of Jerusalem in England. As Milton (1958: 177) himself had put it in 1643, of a world that had seemed to him at that time so quick with promise:

> What could a man require more from a Nation so pliant and so prone to seek after knowledge? What wants there to such a towardly and pregnant soil but wise and faithful labourers, to make a knowing people, a Nation of Prophets, Sages, and of Worthies? We reckon more than five months yet to harvest; there need not be five weeks; had we but eyes to lift up, the fields are white already.

The splendour of that appeal, its generosity, its trust and hope, may have been misplaced; but it is palpable. As Blake (1974: 481) adds in an epilogue to his poem and to the Preface to *Milton*: 'Would to God that all the Lord's people were Prophets'. It is as if he were registering the sequel to Milton's appeal, 16 years on in *The Ready and Easy Way to Establish a Free Commonwealth*; and his biblical reference has its own ironic echo for the British people in the wake of the 1987 sell-out to self-interest and myopia that put the most reactionary government since Lord Liverpool's in Blake's lifetime back into power. 'If the doors of perception were cleansed', Blake (1974: 154) had written in the 1790s, 'every thing would appear to man as it is, infinite'. The problem, then as today, is that 'man has closed himself up, till he sees all things through the narrow chinks of his cavern'.

Of course, the history of England and the fortunes of the English people had gone through a series of irreversible and fateful changes between the 1640s and the 1780s. Milton's great hopes for the Commonwealth and the Republic to which he had committed himself with such pride and magnanimity and which were to appear to be vindicated with the triumph of 'this extolled and magnified nation' over the feudal absolutism of Charles after 1649 – bringing him to a 'pinnacle of personal fame and success in the years 1649–52, when he was a European figure of heroic magnitude who seemed to shed lustre on the English Revolution and the Commonwealth' (Hill 1979: 197) – were to be cruelly and totally reversed in 1660. And he took the impact of this disaster with the fullest awareness of what was being thrown away. As he comments, with a bitter sense of the shock of betrayal, in *The Ready and Easy Way*:

> That a nation should be so valorous and courageous to win their liberty in the field, and when they have won it, should be so heartless and unwise in their counsels, as not to know how to use it, value it, what to do with it, or with themselves; but after ten or twelve years prosperous war and contestation with tyranny, basely and besottedly to run their necks again into the yoke which they have broken, and prostitute all the fruits of their victory for nought at the feet of the vanquished, besides our loss of glory, and such an example as kings or tyrants never yet had the like to boast of, will be an ignominy if it befall us, that never yet befell any nation possessed of their liberty; worthy indeed, themselves, whatsoever they be, to be for ever slaves . . . (Milton 1958: 227).

And from where he stood at the edge of the abyss – witness to this 'strange, degenerate contagion', this 'after-game of folly' which to him seemed fit to 'render us a scorn and derision to all our neighbours' (1958: 224) – Milton was among the few who understood the enormity of the defeat to all that promised an emancipatory future for England and for Europe. As for us, looking back upon that great missed opportunity from where *we* stand now, we can do no more than guess what kind of influence England might have had on the course of European politics if the forces of reactionary privilege and orthodoxy had not been permitted to reverse the gains of the 11-year Republic and to re-establish the monarchy, and if the Commonwealth had been able to maintain the sense of conviction and purpose that marked its first four years. But there can be little doubt that the country would have developed along very different lines.

This, at any rate, was Milton's view, even in 1660. As he saw it, the educative process engendered by a Free Commonwealth would soon have begun to spread 'much more Knowledge and Civility, yea, Religion, through all parts of the land, by communicating the natural heat of Government and Culture more distributively to all extreme parts, *which now lie numb and neglected*'; and this would eventually have made 'the whole Nation more industrious, more ingenious at home, more potent, more honourable abroad' (Milton 1958: 241–2).

But it was not to be. As Williams (1963: 325) has observed of this melancholy turning point, himself citing the above extract: 'Milton's whole argument is a response to the breakdown, not only of his own hopes, but of a kind of society'; and this argument 'carries the fear of an uneducated people, for Milton sees the Restoration as "the general defection of a misguided and abus'd Multitude" '. Indeed, the factions that had regained control of Parliament by 1660 were not interested in the multitude, however 'numb and neglected'. They were those men who (like the King) wanted the people 'kept under' (Milton 1958: 242) and the riches of their world in the hands of the few. And it was the shrewdest and most percipient among these ruling-class groups who, in the crisis generated by the bigotry and arrogance of James II, were to enter into the secret Tory–Whig pact which brought about the Constitutional Settlement of 1689. So that what came to be known in ideological terms as 'the Glorious Revolution' gave them the constitutional and economic grounds to assert the nation's power as an expansive conservative influence upon the whole of Europe, thus retarding the growth of democracy for 200 years, and at the end of the eighteenth century ensuring England's alignment against the libertarian challenge of America and France, and the creation of conditions for a new and deeper enslavement of its own people.

This was the world that Blake was forced to live in. And if we are to understand anything of the urgency and intensity of his vision of reality, we have to understand what it is he was up against – the atmosphere of increasing oppressiveness in which, from 1791 onward, 'the mind of England was visibly clouding' (Bronowski 1972: 71), and reaction was beginning directly to threaten all who drew attention to themselves as radicals. This was the time when Joseph Johnson was prosecuted, with Tom Paine (a friend of Blake) under the 1792 Royal Proclamation Against Divers Wicked Seditious Writings. It was a time, too, of increasing oppression against the people – with press gangs, hanging laws for crimes against property, enforced prostitution, rising infant mortality, famine, mutiny, and the spread of the factory system bringing new sufferings to the poor. Blake (1974: 200) asks in the darkening climate of the time:

> Why trembles honesty, and like a murderer,
> Why seeks he refuge from the frowns of his immortal station?
> Must the generous tremble & leave his joy to the idle, to the pestilence
> That mock him? who commanded this? what God? what Angel?
> To keep the gen'rous from experience till the ungenerous
> Are unrestrained performers of the energies of nature;
> Till pity become a trade, and generosity a science
> That men get rich by; and the sandy desert is given to the strong?
> What God is he writes laws of peace and clothes him in a tempest?
> What pitying Angel lusts for tears and fans himself with sighs?
> What crawling villain preaches abstinence and wraps himself
> In fat of lambs? No more I follow, no more obedience pay!

Blake did not follow, and he refused to accept or to condone the inhumanities of this world. But he did not ignore them, or try to pretend they did not exist. Recognizing what they were doing to his world, he tried to think his way through them and beyond them. For this was that period in the history of England which, defined by the accession of George III and dominated by the Revolution and the Napoleonic Wars and the deepening injustices of land enclosure and the factory system, came to its climax with the triumph of the conservative powers in 1815. It was an age of ideological confrontation, apocalyptic and ruthless, which created conditions out of which the old Utopian instincts were to reassert themselves in the great dream of equality, liberty and fraternity launched by the Jacobin revolutionaries and spreading across Europe to be registered in the work of its great imaginative thinkers and artists, from Blake and Paine and Wordsworth to Hegel, Schiller, Goethe, Pushkin, Beethoven, Mickiewicz and Byron. For the forces which drove it were motivated by common aspirations in its ideas and inventions, its poetry and its politics, its ways of acting and thinking, as polarized by the upheavals brought about by the movement of industry from village to factory and the deadly contentions of ideological and economic warfare.

Blake lived through it all without flinching, in defiant creative witness to its potentialities and terrors, which is why he stands as such a potent example for us today, faced as we are with pressures and shifts and devastating transformations which have shaken our world to its foundations and have unnerved even the most committed among us. As printer, poet and painter, as artisan-craftsman, he has his roots in that history of social and religious dissent which goes back to John Ball in the fourteenth century and which sprang so vigorously to life in the great period of seventeenth-century revolution that produced Milton, Winstanley, Lilburne and Fox – the Diggers, the Levellers, the Fifth Monarchists, the Ranters, the Quakers. And being from the beginning on the side of the dispossessed as a man who had himself suffered neglect and semi-poverty as a consequence of economic deprivation, he thus registers the threat and force of the injustices of his time with peculiar intensity. And he was able to take the shock of what was happening, to him as to others, because he had the gifts and the temperament to respond creatively – setting himself to sharpen those powers of resistance, those interconnected energies of being in the self, that dialectic awareness, which enabled him to recognize and to understand what was at stake in his world, to remain steady under pressure, and to build for a creative alternative.

Indeed, he spent his whole life working to embody his vision of a renewed and healed world against the evidence of degradation and division brought into being by the intolerable system of ruling-class England and the arrogance of its rulers, 'those cool and cruel and insolent men' (Hampton 1984: 404), as Cobbett called them, who had reduced the labouring classes to a condition in which – 'meagre with famine, sullen with despair, careless of a life', in Byron's graphic words, that their masters valued 'at something less than the price of a stocking-frame' (Hampton 1984: 395) – they were 'compelled to starve quietly' (Cobbett 1967: 351).

This, naturally, is not a view likely to be upheld by those who comment on the period from the standpoint of its affluent beneficiaries. No doubt for them, drawing their own conclusions from the activities of such people as one finds in the pages of a Jane Austen novel, it is possible to assume, with A. D. Harvey (1980: 137), that, 'despite the upheavals of the Napoleonic Wars, most English people above the poorer classes led comfortable and essentially stable lives'. But then most people *were* the poorer classes, and if you are not prepared to count them in on the equation, such an assumption is either meaningless or palpably false. For what Cobbett terms 'National Wealth' can make no sense unless it applies, as he says, to

> the whole of the people . . . the *Commonwealth* or *Commonweal*; and these mean the general *good*, or *happiness*, of the people, and the *safety* and *honour* of the *state*; and these are not to be secured by robbing those who labour, in order to support a large part of the community in *idleness* (Cobbett 1967: 350).

Blake had no doubts about this. He was not to be put off by talk of comfort and stability, the propaganda of the affluent. Being among the poorer classes himself, for him, as for Cobbett (1967: 351), it was 'a mockery to talk of their "liberty", of any sort; for the sum total of their state is this, they have "liberty" to choose between death by starvation (quick or slow) and death by the halter'. And in Blake's view, any equation that left these people out of account would have been unthinkable. Through the voice of Enion-Enitharmon, he says

> I will lament over Milton in the lamentations of the afflicted.
> My garments shall be woven of sighs & heartbroken lamentations:
> The misery of unhappy Families shall be drawn out into its border,
> Wrought with the needle with dire sufferings, poverty, pain & woe
> Along the rocky Island & thence throughout the whole Earth;
> There shall be the sick Father and his starving Family, there
> The Prisoner in the stone Dungeon & the Slave at the Mill.
> I will have writings written all over it in Human Words
> That every Infant that is born upon the Earth shall read
> And get by rote as a hard task of a life of sixty years (Blake 1974: 499).

Through the many voices generated from the dramatic narratives of the Prophetic Books, Blake pits himself against the destructive rule of the 'mind-forg'd manacles' of oppressive power, speaking beyond the self in a dialectic of contrary presences, the conflicting 'others' in the self, which he made the instrument of his mental war against singleness of vision and of his visionary concept of a New Jerusalem – man's struggle to create for himself and for

everyone a world in which 'the feet, hands, head, bosom, and parts of love' could
'follow their high breathing joy' (Blake 1974: 142), and honesty and tenderness
would be valued not as attributes of the weak but as the basis of strength and
community. Though he knew he had no power to change the world he lived in,
he recognized the forces that were at work upon it, and through his art did all he
could from a position of increasing isolation to provide his own blueprints for
what had to be done to transform it. Having understood from the start the
terrible contradictions at the heart of his world – with its 'privy admonishers of
men' calling 'for fires in the city, / For heaps of smoking ruins / In the night of
prosperity and wantonness . . . / That the remnant may learn to obey'
(1974: 247) – he knew them to be man-made, and that they had to be fought
within society.

And the weapons of his mental war against the arrogance and cruelty of the
ruling system – issuing as hypocrisy, greed, law, custom, the machine, what
Blake called 'empire' – are Reason and Energy, Imagination and Intellect
working together. The contraries *must*, he stresses, act upon each other.
Separated, they leave man 'a little grovelling Root outside of himself' (Blake
1974: 632), a *false* self, a Spectre. And this false self

>   is the Reasoning Power in Man, & when separated
> From Imagination & closing itself as in steel in a Ratio
> Of the things of Memory, it thence frames Laws and Moralities
> To destroy Imagination, the Divine Body, by Martyrdoms & Wars (1974: 714).

Which is to say that we cannot trust to reason alone, which is merely 'the bound
or outward circumference of Energy', any more than we can to energy alone,
though 'Energy is Eternal Delight' (1974: 149). We need reason and energy
together. And not only these. Human fulfilment can only be achieved by a
fourfold unity of man and woman: Imagination, Sensate apprehension, Feeling
and Intellect, as embodied in the conflicting figures of the three great epics. 'I see
the Four-fold Man', Blake (1974: 635) tells us in *Jerusalem*,

>   the Humanity in deadly sleep
> And its fallen Emanation, the Spectre and its cruel Shadow.
> I see the Past, Present and Future existing all at once
> Before me. O Divine Spirit, sustain me on thy wings,
> That I may awake Albion from his long and cold repose.

It is Blake's purpose in the Prophetic Books to enact the struggle between the
warring energies, the Spectres, of divided humanity, and to delineate his pursuit
of its resolution. As he puts it in *Jerusalem*: 'Our wars are wars of life, & wounds of
love, / With intellectual spears, and long winged arrows of thought' (1974: 664).
For even as this struggle is represented as a struggle within the self, it is also
(beyond this) an unending struggle against the destructive abstracts of Law and
Morality, under the rule of which 'all the Arts of Life' are 'chang'd into the Arts
of Death in Albion', with

>   intricate wheels invented, wheel without wheel,
> To perplex youth in their outgoings & to bind to labours in Albion
> Of day & night the myriads of eternity: that they may grind
> And polish brass & iron hour after hour, laborious task,

Kept ignorant of its use: that they might spend the days of wisdom
In sorrowful drudgery to obtain a scanty pittance of bread,
In ignorance to view a small portion & think that All
And call it Demonstration, blind to all the simple rules of life (1974: 700).

This is a recognition that the world itself is the ground on which the struggle has to be fought, and that in this world there is 'a class of men whose whole delight is in destroying', and whose ideological aim it is to subjugate men and women to their demands, 'Till we can / Reduce all to our will, as spaniels are taught with art' (1974: 323).

These men, the enemies of humanity, 'the oppressors of Albion in every City and Village', are an active embodiment of the realities of Blake's world, thrusting in upon the work at all levels.

They mock at the Labourer's limbs: they mock at his starv'd children:
They buy his Daughters that they may have power to sell his Sons:
They compel the poor to live upon a crust of bread by soft mild arts:
They reduce the man to want, then give with pomp and ceremony (1974: 656).

For this is what he saw at work around him, even as we can see it at work around us in our world today, in Africa, in South America, in the Philippines, in the USA, in Thatcherite Britain – people manipulating the instruments of law and wealth and power to proclaim inequality, social theft, contempt for the majority, war against community.

Blake's poetry repeatedly questions the forms and structures that lead to such institutionalizing of power and its prohibitive laws. Denying people their rights, their freedom to develop, their human potentialities, society can never fulfil itself. It is 'the road of excess leads to the palace of wisdom' (Blake 1974: 150), he writes. To repress is to pervert, to shut down upon people's needs. And in a world in which 'Wisdom is sold in the desolate market where none come to buy, / And in the wither'd field where the farmer plows for bread in vain' (1974: 290), Blake saw it as his great task to register the conditions of the struggle for the opening up of people's minds to the multiple perspectives of their world and its interactive energies. This was an urgent task, and it involved not only content but form – the kind of free and open-ended measure, with 'variety in every line, both of cadences and numbers of syllables' (1974: 621), which he had been experimenting with from at least *Tiriel* (1789) onward, because no shut form could serve his purpose. And this was also no doubt why he chose the image of the city as his model in *Jerusalem*; for cities are multiple and complex; and Blake's Jerusalem juxtaposes the ancient city of the Christian witness with London, the material city of the present, and that which is promised – Jerusalem as London, London-Albion as Jerusalem – a movement in the process of history from Ulro (the material universe) to Utopia, which would bring to fulfilment the diverse potentialities of civilization. And as there was a time, in Blake's mythical scheme of things, as the naked, fallen Jerusalem recalls, when

London cover'd the whole Earth: England encompass'd the Nations,
And all the Nations of the Earth were seen in the Cities of Albion (1974: 720),

so the aim of 'every Christian' must be to 'engage himself openly and publicly before all the World in some mental pursuit for the Building up of Jerusalem' (1974: 717). For this Jerusalem is no mere physical fixed place, but is envisaged as idea, condition, potentiality, and as a living human presence – woman, daughter, sister, voiced and embodied at the heart of Blake's imaginative scheme, his dialectic struggle for the realization of the fourfold unity of being without which there can *be* no New Jerusalem. And it is above all the task of Los, the central figure in this complex interconnected narrative of action, to accomplish that realization out of the distorted actualities of a divided world.

Los appeals to Jerusalem as woman and as sister – 'the soft reflected Image of the Sleeping Man' reposing amid 'Cities not yet embodied in Time and Space' (Blake 1974: 730). For Jerusalem is the key to fulfilment for the multiple presences of Blake's poem – the fallen Albion and his alienated children, the ravished body of England, London, 'blind and age-bent' (1974: 729), 'continually building, continually decaying' (1974: 712). And these presences – the divided selves in their anguished search for answers – are themselves a dramatic embodiment of the process of knowledge as activity, 'the social character of human thinking' (McGann 1988), the many voices of the self generating 'an elemental transformation of the faculties', an interactive witness,

> creating exemplars of Memory and of Intellect,
> Creating Space, Creating Time, according to the wonders Divine
> Of Human Imagination throughout all the Three Regions immense
> Of Childhood, Manhood & Old Age (Blake 1974: 740).

They are there, that is, to give voice to the antagonistic energies that determine the underlying conditions of the struggle, reflecting the peculiar emphasis of Blake's quest, Socratic rather than Platonic – its refutation of the cohesive order of philosophic truth, the 'Abstract objecting power that Negatives every thing' (1974: 629), in favour of the unpredictable conditions that characterize the order of imagination.

Blake's vision of a world remade, of a world modelled on the creative energies of men and women, fully recognizes the difficulty of the struggle that has to be fought for its realization. He knew how powerful the oppressors of Albion were, for indeed they dominated his world and the system he lived under seemed ruthlessly intent upon stifling and suppressing all attempts to break free from its ideologies. Hence Blake's sceptical perception that men and women in society must always fail to achieve his vision of Jerusalem; because no society that he knew could accommodate the multiplicity of people's needs or the perversity of their passions. And hence the relevance of his methods – his dialectic of continual renewal and of incompleteness which refuses to permit the reader to pin down or to separate out the enriching contradictions and ambiguities of the texts. As he saw it, there would have to be many transmutations, many forms of revolutionary change, before society could ever rid itself of its murderously repressive institutions. That was his conclusion, faced with the appalling proofs that surrounded him in the England of Liverpool and Sidmouth and the factory laws. It was a disgrace, and Blake's work condemns the systematic dehumanization of a world that thrived on war and poverty, on unemployment and fear and hatred and oppression, that sought

> To restrain, to dismay, to thin
> The inhabitants of mountain and plain,
> In the day of full-feeding prosperity,
> And the night of delicious songs (Blake 1974: 247).

To have accepted such a world would have been to condone the e.
humanity; and Blake never did that. Though he was forced to recognize
could not escape the bleak realities of that world, he knew that the str.
against it, the 'intellectual war' for knowledge, had to go on, and that it wa
necessity, a condition of existence, because – whether one succeeded or failed –
'to Labour in Knowledge is to Build up Jerusalem, and to Despise Knowledge is
to Despise Jerusalem and her Builders' (1974: 717).

6

s and reaction in the age of
olution: Wordsworth,
Shelley and Burke

In Britain, as on the Continent, the fifty-odd years between the end of the American War of Independence and the 1832 Reform Act were years of unprecedented change and upheaval, dominated, of course, by the momentous events of the French Revolution and the 22 years of war that followed it, but also by the parallel developments of the Industrial Revolution, which laid the foundations for capitalist expansion in the nineteenth-century. This was a period of relentless ideological confrontation and of contradictory struggle between the forces of progress and reaction, with Britain ranged on the side of the counter-revolutionary conservative powers against France and emerging victorious at the Congress of Vienna to impose its own territorial demands upon Europe, if only to find itself afterwards faced with renewed upheavals at home from a working class beginning to organize collectively against crippling poverty and oppression and now expected to endure on top of all that the devastating costs of war.

There had been widespread popular support at first for the Revolution, which had brought together dissenting intellectuals and writers such as Paine, Godwin and Blake, the educated artisans who led the Revolution Societies, and certain elements from among the emergent working class in a direct challenge to the institutionalized forces of English society. But the radical movement was too loosely based to be able to sustain the momentum of opposition for long, let alone to widen the grounds for it against an increasingly repressive state machinery or the ideological onslaught the Pitt government directed at the movement's leaders from 1793 onward. Indeed, by the mid-1790s the radicals had been more or less effectively marginalized or forced into positions of embattled defiance as the forces of entrenched conservatism tightened their grip on the instruments of state power. There was nothing, it seemed, they could do to bridge the gulf between the social vision they were advocating and the actual conditions of their world. Though appearing to be engaged, as Marx (1973b:146) puts it in *The Eighteenth Brumaire*, 'in the revolutionary transformation of themselves and their material surroundings, in the creation of something which does not yet exist', they could only respond according to 'the given and inherited circumstances with which they were directly confronted'. For power was not in their hands; it was the reactionaries who controlled things. And out of what the Revolution had turned into under Napoleon, the barbarism that fed on it, the wars it fomented, a new and aggressive class of men had emerged to open up the Continent and impose its ruthless control upon society in the name of progress. Under the domination of such men and the rapid development of the instruments of production, the capitalist system thrived upon divisiveness and repression, the power of 'institutes and laws hallowed by time' (Wordsworth 1971: 281) for the protection of privilege and property and the degradation of the masses, in a 'universal exploitation of communal human nature' (Marx 1975: 359).

William Godwin had understood the situation clearly enough from his reading of Burke's *Reflections on the Revolution in France*. He knew that the established powers would use every weapon at their command to oppose the Declaration of Rights so recently defined by the Revolution. 'There is a perpetual struggle', he writes in his *Political Justice* (1793), 'between the genuine sentiments of understanding . . . and the imperious voice of government, which bids us reverence and obey' (Willey 1962: 209) the spells and charms of ancient imposture. And now, it seemed to him, 'all prejudices of the human mind are in arms' (1962: 207). For the point is that Godwin's defence of the principles and conclusions of eighteenth-century rationalism was launched at the very moment (February 1793) of incipient reaction – at a time, that is, when the imperious voice of British government was about to come out into the open as the declared enemy of radicalism and emancipation and seize its opportunity to exploit the hysterical anti-French mood of the English upper classes.

For a while, in Hazlitt's words, Godwin 'blazed as a sun in the firmament of reputation . . . and wherever liberty, truth, justice was the theme, his name was not far off' (1969: 35–6). And if this could be said of Godwin, what of Tom Paine, who had already earned the right to claim, writing to Washington from the Paris of 1789, that 'a share in two revolutions is living to some purpose' (Paine 1969: 30)? *His* response to Burke, the first part of *The Rights of Man*, appearing a mere three months after the *Reflections*, became one of the great seminal documents of the radical movement, and was soon being read and discussed among the revolutionary 'corresponding societies' that had sprung up all over the British Isles. And Paine, 'as an American with an international reputation who had lived for close on fifteen years in the bracing climate of experiment and constitutional iconoclasm' (Thompson 1968: 99), was regarded by both enemies and friends as the embodiment of revolutionary sentiment. As he writes in the second part of *The Rights of Man*, which in 1792 had an even greater impact than the first,

> Never did so great an opportunity offer itself to England, and to all Europe, as is produced by the two revolutions of America and France. By the former, freedom has a national champion in the western world; and by the latter, in Europe. When another nation shall join France, despotism and bad government will scarcely dare to appear. To use a trite expression, the iron is becoming hot all over Europe. The insulted German and the enslaved Spaniard, the Russ and the Pole, are beginning to think. The present age will hereafter merit to be called the Age of Reason, and the present generation will appear to the future as the Adam of a new world (Paine 1969: 290).

Such expectancy and assurance (however misplaced) were infectious, encouraging many others – among them Thomas Hardy the shoemaker, Mary Wollstonecraft, Godwin, Blake, Joseph Priestley, John Thelwall, Horne Tooke,

Thomas Muir, Maurice Margorot – to take their stand against the deepening intolerance and panic of the reactionary forces of the establishment in an extraordinary ferment of ideas which echoed that of the revolutionary dissenters – Levellers, Diggers, Ranters, Quakers, Familialists, Fifth Monarchists – of seventeenth-century England.

But it *was* misplaced, perhaps on the mistaken assumption that the enlightened attitudes associated with American independence had taken deeper root. For in England, it was not the iron of revolution that was getting hot, but the iron of the reactionaries. With Pitt invoking draconian decrees to stamp out this alarming threat to ruling-class control, especially after 1793 (when support for the French became treasonable), the repressive forces of authoritarian power were brutally to impose their will. Trading on fear and hatred of the external enemy, the Pitt government had issued a Royal Proclamation against Seditious Publications (May 1792), outlawed Paine in his absence, and condemned *The Rights of Man* as seditious libel (December 1792). And the outbreak of war in February 1793 signalled the start of systematic legal prosecutions against the Jacobins, including the suspension of *habeus corpus* (1794), the Seditious Meetings and Treason Acts (1795) and the Combination Laws of 1799. In the darkening atmosphere of counter-revolutionary oppression, many radicals were arrested, arraigned for treason and imprisoned in the notorious treason trials of the mid-1790s, though Hardy, Horne Tooke and Thelwall (skilfully defended by Thomas Erskine) were acquitted to the acclaim of excited crowds of well-wishers.

The scandalous mockery of justice presided over by Lord Braxfield against the Scottish Jacobins in 1793 set the tone. And the harshness of Braxfield's sentences – Muir, Skirving, Margorot and Gerrard got 14 years' transportation – had the full support of the English government in the House of Commons, no doubt on the assumption (as Braxfield put it in his address to the jury at Muir's trial) that 'the British constitution is the best that ever was since the creation of the world, and it is not possible to make it better' (Thompson 1968: 136). In other words, an ideological process was at work in Britain which, bred upon the imperious rhetoric of Burke, and fuelled by war, justified and reinforced the repressive order of the state as essential to the stability and survival of human society. According to Burke, in his *Reflections*, a mysterious divine law – a law that human beings have no right to question – rules and ordains the contracts of society. And under the terms of this law, every society is

> but a clause in the great primeval contract of eternal society, linking the lower with the higher natures, connecting the visible and invisible world, according to a fixed compact sanctioned by the inviolable oath which holds all physical and all moral natures, each in their appointed place (Burke 1968: 195).

In such terms, the contract of society is *unalterably* fixed, an absolute determined by the 'manuscript-assumed authority of the dead', as Paine (1969: 64) scornfully comments, and therefore in fact no contract at all. The masters have their appointed place and the servants have theirs – presumably fixed for them by some sort of all-embracing Divine Authority embodied in the rights of kings; and not one of us has any choice but to accept and to submit, since apparently we are bound to do so by 'inviolable oath': by an oath we swore, that is, before we were born. This, of course, is confirmed by the 1688 declaration of

Parliament to William and Mary: 'We do humbly and faithfully submit ourselves, our heirs and posterities, for ever' (Burke 1968: 108). For these are the sorts of 'parliamentary clauses', in Paine's view, 'upon which Mr. Burke builds his political church' (1969: 66) in his attempt to 'set up an *assumed, usurped* domination over posterity' (1969: 67). And what such clauses actually signify when reduced to comprehensible human terms is that the 'lower natures' are bound by their inviolable oath and 'by consent of force' to obey the 'higher natures'; and that if these lower natures should dare to go against their oath

> the law is broken, nature is disobeyed, and the rebellious are outlawed, cast forth from this world of reason, and order, and peace, and virtue, and fruitful penitence, into the antagonistic world of madness, discord, vice, confusion, and unavailing sorrow (Burke 1968: 195).

Thus do protest and resistance – the kind of protest and resistance Burke himself saw with such shocked outrage in the upheavals of the French Revolution – threaten to destroy the absolute, God-ordained balance of the hierarchic order of the masters, and to replace it with a *dis*order and a chaos that sound very much like a Burkeian definition of hell. Indeed, the judgement carries more than an echo of God's outraged response to Adam's claim to rational participation in the resources of Eden: 'Behold, the man is become as one of us, to know good and evil' (Genesis 3: 22), and what follows it – the command that he be driven out and kept from tasting further of the delight of the knowledge of paradise.

It was just such a concept of social order – authoritarian, rigid, fixed, appealing to divinely-appointed absolutes which are ultimately indifferent to the rights and sufferings of those they oppress – that Marx set out to attack in his exposure of the 'crass materialism' underlying Hegel's doctrine of the state. For though in Burke's scheme of things the higher natures are made to seem a breed apart – embodying the 'necessity that is not chosen, but chooses', 'that admits no discussion and demands no evidence' (Burke 1968: 195) – what actually enables them to maintain their superior positions in society is what Burke insistently obscures – their ideological control of the institutions of society; a mystification based upon control of the material forces of production and, therefore, of other people.

As for these others, the lower orders – their station fixed by the inviolable pre-natal oath of their contract – they had no choice but to accept the conditions they were born to, as a sort of servant race, an insect species. Or rather, in the words of Davies Giddy, patron of science, later President of the Royal Society, it was firmly believed that to educate such people

> would in effect be found to be prejudicial to their morals and happiness; it would teach them to despise their lot in life . . . render them factious and refractory . . . enable them to read seditious pamphlets, vicious books, and publications against Christianity; it would render them insolent to their superiors; and in a few years the result would be that the legislature would find it necessary to direct the strong arm of power towards them, and to furnish the executive magistrate with much more vigorous laws than were now in force (Bronowski 1972: 149).

Under these conditions – the terms of reactionary conservatism defined by Burke, which were to dominate the politics of Britain till at least 1832 – the lower natures were required to remain anonymous, humble, passive, a neutral and obedient workforce, bound to their appointed place (poverty producing plenty) by the fixed laws of the great primeval contract of eternal society. Their rulers did not require them to feel, to display emotion, to have ideas; their natural role was to obey. Thus, Burke and his peers were particularly shocked that these lesser creatures should believe they had the right to question the order of things or to harbour resentment against their betters. They considered such liberties irresponsible and destructive. And as for the revolutionary activity of the French people, and what Burke (1968: 182) calls their 'paltry and blurred sheets of paper about the rights of man', this was a blasphemy against the very essence of the civilizing process, the 'moral and physical disposition of things', the fundamental laws of nature, 'to which man must be obedient by *consent of force*' (1968: 195).

In face of the palpable irrationality of this dogma, in an atmosphere as threatening as that which increasingly dominated Europe at the turn of the century, it was not to be wondered at that impressionable men like Wordsworth, Coleridge and Southey should have begun to find the support they had given to the principles of liberty and justice and humanitarian politics turning sour on them. From the evidence available, it could be argued that the romantic nature of their support for Godwinian ideals and the spirit of the Revolution had only the shallowest of roots; that their enthusiasm was no more than the enthusiasm of youth, the 'bigotry . . . of a youthful patriot's mind' (Wordsworth, *Prelude*, Bk IX. 499–500), as Wordsworth defines it, and formed no part of the deeper convictions of the bounded self; that it was little more than an intoxication of the moment, a spell cast by the excitements of the time; a transitory mood of the soul.

Nevertheless, Wordsworth himself *had* given a great deal of energy and commitment to the issues of the Revolution and its challenge; and his sense of indignation and outrage seemed passionately convinced, driving him even to the point of considering whether an *English* revolution might not be necessary to rid the country of a villainous government. It is all the more disconcerting, therefore, to note the completeness with which such ardent and generous political sentiments could collapse before the pressure of events and be rejected as 'an idle dream' associated with 'the meddling intellect' (*The Tables Turned*). Even taking into account Wordsworth's own record – the depth of disillusionment he suffered at the way the Revolution had gone wrong, his awareness of the 'terrific reservoir of guilt / And ignorance filled up from age to age' (*Prelude*, Bk X. 437–8, 477–8), his sense of 'all things tending fast / To depravation' (X. 806–7; XI. 223–4) – it is hard to credit. Surely, one asks, rational convictions of the sort the poet held during the five years up to 1795 are not so easily surrendered? Study of human nature may well have suggested the

> awful truth, that, as . . . sin and crime are apt to start from their very opposite qualities, so there are no limits to the hardening of the heart, and the perversion of the understanding to which they may carry their slaves (Wordsworth 1969: xxxii).

But that is not the whole of it; for there are other kinds of truth it may suggest. The study of human nature is not *exhausted* by observing man's capacity for perverting his idealism into sin and crime. What, one might ask, of that perversion of the understanding which had brought about the Revolution, defined by the spells and charms of a social order in which 'the man who is of soul / The meanest thrives the most'? (IX. 353–4, 346–7). What about the capacity of the few to harden their hearts against the sufferings of the oppressed? Is this sort of perversion to be accepted as a preferable alternative and the struggle against it to be renounced as invalid?

One can, of course, explain Wordsworth's retreat from involvement in personal, psychological terms – as a kind of breakdown, a loss of nerve, a form of emotional dissociation (even connected, perhaps, with the deepening frustrations of his separation from Annette Vallon, the girl he had fallen in love with and left in France) which left the poet unable to deal either emotionally or intellectually with the onslaught, or to keep the distinctions clear between tyranny and oppression abroad and the proofs of it at home. He was gripped, as he says, by fear – 'the fear that kills; / And the hope that is unwilling to be fed' ('The Leech Gatherer') – and by an ominous sense of negation. 'We poets', as he writes in 'The Leech Gatherer', 'in our youth begin in gladness / But thereof come in the end despondency and madness'.

However, such pessimism is more than simply personal. It is symptomatic also of the underlying social (and class) assumptions on which Wordsworth's conception of the world was grounded, his traditionalist view of the sanctities of human intercourse as dictated by long-established myths of organic rural life and popular culture, 'the instincts of natural and social man' (Thompson 1968: 378), rooted in a paternalistic Burkeian vision of society. And if he was at all aware of the deepening contradictions of a class society in action, he showed little interest in understanding what was happening. This was not a context he was equipped either by upbringing or by predilection to cope with; his was a philosophy of universal and universalizing principle, of man in nature, and of mystical 'Faith in life endless, the sustaining thought / Of human Being, Eternity, and God' (*Prelude*, 1850: Bk XIV. 204–5).

This, at least, is what it came to in the end – though there had been a time when, faced with the terror of the abyss, the void surrounding him, his mind 'both let loose, / Let loose and goaded' (*Prelude*, Bk X. 863–4; XI. 272–3), it seemed there could be no way forward. Then, at the point of crisis, it had seemed 'the human Reason's naked self' served only to oppress, to attack and to impair the findings of the mind and feelings; to excite 'morbid passions'. The consequence was that, 'endeavouring . . . to probe / The living body of society', he found himself

> Dragging all passions, shapes of faith,
> Like culprits to the bar, suspiciously
> Calling the mind to establish in plain day
> Her titles and her honours, now believing,
> Now disbelieving, endlessly perplexed
> With impulse, motive, right and wrong, the ground
> Of moral obligation, what the rule
> And what the sanction, till, demanding proof,
> And seeking it in everything, I lost
> All feeling of conviction, and, in fine,
> Sick, wearied out with contrarieties,
> Yielded up moral questions in despair (X. 890–901, 294–305).

In other words, Wordsworth found himself unable to sustain the harshness of that dialectic vision of reality without which the contrary states of being cannot be reconciled – the tension between subject and object, self and society, intellect and imagination, reason and energy, the struggle for the self and the Other in the self, the dialogic interchange that sets up connections. Not that he did not try. But what he saw as the 'degradation' of the age was too much for him. Turning to 'Nature's self', he turned his back on the 'gewgaw' process of history, the injustices and wholesale mutilations that were disfiguring the life of England and the Continent, and retired into the country, to Racedown and Alfoxden and the Lake District, for 'a saving intercourse', as he phrased it, with his 'true self' (x. 915–16).

In confirmation of this view of Wordsworth's change of heart, it has been suggested that it was not intellectual conviction at all but only a kind of 'hypochondriacal graft of his nature' that led him in the first place to take up with Godwin's radical ideas. But this is obviously an inadequate explanation. More to the point is the observation of Coleridge, who knew him intimately, that 'certain beliefs, at any rate by men of Wordsworth's stamp, are sickness', and 'with the restoration of vitality and the influx of joy they disappear' (Willey 1962: 216).

The pity is that such restoration, such influx of joy, and with it much of his best poetry (written in the years immediately succeeding his withdrawal, between 1795 and 1805), should have been gained at such cost in perspective. It is as if, for Wordsworth, sickness had its roots in the stirrings of that conscience which had urged him towards involvement, and health its roots in escape from 'the dreary intercourse of daily life' (*Tintern Abbey*), retreat into the self and a glorification of the 'renovating power' of Nature – which he looks upon with the longing of a sick man for the *sources* of health. This is the illusion that undermined his life. Though at one time, it seems, the world was too much with him – so that 'getting and spending we lay waste our powers' (Sonnet, 'The World is Too Much With Us') – after 1805 he came to settle for too little of it, to begin to see people and things as fixed and unchanging and to turn a blind eye to the ugliness and inhumanity, the 'fretful stir' and change, around him, having by then convinced himself that 'pure intellectualism in morals was more likely to produce or justify crime than virtue', and that the healing power of Nature was an adequate substitute for 'all the ways of men, so vain and melancholy' ('The Leech Gatherer').

It is a devastating commentary on the oppressive and illiberal atmosphere of the time and the ways in which its perversions and dichotomies undermined and broke the resistance of the radicals that Wordsworth should have been driven to making such a choice and to withdraw from the field of urban (and rural) struggle, of social crisis, of political and social challenge. Clearly, with the forces of reactionary power in England brutally intent on crushing 'the enemy' at home and engaged in full-scale war with the enemy abroad, the pressures were too great for him. The generous sentiments of the idealist were no match for the repressive violence of a militarized state order or the ideology that legitimized it. Resisting such violence demanded a tougher humanism than Wordsworth's, grounded on experience, the obstinacy and outrage of a Cobbett or the harsh realism of those among the oppressed working class who suffered most. For the fact is that the confirmed supporter of republican France in the 1790s was to become by 1803, as his sister writes, 'a determined hater of the French'. And the passionate defender of the 'government of equal rights and individual worth' who had urged in his 1793 *Letter to the Bishop of Llandaff* the use of violence to overthrow despotism, the claims of manhood suffrage, abolition of the law of inheritance, and equality of income, was to speak out 16 years later in his pamphlet on the *Convention of Cintra* (1809) as a powerful voice for conservatism and nationalism, and in 1818 to contradict every single principle and sentiment so solemnly affirmed in 1793.

Such is the manner in which superior force can crush people's hopes and turn them against themselves to diminish and betray. In one way or another, Wordsworth seemed to find all paths forward blocked; and, appalled by the contradictions that confronted him, he faltered, lost courage, and drew back, to try to salvage for himself those parts of his world he knew best and could trust.

To Shelley, writing in 1816, this was sufficient cause for lament. The poet who had stood 'like to a rock-built refuge ... Above the blind and battling multitude: / In honoured poverty' weaving 'Songs consecrate to truth and liberty' (Shelley 1934: 526), had deserted the field; and his withdrawal was not to be taken lightly. But it was not enough to lament. There were lessons to be learnt from this – warning as much against what Keats (1952: 226) had called the 'egotistical sublime' as against the vulnerability of an idealism that could lead to such collapse of hope, such 'gloom and melancholy'. In other words, as Shelley saw it, stronger foundations were needed, a deeper resistance to the negative forces at work in society and the momentous changes taking place in Europe, with wealth as 'a power usurped by the few to compel the many to labour for their benefit' (Shelley 1934: 805) in a system which left the manufacturing classes 'famished, without affections, without health, without leisure or opportunity for ... instruction' (Shelley 1951: 1012). He did not need to be told what had to be done. Though it was too early for him to be in any position to recognize the full significance of the industrial transformation being engineered by capitalist organization of the factory system, he (like Byron) had written about the Luddite machine-breakers, and understood the need for some sort of objective commitment to social change and for poetry as an active instrument in the struggle for it.

Indeed, having been brought up in an England at war, and denouncing the callousness and hypocrisy of his class, its 'kings and parasites' (Shelley 1934: 772), he considered it the poet's place and duty to speak for the people, those 'without whom society must cease to subsist' (1934: 805), against their oppressors, and to equip himself to resist the tyrannies of his age. Hence his dismay at Wordsworth's retreat. He had taken the trouble to think through Godwin's concept of political justice, and to build on it, to absorb the lessons it offered – as the notes to *Queen Mab*, very early on, and the prefaces he wrote to a number of the mature poems, and the poems themselves, clearly demonstrate. For there were vital theoretical issues at stake here, which set up the closest links between the imperative concerns of the outer world and his own aesthetic aims as a poet. In the Preface to *The Revolt of Islam*, Shelley (1934: 32) writes:

> I have sought to enlist the harmony of metrical language, the ethereal combinations of the fancy, the rapid and subtle transitions of human passion, all those elements which essentially compose a Poem, in the cause of liberal and comprehensive morality; and in the view of kindling within the bosoms of my readers a virtuous enthusiasm for those doctrines of liberty and justice, that faith and hope in something good, which neither violence nor misrepresentation nor prejudice can ever totally extinguish among mankind.

And much of his poetry bears compelling witness to this struggle, and to his perception of the links between revolutionary activity in the external world and the mind's activity, as an irrepressible collective energy contained by repressive power.

In the works of his last three years – poems like *The Mask of Anarchy, Prometheus Unbound, Hellas* and *The Triumph of Life* – he makes a sustained attempt to embody the contradictory terms and conditions of a radical Utopianism and the disturbing issues it confronted him with, as a cosmic phenomenon centred upon the struggles of humanity. Not that there was any question of Shelley being free to translate his vision of things into social action; for he had already been effectively marginalized. Nevertheless, he saw his art as an instrument of change ('the trumpet of a prophecy') and as giving concrete form to the controversial ideas and feelings from which social action springs. Even if he was sometimes guilty of drifting off into the 'intense inanc' of Platonic contemplation, he did so in search of answers to the questions and doubts and contradictions of actuality, not to evade them, as Wordsworth did. With Shelley politics and culture, society and the individual, the interests of people and the interests of literature, were aspects of an interactive dialogic process that was everybody's business. Though Arthur Hallam was later to argue that a poet like Tennyson had the advantage over Shelley because 'he came before the public unconnected with any political party or peculiar system of opinions', it is precisely Shelley's commitment, his refusal to separate social and aesthetic issues, his conviction that politics mattered and could not be ignored without ignoring other crucial issues, that make him a more significant, if not a better, poet than Tennyson. But then for Shelley politics was to be equated not with the paraphernalia of political *parties* (and there was no political party in England radical enough for him, since they had all been outlawed) but with the clash of ideas and feelings and the sharpening influence of ideas upon the mind and the sensibility. And perhaps most of all, for him politics meant raising the level of awareness to a maximum attentiveness to alert people to the oppressive conditions they were faced with and to incite them into open conflict and rebellion against their enemies in the struggle for emancipation and freedom. It may be that the inspired Utopianism of this quest was often pitched at too high a level. But Shelley knew that inspiration was not enough. The challenge, at a time of singular difficulty for the oppressed, was to put that inspiration to use – to feed it with ideas that would match his instinct, to risk himself and make his words a concentrated voice for the needs of others.

In fact, at its best his poetry is a delicate impassioned tribute to the creative spirit of his age, shot through with tenderness and poetic insight drawn, as he puts it, 'from the operations of the human mind, or from those external actions by which they are expressed', and, like Prometheus, using 'knowledge as a weapon to defeat evil' (Shelley 1934: 205). Not that he was foolish enough to believe that the possession of such knowledge could in itself bring about the necessary changes. Though he tended to idealize the real, he knew what people were up against – a world ruled by 'Force and Fraud: Old Custom, legal Crime, / And Bloody Faith the foulest birth of Time' (1934: 527). In such words there is a harsh unillusory awareness of the inhibiting powers that block the paths to freedom and fulfilment. It is the kind of awareness which, in *The Mask of Anarchy*, calls upon the common people to rise, as at some vast Peterloo, against the institutionalized hierarchies of ruling-class England – bluntly denounced in the names of government ministers (Castlereagh, Eldon, Sidmouth and

Liverpool) as Murder, Fraud and Hypocrisy, with Anarchy embodied as 'God, and King, and Law' – to

> Rise like lions after slumber
> In unvanquishable number –
> Shake your chains to earth like dew
> Which in sleep had fallen on you –
> Ye are many – they are few.

Such revolutionary implications – which characteristically incite the people to *non*-violent resistance to the forces of violence in society – are fully consistent with Shelley's underlying philosophy. One could argue that this naively underestimates not only the ruthless determination of the ruling class to maintain its domination, but also the power which violence has to command obedience and to crush the will. To which Shelley might well have answered that even violence cannot prevail against an undivided people – that if *all* the people were to rise against their masters, there would be no stopping them. And that is the Utopian aim he has. For his particular vision of things is the embodiment of myths which give momentum and focus to the desired, the possible, to things as yet unrealized, the 'change beyond the change' – thus provoking a revolutionary attitude towards reality itself. 'Mistake me not!' cries the old Jewish prophet in *Hellas*.

> All is contained in each.
> Dodona's forest to an acorn's cup
> Is that which has been, or will be, to that
> Which is – the absent to the present. Thought
> Alone, and its quick elements, Will, Passion,
> Reason, Imagination, cannot die;
> They are, what that which they regard appears,
> The stuff whence mutability can weave
> All that it hath domination o'er, worlds, worms,
> Empires, and superstitions (Shelley 1934. 471).

And out of the awakened consciousness, which sees the future 'shadowed on the Past / As on a glass', will emerge the recognition of the necessity of the struggle for the future and the challenge of the new conditions to be made from it, the promise of a world in which the tyrants of humanity shall be vanquished and left to 'rule the deserts they have made' (1934: 476).

Such a concept of the future, envisaged here in the immediate context of the 1821 rising of the Greek people against their oppressors, is an essential precondition to social action. For in order to be able to reject the 'stagnant and miserable' conditions that hold them back, people must be given the incentive to look beyond these conditions. It is not enough, because it has to be linked to the contradictory material conditions, the driving forces of history, that are the grounds for progressive action and social change; but it generates the will to act. And Shelley (1934: 206), as part of the history of his time, put himself consciously on the side of the people as one of the 'forerunners of some unimagined change in our social condition'. And his commitment to the struggle he saw taking place around him, in Spain, Italy and Greece, is nowhere registered more unequivocally than in the paragraph from the

Preface to *Hellas* which all editions till 1892 suppressed as offensive to the tastes of public men:

> Should the English ever become free, they will reflect upon the part which those who presume to represent their will have played in the great drama of the revival of liberty, with feelings which it would become them to anticipate. This is the age of the war of the oppressed against the oppressors, and every one of those ringleaders of the privileged gangs of murderers and swindlers, called Sovereigns, look to each other for aid against the common enemy, and suspend their mutual jealousies in the presence of a mightier fear. Of this holy alliance all the despots of the earth are virtual members. But a new race has arisen throughout Europe, nursed in the abhorrence of the opinions which are its chains, and she will continue to produce fresh generations to accomplish that destiny which tyrants foresee and dread (1934: 448).

No one can doubt from this where Shelley stood or what he believed had to be done. But there is another passage – the prose statement he makes in the Preface to *The Revolt of Islam*, recording his response to the French Revolution, the greatest event of the age – in which the cogency of the argument gives particular weight to the maturity of Shelley's powers of judgement and perception. It is worth quoting from at length because of the illuminating commentary it provides upon the psychological context that defined the position of men like Wordsworth, Coleridge and Southey:

> The French Revolution may be considered as one of those manifestations of a general state of feeling among civilized mankind produced by a defect of correspondence between the knowledge existing in society and the improvement or gradual abolition of political institutions. The year 1788 may be assumed as the epoch of one of those most important crises produced by this feeling. The sympathies connected with that event extended to every bosom. The most generous and amiable natures were those which participated the most extensively in these sympathies. But such a degree of unmingled good was expected as it was impossible to realize. If the revolution had been in every respect prosperous, then misrule and superstition would lose half their claim to our abhorrence, as fetters which the captive can unlock with the slightest motion of his fingers, and which do not eat with poisonous rust into the soul. The revulsion occasioned by the atrocities of the demagogues, and the re-establishment of successive tyrannies in France, was terrible, and felt in the remotest corner of the civilized world. Could they listen to the plea of reason who had groaned under the calamities of a social state according to the provisions of which one man riots in luxury whilst another famishes for want of bread? Can he who the day before was a trampled slave suddenly become liberal-minded, forebearing and independent? This is the consequence of the habits of a state of society to be produced by resolute perseverence and indefatigable hope, and long-suffering and long-believing courage, and the systematic efforts of generations of men of intellect and virtue. Such is the lesson which experience teaches now. But, on the first reverses of hope in the progress of French liberty, the sanguine eagerness for good overleaped the solution of these questions, and for a time extinguished itself in the unexpectedness of their results. Thus, many of the most ardent and tender-hearted of the worshippers of public good have been morally ruined by what a partial glimpse of the events they deplored appeared to show as the melancholy desolation of all their cherished hopes. Hence gloom and misanthropy have become the characteristics of the age in which we live, the solace of a disappointment that unconsciously finds relief only in the wilful exaggeration

of its own despair. This influence has tainted the literature of the age with the hopelessness of the minds from which it flows (Shelley 1934: 33–4).

Such, in Shelley's view, was the effect of his age on the sensibilities of sensitive men. That he himself was not seduced is due as much to his objective grasp of the issues involved as to his ability to see beyond the confusions and threats of the time to a concept of community in which the 'loathsome mask of tyranny' will have fallen. But Wordsworth was one of those who did yield, and Shelley must surely have had him in mind in the writing of this passage. He had been reduced to his lowest ebb by the enmities of the tyrant powers of England and France, with 'the lordly attributes / Of will and choice' made a mockery of, 'the dupe of folly, or the slave of crime' (Wordsworth, *Prelude*, Bk XI. 309–10). And Shelley's assurance of 'a slow, gradual, silent change' (1934: 34) for the better, of a 'reflux in the tide of human things' (1934: 33) to be brought about by 'the systematic efforts of generations of men of intellect and virtue', was not available to Wordsworth. Shattered and appalled by the record of 'human ignorance and guilt', he could not see beyond it. The world *had* become too much for him. Seeing only

> Presumption, folly, madness, in the men
> Who thrust themselves upon this passive world
> As rulers of the world;

seeing in their plans concepts 'bottomed on false thought / And false philosophy', and from this 'the utter hollowness of what we name / The wealth of nations', its betrayal of 'the dignity of individual man' (XII. 66–81), he recoiled in horror and dismay. There was no question, it seemed, of fighting such despair; it had incapacitated him. And that saving intercourse with 'Nature's self' to which he turned was the consequence of that despair, his solace and his refuge, what in *Tintern Abbey* he calls 'the anchor of my purest thoughts'.

And, of course, it is in this anchor that we recognize the peculiar quality of Wordsworth's genius, what we call the Wordsworthian experience — that reversion to a transcendental mystical view of nature which has its echoes in the Burkeian concept of the social process —

> that blessed mood,
> In which the burthen of the mystery,
> In which the heavy and the weary weight
> Of all this unintelligible world
> Is lightened

until a state is attained in which

> With an eye made quiet by the power
> Of harmony, and the deep power of joy,
> We see into the life of things (*Tintern Abbey*, 38–50).

This is what we are accustomed to think of as the essential Wordsworth. Its peculiarity is the extraordinary impact upon Wordsworth of the natural world, 'the ghostly language of the ancient earth', from which he drank in 'the visionary power' (*Prelude*, Bk II. 328–30). As he says in a revealing note:

> I was often unable to think of external things as having external existence, and I communed with all I saw as something not apart from, but inherent in, my own immaterial nature. Many times while going to school have I grasped at a rock or tree

to recall myself from this abyss of idealism to the reality (note to the *Ode: Intimations of Immortality*, 1843).

The phrasing is significant – that in fact 'idealism' represents an 'abyss', an abyss for the self; that Wordsworth was, in other words, aware of the danger of an imbalance in himself between idealism and reality, and of the difficulty of reconciling the two, of maintaining an interconnection between them. This was his dilemma: how to cross or to span the abyss, or to find the means to transform it – for it was, after all, no physical *space* but the recognition of a psychological area in the self, a sense of the void that he feared – the void he recognized even between himself and the world outside him, between the adult and the child, the internal self and the external presence, the actuality of the self and that being rooted in the echoes of a former self. And it may be that in withdrawing from the 'abyss of idealism' which had defined his involvement in the revolutionary events of his time, and attempting to recall himself to what he thought of as the reality, *his* reality, he was actually sharpening the divisions in the self rather than reconciling them.

In one of the most revealing passages from *The Prelude*, we find him seeking some kind of resolution to this dilemma which will enable him to reconstitute an undivided self out of the estranged parts of being. As he puts it, attempting the connection, reaching across the abyss,

> feeling comes in aid
> Of feeling, and diversity of strength
> Attends us, if but once we have been strong.
> Oh! mystery of man, from what a depth
> Proceed thy honours. I am lost, but see
> In simple childhood something of the base
> On which thy greatness stands; but this I feel,
> That from thyself it comes, that thou must give,
> Else never canst receive. The days gone by
> Return upon me almost from the dawn
> Of life: the hiding-places of man's power
> Open; I would approach them, but they close.
> I see by glimpses now; when age comes on,
> May scarcely see at all; and I would give,
> While yet we may, as far as words can give,
> Substance and life to what I feel (XII. 269–84).

There is a sense here that the poet is aware of the nulling effect of the abyss, of the void surrounding him or within him, of his isolation from the world. He is lost, he says, but he is at the same time obscurely conscious of sources of replenishment which, if they could be got at, might give him back his subjective sense of place and identity, of recognition, of assurance. But the quest has become elusive, a groping back into the past, perhaps most of all because it lacks the necessary context, the objective social reality Wordsworth has turned away from. It is a quest for the interconnections of the outer world and the inner, that process of giving and receiving which is the condition of self-knowledge; and Wordsworth makes his supreme attempt in *The Prelude* to maintain the balance between the complementary opposites, but with an increasing sense of the difficulty of standing up to the pressures of the outer world. Drawing, that is, upon the mystery he has felt and the strength he has known, against the fear of dispossession, the intuition of loss, he seeks a renewed equilibrium at the roots of his own world. And it could even be said of this, and of Wordsworth's work at the time he was writing (or finishing) the first version of *The Prelude*, that he sensed the very intensity of the need to give substance and life to what he felt as a direct consequence of the intensity of his physical and emotional reaction to the great crisis of spirit he had lived through, the stress and turmoil of revolutionary Europe. Though he had already by this time turned away from involvement and from his own radicalism, the experience still remained as a motivating charge of energy, in the sense in which the imagination is most likely to develop 'that intensity of application which is the poetic vision' under conditions of stress and conflict (Read 1938a: 172). Perhaps this is what Hazlitt (1969: 138) meant by hailing Wordsworth's work as 'a pure emanation of the Spirit of the Age'.

If so, he had a bitter price to pay for his withdrawal, his rejection of the dialectic issues of the historical struggle, his acceptance of a one-sided subjective status quo. For by cutting himself off from the channels through which the antagonistic energies flow and meet, and settling finally for what had given him back his 'settled judgement', he cut himself off from the very sources of replenishment and of creative conflict that had given such charge of intensity to his work. The gradual decay of his poetic powers was the inevitable consequence, already apparent in the writing of *The Excursion*, which he had planned as a sequel to *The Prelude*. Unable or unwilling to come to terms with the material conditions of an industrial age or the stress and challenge of the political process in any active sense, feeling himself sapped and threatened by it, he opted for the false quiet and repose, the illusory peace, of Nature, and a steady retreat from even such vitality as Nature gave him towards 'Duty' and 'Faith'. In Kiernan's words:

> Things cooled down into separate, inert blocks, fundamentally because he came to see the structure of society as a rigid hierarchy of classes. Human nature, having no warmth of action to transform it, was unalterable; duty abstract and changeless; suffering irremediable. No room was left for imagination as an active, working force. It came down to merely laying a varnish of verse over a worm eaten surface (1975: 196).

After 1814 the atmosphere became increasingly one of 'domestic tyranny and provincial narrowness; of decaying sensibility and the slow growth of a thick shell of convention – conventional religion, conventional morality, and worst of all, conventional poetry' (Read 1938b: 152).

Wordsworth was one among the many who were to come under the spell of Burke's arguments against radicalist and revolutionary principle and to find them persuasive. No doubt this was because they confirmed his own innate conservatism, his love of Nature, his longing for stability, his rejection of the principles of change and progress. But these arguments – forewarning, denouncing, launching forth in keen ridicule 'against all systems built on abstract rights' (*Prelude*, 1850: Bk VII. 524) – were the very arguments which the forces of intolerant ruling-class power were using to hold the people of Britain in thrall and to subject them ruthlessly to the cruelties and miseries of war and of economic enslavement, as mere instruments for the production of wealth. 'The times', as Wordsworth says, 'were big / With ominous change' (1850: VII. 534–5); and Burke was to do much with his eloquent appeal to irrationality and divisiveness – invoking God as the authoritarian Author and Nature as God's assistant – to shape the prevailing ideology.

'By a constitutional policy working after the pattern of nature', Burke (1968: 120) has it, 'we receive, we hold, we transmit our government and our privileges, in the same manner in which we enjoy and transmit our property and our lives'. The tone of autocratic assertion, where even the pronoun has the flavour of a royal plural, is at once apparent; for this is the voice of a governing elite uttering prescriptive absolutes and dispensations to a deferent multitude, which in obedience to the laws of the Divine Author, knows that our political system is 'placed in a just correspondence and symmetry with the order of the world . . . by the disposition of a stupendous wisdom [that moulds] together the great mysterious incorporation of the human race' (1968: 120). From which it follows, unalterably, that the 'we' that rules enjoys the luxuries of privilege and property as a *natural consequence* of the divinely constituted political system. And this minority of the favoured, those who (like Braxfield and Eldon and Sidmouth and Pitt) hold commanding positions in the hierarchy, are themselves, of course, no more, in Burke's opinion, than humble instruments chosen by natural selection to preserve 'the method of nature in the conduct of the state' (1968: 120).

It was, therefore, regarded as virtually treasonable to suggest that the natural order of things might be differently constituted; that those who had been appointed to govern might have *engineered* or *perverted* the laws of Nature to preserve their privileged positions and their power over others. Human society functions, as Burke (1968: 195) reminds us, 'according to a fixed compact . . . which holds all physical and moral natures, each in its appointed place'. And this compact is itself a fundamental law, which 'is not subject to the will of those who, by an obligation above them, and infinitely superior, are bound to submit their will to that law'. Apparently we have no choice in the matter. Either we agree to remain inside the closed circle of this natural order, or 'the law is broken, nature is disobeyed'. And Nature demands that we bind up 'the constitution of our country with our dearest domestic ties; adopting our fundamental laws into the bosom of our family affections' (1968: 120). We do not question whose interests that binding familial process is intended to serve; for that would be to raise the question of the deprived and mutilated masses, the women and children in the mills, the so-called beneficiaries of the Poor Laws, the Corn Laws and the Factory Laws. Working after the pattern of Nature, we simply accept the justice of our political system, with its 'protected, satisfied, laborious, and obedient people, taught to seek and to recognize the happiness that is to be found by virtue in all conditions' (1968: 124). For as Burke (1968: 182) affirms: 'Atheists are not our preachers; madmen are not our lawgivers'. English society, in other words, is ruled by wise and humane people who

> fear God . . ., look up with awe to Kings; with affection to parliaments; with duty to magistrates; with reverence to priests; and with respect to nobility. Why? Because when such ideas are brought before our minds, it is *natural* to be so affected.

And what if we find ourselves confronted, in the words of Shelley's 'Sonnet: England 1819', by

> An old, mad, blind, despised and dying king –
> Princes, the dregs of their dull race, who flow
> Through public scorn – mud from a muddy spring –

Rulers who neither see, nor feel, nor know,
But leech-like to their fainting country cling,
Till they drop, blind in blood, without a blow . . .?

This, presumably, would be dismissed with scorn, even as Burke (1968: 212) dismissed the 'political Men of Letters' in 1790 for attempting to carry 'the intolerance of the tongue and the pen into a persecution which would strike at property, liberty, and life'. For such people, in Burke's view, 'are rarely averse to innovation' (1968: 211); whereas

> we know that *we* have made no discoveries; and we think that no discoveries are to be made in morality; nor many in the great principles of government, nor in the ideas of liberty, which were understood long before we were born (1968: 182).

Which is to say that the wisest among us are those who have the magnanimity to leave things as they are – to accept the cruelty and injustice of the system, 'a people starved and stabbed in the untilled field' (1968: 575), for the sake of the great principles of conservative government, as determined by the laws of Nature. Furthermore, since it is by the laws of Nature and of God that the wise receive, hold and transmit their government and their privileges, it is apparently quite natural that the laws *they* make should happen to fall with crushing weight upon the poor. For it is Burke's contention that we must submit to the conditions established by Nature's benign rule and thus to the authority of her obedient higher servants – who are there to ensure that we all remain in our appointed places, rich and poor, great or small, wise or ignorant, for ever.

This is the kind of psychology which – emerging out of the mystifying terms of the Divine Right of Kings, and building irrationality, prejudice and intolerance into a weapon of authoritarian control – had re-established its hold upon, and re-entered into the substance of, the social structures of European society from the mid-1790s onward, and was to triumph in 1815. When the superior virtue of prejudice over reason can be argued as a means of organizing society, 'because prejudice, with its reason, has a motive to give action to that reason, and an affection which will give it permanence' (Burke 1968: 183), we are already in the presence of a consciousness dislocated and crippled by its incapacity to look its mystifying abstractions in the face. Why should such a system, if it believed in its own nature, as Marx (1975: 247) ironically asks, attempt 'to hide that nature under the *appearance* of an alien nature and seek its salvation in hypocrisy and sophism? The modern *ancien régime* is merely the *clown* of a world order whose *real heroes* are dead'. Because what it argues is blind adherence to established institutions (however inhumane, however bankrupt) as the tried and tested instruments of social intercourse sanctioned by the inviolable laws of nature.

In this way it was possible to justify the system of intolerance and inhumanity that prevailed, by a species of deception under the influence of which many of its functionaries were even convinced that they were supporting the very foundations of tolerant and humane government. Here we see embodied the Hegelian inversion which became the focus for Marx's penetrating dialectic. Nature, the universal abstract, has been placed in the position of man the subject, and man himself turned into an object upon which 'Nature' operates as a mystical authority – though it is still, of course, men who take it upon themselves to act as Nature's obedient agents.

This enthronement of Nature as the source of social order represents the manner in which, in the Burkeian sense, the separation of the classes was determined afresh at the end of the eighteenth-century, and the oppression of the many by the few was justified and systematically pursued. Defined in terms of 'entailed inheritance', 'wisdom without reflection' (Burke 1968: 119), reverence for civil institutions and the rights of property, it was to become the ideology which asserted the ruthless cut-throat principles and the sickening hypocrisies of nineteenth-century capitalism, and, with the expansion of competitive war into an imperialist game of power, the appalling carnage of the First World War.

Marx understood what was happening from the start. He saw that the tools of thinking had become perverted by abstraction – hence the urgency of his early call for a merciless criticism of the existing order, and of all forms of 'mystical consciousness', religious and political. The essential task was to make people aware of the real conditions of the struggle for the future, to unmask the deceptions that ruled, and thus to clear the ground for the re-establishment of the links between theory and practice, the historical contradictions of material existence, and its class terms. Nature is not a mysterious divine law, but a complex set of conditions and energies which determines materiality. And as Nature is 'the immediate object of the science of man', so 'man's first object – man – is nature, sense perception'. Accordingly, even 'the element of thought itself, the element of the vital expression of thought – language – is sensuous nature' (Marx 1975: 355–6), since it is rooted in and dependent upon the sensuous animal existence of man. Any process, therefore, which separates or abstracts thought from its material context – such as that which led Hegel to exalt Nature into an abstract mysterious power – constitutes a threat to the interaction between men and women and the changing material conditions of their existence, the history of their struggle for solvency and fulfilment.

Quite simply, in the objective and unmystical terms of Marx's argument, man – that is to say men and women – 'is directly a *natural* being. As a natural being and as a living natural being he is on the one hand equipped with natural *powers*, with *vital* powers, he is an *active* natural being; these powers exist in him as dispositions and capacities, as *drives*' (1975: 389–90). And at the same time he is 'a suffering, conditioned and limited being like animals and plants. That is to say, the *objects* of his drives exist outside him as objects independent of him'; and these objects are 'indispensable to the exercise and confirmation of his essential powers'. But beyond this, and including this, he is also an objective *social* being. And as a social being it is he who in fact creates and organizes the structures and systems of society, which ought to function as the objective complements to his sensate human powers. In other words, in the rational and objective sense that is continually being perverted by the imposition of abstract alien powers directed against people: 'I am *socially* active because I am active as a *man* [or *woman*] . . . What I create from myself I create for society, conscious of myself as a social being'; and 'my *universal* consciousness is only the theoretical form of that which has its living form in the real community' (1975: 350).

What, then, is this mysterious higher power that sanctions everything for us by some preordained plan, according to Burke's philosophy? Should we, as fallible finite beings, each with his own constricted view of things, his small 'private stock of reason' (Burke 1968: 183), submit unquestioningly to it as to the guiding spirit of God and his omniscient authority? Are we to be expected to remain its blind obedient subjects, without even the right to know what its powers are? Forbidden forever, as Milton's Satan asks, 'from achieving what might lead / To happier life, knowledge of good and evil?' (*Paradise Lost*, Bk IX. 696–7). In Burke's hierarchic view of Nature's disposition of powers, most (if not all) people are condemned from the start to servitude, deprived of choice. 'Ah', we might object, with Adam, 'why should all Mankind, / For one man's fault, thus guiltless be condemned, / If guiltless?' (*Paradise Lost*, Bk X. 822–4).

Marx (1975: 357) deals with the issue in characteristically convincing manner (though justice demands that we think and read 'woman' wherever he uses the word 'man'):

> To the question: 'Who begot the first man, and nature in general?' I can only answer: Your question is itself a product of abstraction. Ask yourself how you arrived at that question. Ask yourself whether your question does not arise from a standpoint to which I cannot reply because it is a perverse one. Ask yourself whether that progression exists as such for rational thought. If you ask about the question of nature and of man, then you are abstracting from nature and from man. You assume them as *non-existent*, and you want me to prove to you that they *exist*. My answer is: Give up your abstraction and you will then give up your question. But if you want to hold on to your abstraction, then do so consistently, and if you assume the non-existence of nature and of man, then assume also your own non-existence, for you are also nature and man ... You can reply: I do not want to assume the nothingness of nature, etc. I am only asking how it arose, just as I might ask the anatomist about the formation of bones, etc.
>
> But since for socialist man the *whole of what is called world history* is nothing more than the creation of man through human labour, and the development of nature for man, he therefore has palpable and incontrovertible proof of his self-mediated *birth*, of his *process* of emergence. Since the essentiality (*Wesenhaftigkeit*) of man and of nature ... has become practically and sensuously perceptible, the question of an *alien* being, a being above nature and man – a question which implies an admission of the unreality of nature and of man – has become impossible in practice.

It is clear that such a defiantly subversive and demystifying view of the place of people in their world would have been able to do as little to influence the mood or the consciousness of Europe in the 1790s as it was able to in the 1840s. The elitist, violently divisive course of capitalist development had been set, for the men who ruled or were about to rule Europe seemed proof against any sort of social logic that argued the rights of the oppressed. In Hazlitt's words, written in 1826: 'The spirit of monarchy was at variance with the spirit of the age. The flame of liberty, the light of intellect, was to be extinguished by the sword – or with slander, whose edge is sharper than the sword' (Rickword 1978: 247). Those who dictated conditions were intent upon the preservation and the extension of power and property. Motivated now by fear, now by greed, now by superior wisdom and contempt for the anarchic reactions of the 'mob', the 'riotous' and 'beer-swilling masses', they would have heard nothing of the authentic appeal to unanswered human needs in the arguments of the Jacobins, let alone in Marx; only the note of subversive challenge that held out its threat to the mysteries of the sacred framework of the social order that confirmed their place in the system.

In fact, from the mid-1790s onward, with war being waged abroad and industrialism ruthlessly implemented at home, all signs of dissent or of revolt by the people against deepening distress and deprivation were suppressed with a

savagery and vindictiveness that virtually strangled the revolutionary impulse.
In the words of Thompson (1968: 194–5):

> the counter-revolutionary panic of the ruling classes expressed itself in every part of
> social life; in attitudes to trade unionism, to the education of the people, to their
> sports and manners, to their publications and societies, and their political rights. And
> the reflex of despair among the common people can be seen, during the war years, in
> the inverted chiliasm of the Southcottians and the new Methodist revival. In the
> decades after 1795 there was a profound alienation between classes in Britain, and
> the working people were thrust into a state of *apartheid* whose effects . . . can be felt to
> this day. England differed from other European nations in this, that the flood-tide of
> counter-revolutionary feeling and discipline coincided with the flood-tide of the
> Industrial Revolution; as new techniques of industrial organization advanced, so
> political and social rights receded.

There had been risings of the people throughout this period, culminating in
the 'Swing' riots of 1830 which – described by Cobbett as a 'rural war' – brought
to an end not only a distinctive phase in the formulation of the working class but
also, with the death of Blake in 1827, a great epoch of intellectual dissent. For by
1830 the new conditions of industrial development had brought new kinds of
oppression and of servitude, and were to demand new kinds of organized
response. And at this moment of transition, there is no one who more aptly
registers the uncertainty of the time than John Clare, who, as a voice for 'the
otherwise silent peasantry of the enclosure years' (Clare 1966: xv), speaks from
first-hand experience of *England, 1830*:

> These vague allusions to a country's wrongs,
>   Where one says 'Ay' and others answer 'No'
> In contradiction from a thousand tongues,
>   Till like to prison-cells her freedoms grow
> Becobwebbed with these oft-repeated songs
>   Of peace and plenty in the midst of woe –
> And is it thus they mock her year by year,
>   Telling poor truth unto her face she lies,
> Declaiming of her wealth with gibe severe,
>   So long as taxes drain their wished supplies?
> And will these jailors rivet every chain
>   Anew, yet loudest in their mockery be,
> To damn her into madness with disdain,
>   Forging new bonds and bidding her be free? (Clare 1965: 194).

The new bonds were even then, as Clare knew, being forged, through the
Reform Act of 1832, the Tolpuddle transportations and the Poor Law of 1834,
the rejection of the Chartist Petitions of 1839 and 1842, the Bank Charter Act of
1844 and the institution of *laissez-faire*, and so on. So that when the revolutions of
1848 broke out in city after European city to present once again a seemingly
direct challenge to the bastions of inequality, what they achieved was in fact a
confirmation of the power struggle fought through in the France of 1789–94,
but this time to assert the domination of the bourgeois capitalists, who had seized
their opportunity by linking up with and manipulating the urgent needs of the
working classes to strengthen their control. The end-result of these major
uprisings of the people was increased power for the institutional structures of
the system, an immediate deepening of the alienating conditions of labour, and

renewed oppression for the working classes, as characterized by the two stages of the Paris Revolution – the February triumph of the literary spokesmen, and the June defeat of the workers on the barricades – and the humiliating failure in London of the Third Chartist Petition.

The bourgeoisie, having taken power by challenging and thrusting aside, as the *Communist Manifesto* puts it, 'the motley feudal ties that bound man to his "natural superiors"', was now in a position to utilize the newly unleashed resources of society to the demands of the 'naked self-interest' that was the motivating principle of its thirst for power. And in the ruthless embodiment of this mode of production, what it did was to resolve 'personal worth into exchange value, and in place of the numberless indefeasible chartered freedoms' characteristic of the system it had (at least in France and England) overthrown, to 'set up that single, unconscionable freedom – free trade' (Marx 1973a: 70). The process of development thus unleashed exploded in every direction in a feverish quest for new markets, new sources of exploitation; for what distinguishes the bourgeois epoch from all earlier ones is its

> constant revolutionizing of production, [its] uninterrupted disturbance of all social conditions, [its] everlasting uncertainty and agitation . . . All fixed, fast-frozen relations, with their train of ancient and venerable prejudices and opinions, are swept away, all new-formed ones become antiquated before they can ossify. All that is solid melts into air, all that is holy is profaned, and man is at last compelled to face, with sober senses, his real conditions of life, and his relations with his kind (Marx 1973a: 70–1).

But at the same time 'the need of a constantly expanding market for its products chases the bourgeois over the whole surface of the globe. It must nestle everywhere, settle everywhere, establish connections everywhere' (1973a: 71). Hence the inexorable development of those forms of competitive nationalism which were increasingly to dominate the politics of Europe and to take Britain, France and Germany into the obscurest corners of the world in the race for power and influence and territorial acquisition. And all this, it was predicted, could lead in one direction only: from crisis to crisis, an intensification of the class struggle and the sharpening of the contradictions and dichotomies of the system, to its eventual breakdown and the triumph of a revolutionary working class. That, at least, was how it looked to Marx and Engels at the time. Against the apparent logic of such a view, history has added new and unforeseen perspectives of development and change.

7

Matthew Arnold:
culture and the established order

Beyond the middle of the nineteenth century, with industrial capitalism transforming British society wholesale, new and profound divisions had opened up between the classes, which set them further apart than ever on opposite sides of a seemingly impassable gulf. Increasing luxury and privilege were being bought at the cost of increasing deprivation and impoverishment. There was, in William Morris's words, the 'terrible spectacle . . . of two peoples, living street by street, and door by door – people of the same blood, the same tongue, and at least nominally living under the same laws – but the one civilized and the other uncivilized' (1973: 111).

This was the world in which Matthew Arnold wrote *Culture and Anarchy*. It was a world that had been organized and harnessed to make the acquisitive powers of property and capital available to the most active and ambitious new men of the middle class – entrepreneurs, managers, employers, businessmen – the Brocklebanks and Bounderbys and Veneerings of the age, the practical men of affairs who had been enfranchised by the Reform Act of 1832, and provided with the necessary grounds for unlimited expansion by the success in 1846 of the Cobden–Bright campaign for free trade and the establishment of favourable conditions for the rapid development of industrial capitalism after 1848. As Marx (1972: 273–4) puts it, commenting on this world in the 1860s:

> No intelligent observer can fail to see that capitalist production (though, historically considered, it dates but from yesterday) has already sapped the vital energy of the people at the root; that the degeneration of the industrial population is only kept in check by the absorption of fresh and vigorous elements from the rural districts; and that even agricultural workers, though they live in the open air, . . . are already passing into a phase of incipient decay. The capitalists have such good reason for denying the suffering of the legions of workers who surround them, that in practice they are no more moved by the prospect of the coming degeneration and final disappearance of the human race than they are disturbed by the prospect that the earth may one day fall into the sun. When there is a boom on the stock exchange, everyone who takes part in the swindle knows that sooner or later the crash will come, but each man hopes that the disaster will involve his neighbours, after he himself has taken safe refuge with a goodly share of loot. 'After me, the deluge!' is the watchword of every capitalist and of every capitalist nation.

Was this the same world in which Arnold himself could talk of 'the very framework and exterior order of the State, whoever may administer the State' as 'sacred'? If it was, clearly the new leisured class had a very different view of it in their pursuit of art and culture from those whose task it was to produce the wealth which made that pursuit possible. Of course, there were those among the privileged who recognized the intolerable nature of the contradictions that disfigured their world. But for the most part the middle class was intent on justifying its ruthless expansionary practice, and its intellectuals were culturally distancing themselves from the crudities of material exploitation, surrounding themselves with the consoling and protective luxuries that confirmed their place in society. One is reminded of the myopic certainties of Kenge in *Bleak House* (Chapter 62), proclaiming 'a very prosperous community . . . a very great country', and 'gently moving his right hand as if it were a silver trowel with which to spread the cement of his words on the structure of the system, and consolidate it for a thousand ages'.

This was the England that Marx found himself commenting on in 1864 in the course of his inaugural address to the International Working Men's Association – a country 'unrivalled for the development of its industry and the growth of its commerce' (Marx 1974: 73). It had produced, as Marx scathingly reports from Gladstone's 1863 budget speech – the Chancellor 'dazzled by the "Progress of the Nation" statistics dancing before his eyes' – a growth in taxable income 'so astonishing as to be almost incredible'. And '"This intoxicating augmentation of wealth and power", adds Mr Gladstone, "is entirely confined to classes of property"' (Marx 1974: 75) – at a time, that is, when 'death by starvation' had risen almost to the rank of an institution . . . in the metropolis of the British Empire' (1974: 78).

What makes it possible to separate or to conceal such shaming contrasts is what Tawney (1964: 190) calls the 'decorous equivocation' of ruling-class control, interposing

> a veil between men's minds and the realities, which though not too opaque to allow the latter to be seen, changes their colour and proportions, and, while revealing their existence, conceals their significance. Thus . . . the rulers of mankind [!] are enabled to maintain side by side two standards of social ethics, without the risk of their colliding. Keeping one set of values for use, and another for display, they combine, without conscious insincerity, the moral satisfaction of idealistic principles with the material advantages of realistic practice.

This is an ideological process which the ruling classes of Victorian society brought to perfection during the second half of the nineteenth century, not only to ensure that they would continue to control the 'intoxicating augmentation of wealth and power' that was in their hands, but also to justify their possession of it. And it is no accident that 1848 should have the significance it does. For 1848 defines with singular intensity, in the revolutionary collisions that occurred all over Europe, the triumph of industrial capitalism, and a deepening of the divisions between the privileged and the dispossessed, the educated and the ignorant, the rich and the poor, which became so marked as to set up two seemingly incompatible orders in society. So that only now is it possible to speak of middle-class intellectuals putting 'a veil between men's minds and the realities' and detaching themselves from 'the rough and coarse actions' (Arnold 1932: 73) going on around them while living on the proceeds of these actions. Only now is it 'possible to speak of classical culture becoming the preserve of the apolitical aesthete', since 'it is only now that culture and politics . . . become separate spheres' and 'the "pure spirit" can renounce all attempts to penetrate and change the world', giving way to 'the spirit of profundity and inwardness, the silent spirit purified of 'rhetorical dross', the 'babble of civilization', and of 'literary jacobinism' (Jens 1973: 74–5).

This is the context in which Matthew Arnold's *Culture and Anarchy* has its place. It is the work of a man who, educated at Rugby and Oxford, aged 20 at the time of the Second Chartist Petition of 1842 and the great risings of the working class in the North of England, had absorbed the changed (and spiritualized) aspirations of the affluent middle class after the watershed of 1848. One might have thought that his work as an HM Inspector of Schools would have given him a deeper insight into the contradictions and dichotomies of his time, and strengthened his will to resist the drift towards pessimism that took over. But in the changed conditions of the world he found himself living in after 1848, 'wandering between two worlds, one dead, / The other powerless to be born' (Arnold 1949: 151), it seemed to him – infected by the 'strange disease of modern life, / With its sick hurry, its divided aims' (1949: 147) – there was no way forward. Though his brother Tom had argued at the time that this was a world made intolerable by 'the total distortion of human relationships caused by the systematisation of selfishness manifest above all in the "class of capitalists"' (Lucas 1971: 59), and had to be changed, Arnold disdainfully rejected the possibility. As he saw it, to change the world was to do no more than tinker with a dream (Lucas 1971: 57). So that in the end even his preoccupation with religion, with the classics of philosophy and literature, served only to reinforce the sense of disillusionment and self-defeat that coloured all his poetry, and to confirm, through the contemplative and ahistorical terms on which his concept of literature and culture was to be defined, his support for the established order.

Arnold published *Culture and Anarchy* in 1869. He describes it as 'an essay in Political and Social Criticism' (Arnold 1932: 1), and clearly invites us to judge it in these terms. Its immediate background was the series of huge working-class demonstrations, organized by trade unions and radicals with the help of the International, which occurred in towns and cities all over Britain from the spring of 1866 in support of Gladstone's Reform Bill, and with increasing momentum following the Bill's defeat in the summer and the public insults of men like Robert Lowe about workers having 'no sense of decency or morality' (Briggs 1965: 251) and therefore being unfit for the franchise. But the book was actually written in direct response to the mass demonstrations held in Trafalgar Square and Hyde Park to protest against the formation of a Tory government, which had been denounced by John Bright as 'a declaration of war against the working classes' (Briggs 1965: 238); and it reflects the alarm of many ruling-class observers about what they called working-class anarchy and its threat to the state – the substanceless Tory belief that England was on the verge of revolution, though this eventually forced Disraeli to take his 'leap in the dark' and put forward a Reform Bill of his own in 1867.

Arnold's specific purpose thus seems to have been, on the one hand, in Lionel Trilling's words, to attempt 'to allay the hysterical fears of the upper classes' (Arnold 1949: 434) and, on the other, to appeal to a largely philistine middle-class public to stir itself from its narrow sectarian preoccupations and take a more disinterested, informed and civilized attitude to the pressing problems of society. It is in these terms, and as a *remedy* for the 'diseases of his time' and its 'anarchic' tendencies, that he sets out to argue his case for culture.

It is not a very convincing case; and this has at least as much to do with its failure to define the basic conditions at issue and thus to get to grips with the underlying causes of the social divisiveness of the period as with the manner in which it is argued. Indeed, it reads more like a piece of special pleading than an analysis, grounded on the comfortable assumption that a middle-class concept of culture actually has the power to provide some sort of solution to the complex problems of social conflict. And its logic is deeply flawed by the disingenuous terms of reference one meets with on almost every page of the book, whether these take the form of a general plea for 'inaction' aided by 'right reason' and 'the will of God' (Arnold 1932: 33) in the 'study of perfection', 'the best that is thought and said in the world' (1932: 6), or of propositions invoking 'sweetness and light' as 'characters of perfection' (1932: 54). And it is obsessed to the point of tedium with culture. For culture is everywhere Arnold's primary concern – culture in the abstract, culture as a thing in itself, as an autonomous pursuit of the mind, as freedom from constraint; culture against 'machinery' and 'anarchy', the anarchy of machinery and 'faith in machinery' (1932: 49) – since 'he who works for machinery, he who works for hatred, works only for confusion', whereas 'culture looks beyond machinery, culture hates hatred' and 'has one great passion, the passion for sweetness and light' and 'for making them prevail' (1932: 69). From all of which it must inevitably follow that culture is the key to social health, and is to be found embodied in the 'civilizing' institutions of the established order.

In the context of the actual conditions of the time, the inequality and divisiveness and exploitation of a system that held millions, in Milton's words, 'numb and neglected', and the contradictions even then being exposed by the rigorous dialectical methods Marx was employing in his analysis of the capitalist economy (Volume One of *Capital* was published in 1867) – not to mention the fundamental questions being raised by men like Darwin, Ruskin and Mill – the Arnoldian thesis begins to look decidedly parochial and one-sided. And ludicrous though it may be to compare Arnold with Marx, the comparison does after all have a certain validity, since not only were they near contemporaries, but Arnold's second language was German, and Marx himself was living in London at the very time when *Culture and Anarchy* was being written, as he had been for nearly 20 years. Furthermore, Marx, too, had concerned himself with the political and social problems of England in various newspaper articles published in the 1850s and 1860s as well as through his involvement with the International Working Men's Association from the 1860s onwards; so there is little excuse for Arnold not to know what was going on. But, of course, the question is whether, if he had known, it would have made any difference. In the light of his reaction even to men like Bright and Frederick Harrison, one has to doubt it. For Marx, after all, *begins* with the unacceptable premiss that theory, 'the reality and power of thought', must be demonstrated in practice (as 'practical, human-sensuous activity') (Marx 1975: 422), and he made it his great task to investigate the inescapable material conditions on which the capitalist system functioned – to get at the sources, the grounds; to make

> the essential connection between private property, greed, the separation of labour, capital and landed property, exchange and competition, value and the devaluation of man, monopoly and competition, etc. – the connection between the entire system of estrangement and the money system (1975: 323).

And Arnold would have recoiled from any such investigation. It would have meant questioning the very institutions he supported and accepting that *all* cultural manifestations are to be thought of not as 'independent', 'universalizing', 'autonomous' but as an 'outgrowth of the conditions of capitalist production and capitalist property' (Marx and Engels 1968: 49) – that they do not have a life of their own but are material products determined by the contradictions of material reality as formulated by the pressures of history, 'the existing conflict between the social forces of production and the relations of production' (Marx and Engels 1968: 182). And this would have meant accepting that culture was involved in a historical struggle for rights, needs, and living conditions; and that this struggle was a *class* struggle. And to do that he would have had to think his whole conception of society back to its roots, and start from scratch. He would have had to break through the barriers of his class conditioning and call the whole system into question in a 'ruthless criticism of the existing order' (Marx 1975: 207).

And Arnold was simply not equipped for such a task. His prescriptive terms for social health, rooted as they are in the rigidities of the class structure, reflecting an ideological apparatus determined by the underlying material conditions of the capitalist system at work, merely serve to reinforce the very myths of consciousness that Marx was seeking to unmask. They are, in other words, directed towards justifying the psychological assumptions of a leisured class and maintaining its privileges and rights, rather than (in any sense) towards creating conditions for the resolution of real problems. To suggest, with Eagleton (1976: 104), that Arnold had a logically considered programme for the 'radical realignment of class-forces within the ruling bloc of Victorian England, so as more effectively to incorporate the proletariat', is to credit him with an understanding of the historical process (and of the economic-material forces it involved) which the terms of the argument of *Culture and Anarchy* clearly demonstrate he did not have. Indeed, one questions the claim with astonishment – the more so because Eagleton (1976: 105) compares this programme with Gramsci's concept of *hegemony*, declaring that 'what Antonio Gramsci demands for the modern proletariat ... Matthew Arnold seeks for the Victorian bourgeoisie'. But on what grounds can Arnold's appeal for culture, for the cultivation of the mind, the pursuit of 'harmonious perfection', be considered a feasible objective in a society so deeply rooted in class division and economic subordination as to force a great majority of its citizens to spend most of their lives struggling for the bare necessities? Who, one asks, beyond a tiny minority of privileged people at the time, would have had the leisure or the energy, let alone the incentive, to cultivate what can 'only be won by unreservedly cultivating many sides in us' (Arnold 1932: 20)?

The disabling fact is that this harmonious perfection was to be sought not by improving the *material* conditions of people's lives, or by trying 'to teach down to the level of inferior classes' (1932: 70), but simply by *rising above* or *doing away with* class altogether through 'culture and poetry' and through religion, which (in 'its instinct for perfection') apparently 'supplies the language to judge it' (1932: 56). In other words, the pursuit of perfection is bound up with religion, the *idea* of religion, as 'the greatest and most important of the efforts by which the human race has manifested its impulse to perfect itself' (1932: 47). In the sense that 'religion says: the kingdom of God is within you', so 'culture, in like manner, places human perfection in an internal condition, in the growth and predominance of our humanity proper, as distinguished from our animality' (1932: 47).

These are fine sentiments for the affluent. But being the product of that world of 'inverted consciousness . . . whose spiritual aroma is religion' (Marx 1975: 244), they can afford to ignore the record of history which created the class divisions conducive to such manifestations. And to a man or woman denied basic (perhaps merely animal) rights and caught in the trap of a ruthless economic system, they remain little more than a repressive formula.

On such grounds, it is not to be wondered at that there should have been people telling Arnold (1932: 22) that spirituality, and sweetness and light are, all moonshine'. The very possibility that ideas which 'divest knowledge of all that [is] harsh, uncouth, difficult, abstract, professional, exclusive' (1932: 70) for the sake of 'an inward spiritual activity' (1932: 64) could be put forward as a means of resolving the momentous inequities and injustices of mid-Victorian society must have seemed to those who were seriously involved in the struggle for change some sort of grim joke. How could spirituality and sweetness and light, they might have asked, be any answer to the harsh, uncouth, difficult and material contradictions that confronted people in this world – in terms of which, as Marx (1973b: 300) pointed out in 1856, 'all our invention and progress seem to result in endowing material forces with intellectual life, and in stultifying human life into a material force'?

Arnold seems to be aware of the difficulty, for in dealing with culture as a concept he deplores the fact that it has come to be associated with 'a notion of something bookish, pedantic and futile' and that 'we cannot use a word more perfectly free from all shadow of reproach' (Arnold 1932: 6). So one would expect him to extend the context. Instead, he immediately defines the word bookishly. It is, as he puts it, the

> pursuit of our total perfection by means of getting to know, on all matters which most concern us, the best which has been thought and said in the world; and through this knowledge, turning a stream of fresh and free thought upon our stock notions and habits, which we now follow staunchly but mechanically (1932: 6).

This is surely an inadequate definition for a word that ought properly to convey some awareness of the range and diversity of the activities people engage in to the enrichment of society, including a great many that have nothing to do with thinking and reading. Conceived in such narrow terms, as an intellectual process pursued and refined upon by the educated few – those who have the freedom and the leisure to cultivate detachment – it is bound to remain inadequate, class-bound, elitist, exclusive, and condescending towards all that is linked to the basic work process, the 'stock notions and habits' of 'the raw and uncultivated many' (Arnold 1932: 76).

Thus, Arnold's culture becomes a sort of absolute guide and rule, independent of and uncontaminated by 'practice, politics, and everything of the kind' – a source of superior judgement capable of getting up and acting of its own accord, of 'disinterestedly trying . . . to see things as they really are' (1932: 30) and of showing 'its singleminded love of perfection, its desire simply to make reason and the will of God prevail' (1932: 60), though it is actually incapable of seeing or desiring or being single-minded about anything. Furthermore, the abstracts it is conceived in terms of are derived from the ethical ideals of Christianity. For while Arnold (1932: 30) is happy enough to accept that 'the religious side in man' is 'not the whole of man', he is clearly convinced that

> it would still have been better for a man, during the last 1800 years, to have been a Christian and a member of one of the great Christian communions, than to have been a Jew or a Socinian; because the being in contact with the main stream of human life is of more moment to a man's total spiritual growth, and for his bringing to perfection the gifts committed to him, which is his business on earth, than any speculative opinion which he may hold or think he holds (1932: 30).

The sectarian ethnocentric assumptions implicit in this declaration reveal a central inconsistency in Arnold's concept of culture, 'by which superiority and power are lodged both in a rhetoric of belonging, or being "at home", so to speak, and in a rhetoric of administration' (Said 1984: 13). For in distinguishing between those who belong and those who do not, it suggests that neither Jews nor Socinians – nor for that matter followers of any other religion – can hope to 'bring to perfection the gifts committed to them', because they are not in contact with the main stream of human life. This is a very strange argument for a creed that urges reconciliatory virtues, since even as it 'enjoins' and flexibly 'affirms' a greater and more 'disinterested' intelligence, it seems to be asserting that it is only in the parish of mainstream Christianity that a man can bring his gifts to perfection.

Under these conditions one has to ask whether there *is* a case to be made for Arnold's advocacy of culture as a weapon of enlightenment, and for his avowed mission, which was to transform a nation of philistines into a nation based upon 'an inward working' by means of 'the best art and poetry of the Greeks' with 'the moral and religious fibre' (Arnold 1932: 54–5) of the Hebraic European impulse – the ideals of the man of science and poetry with the virtues of the Puritan. For the critical and descriptive terms he employs toward this laudable end leave so many questions unanswered and beg so many others that one wonders how he could even have begun to think them adequate. To argue, for instance, that culture 'knows that the sweetness and light of the few must be imperfect until the raw and unkindled masses of humanity are touched with sweetness and light' (1932: 69) – and, beyond this, in a feeble echo of Marx, that culture even 'seeks to do away with classes, to make the best that has been thought and known in the world current everywhere' (1932: 70) – is to argue in face of all that the divisive institutions of society appeared most anxious to perpetuate. And if Arnold's idea of culture, nourished on Church and school and university as breeding-grounds of middle-class ideology and discrimination, had any such intent, it fails to tell us how this was to be achieved without some sort of revolutionary struggle against its own interests. On the contrary, Arnold's (1932: 212) aim was to turn people into 'docile echoes of the eternal voice, pliant organs of the infinite will'

(1932: 212), passive upholders of the status quo. Which is to suggest that his words were not intended to mean 'doing away with classes' at all, but rather 'smoothing over the differences between' or 'rising above' or by-passing them or simply 'dismissing them as irrelevant'.

He seems to believe that if his plea for sweetness and light and for people who will carry the great inward message of culture 'from one end of society to the other' is repeated often enough, it will miraculously eradicate the class conditions that stand in its way. This being so, it is hardly surprising that Arnold (1932: 96) should be accused of 'keeping aloof from the work and hope of a multitude of earnest-hearted men, and of merely toying with poetry and aesthetics', as he says he is. You cannot expect to satisfy such accusations by suggesting a little 'inaction' to enable us to 'lay in a stock of light for our difficulties' against 'the rougher and coarser actions going on' (1932: 73) around us. For that still leaves unanswered the problems of 'ignorance and anarchy' among 'the raw and uncultivated masses'. And though Arnold suggests that a possible solution for such difficulties might be to conscript the whole populace into military service, where they would at least be taught 'the idea of public duty and discipline' (1932: 76), he seems almost at once to recognize the barbarity and injustice of this method of countering the threat to culture by reporting a remark made to him by the manager of the Clay Cross works during the Crimean War: that 'sooner than submit to a conscription the population of that district would flee to the mines, and lead a sort of Robin Hood life under ground' (1932: 76).

Not that we should deceive ourselves into thinking that Arnold approved of this sort of action. On the contrary, it seems to him a characteristic instance of the ways in which the people so often sought to evade the demands of public duty and discipline. It is an assertion, in other words, of what he mockingly describes as 'the prime right and blessedness of doing as one likes' (1932: 76) – which is an idea Arnold clearly finds attractive in spite of its gestural vagueness for he exploits it to the full, giving it a chapter to itself. Thus 'doing as one likes' becomes a kind of refrain, constantly varied and reiterated, and applied with particular derision to what he takes to be the indulgent activities of the working class as a whole. 'This class, pressed constantly by the hard daily compulsion of material wants', as he puts it, 'is naturally the very centre and stronghold of our national idea, that it is a man's ideal right and felicity to do as he likes' (1932: 75). The dubious logic and imbalance of the proposition – that men and women so deeply oppressed by such harsh and relentless compulsion are in any position to do as they like – does not seem to matter.

But this, of course, is not what Arnold has in mind. He means that when the working man takes it into his head to dare to protest against the conditions under which he has to work he is acting irresponsibly and making himself a threat to society. The assumption that a working class with too much time on its hands must inevitably tend towards anarchy, or worse, towards revolutionary action. Nervously, and with a tenuous grasp of logic, he states:

> More and more, because of our blind faith in machinery, because of our want of light to enable us to look beyond machinery to the end for which machinery is valuable, this and that man, and this and that body of men, all over the country, are beginning to assert and put in practice an Englishman's right to do as he likes; his right to march

where he likes, meet where he likes, enter where he likes, hoot as he likes, threaten as
he likes, smash as he likes (1932: 76).

It is Arnold's view that the working man, the 'Hyde Park rough', as he is called,

has no idea of a state, in its collective and corporate character controlling, as
government, the free swing of this or that one of its members in the name of the
higher reason of all of them . . . He sees the rich, the aristocratic class, in occupation
of the executive government, and so if he is stopped from making Hyde Park a
bear-garden or the streets impassable, he says he is being butchered by the aristocracy
(1932: 80–1).

One notes the sense of mounting alarm conveyed by these two passages, and
the refusal even to countenance that the working man could have any alternative
concept of government and hence any serious purpose in demonstrating in the
streets or in the parks, as Marx suggests he had, and the history of the
working-class movement proves he had. He is little more than a 'rough' who 'has
not yet quite found his groove and settled down to his work, and so he is just
asserting his personal liberty a little' (Arnold 1932: 80), and in the process
turning Hyde Park – normally set aside on Sundays for the civilized parades of
high society – into a 'bear-garden'. And because he insists on behaving in a
thoroughly uncivilized manner, he must therefore be unflinchingly discouraged
in the interests of stability, 'right reason' and the 'light' that culture provides. For
it is clear, at least to Arnold, that these raw and uncultivated people,
demonstrating 'the anarchical tendency of our worship of freedom' (1932: 76),
are not interested in reason, and consequently have no right to claim even a little
of the leisure or the wealth that are the basis for it.

Such an argument is difficult to reconcile with any idea of a society worth living
in. Not only does it misrepresent and trivialize the gravity of the claims being
made by working-class men and women; in denying that they have any right to
agitate for a proper share in the benefits of society, it makes a travesty of social
justice. And if this is what Arnold means by 'giving the best help towards finding
some lasting truth to minister to the diseased spirit of the time', one can only say
that he has strange ways of going about it.

His appeal is launched, of course, with the best of liberal intentions. It is an
attempt to argue for 'the intelligible law of things in pursuit of the progress of
humanity towards perfection' (1932: 202) and to apply these general and
universal standards of value and truth to the problems, as he puts it, of 'that
Thyestean banquet of clap-trap which English public life for these many years
has been' (1932: 210). The trouble is these intentions are confused by the naive
and unhistorical assumptions on which they are based – a process of thinking
which, because it functions in terms of the ideology of a class-divided world, is
only able to reproduce distorted reflections of the underlying conditions,
presenting partial truths as if they were universal laws in a vague Parnassian
concept of reality which in effect confirms the mystifying abstracts of the
established order. And with Arnold's constant appeal to the 'beautiful', to the
aesthetics of contemplative detachment, one is reminded of Marx's distinctions
concerning the events in Paris in 1848:

The February revolution was the *beautiful* revolution, the revolution of universal
sympathy, because . . . it existed only as a phrase, only in words. The June revolution

is the *ugly* revolution, the repulsive revolution, because realities have taken the place of words (1973a: 131).

Indeed, the very language Arnold uses to define the superior attributes of culture is so resonant with acceptance of the authority of the established order – the patriarchal state as the 'centre of light and authority' (Arnold 1932: 94), and organ of the 'collective best self' (1932: 96) – as to leave him almost disabled as a critic. Faced with the ideological suppression of inconvenient (and sometimes ugly) facts, the 'rough and coarse actions' of the real world, one finds oneself continually questioning his notions, and wondering whether he actually understands the implications of what he is arguing. It is all very well to believe in 'right reason' and 'the progress of humanity towards perfection', but you cannot build anything solid on such questionable grounds. Yet Arnold (1932: 204) hopes that somehow they will 'come gradually to fill the framework of the State', even though he defines the normal procedures of those who administer this framework as a 'banquet of clap-trap'. The suggestion is that clap-trap can be modified and *transformed* by 'faith in the progress of humanity towards perfection' (1932: 204), and that people who indulge in clap-trap are to be considered as likely candidates to fill the framework of the state with the high abstract concepts of culture!

Naturally the working class has to remain outside this framework because 'from the very nature of its condition' it does not 'have a sufficiency of light which comes by culture' (1932: 93); and so long as it persists in clamouring against the authority of the state, it can have no part to play inside it. Quite the reverse. For the preservation of culture and the state, Arnold would have the instruments of law and order, as he asserts in a truly Thatcherite injunction, used 'unflinchingly' to suppress the riotous instincts of the working class, because 'in our eyes, the very framework and exterior order of the State, whoever may administer the State, is sacred' (1932: 204). He would urge it as a duty to stand behind the state's administrators 'steadily and with undivided heart . . . in repressing anarchy and disorder; because', as he stresses, 'without order there can be no society, and without society there can be no human perfection' (1932: 203).

This may be an argument for protecting the privileged. But in denying others their right to challenge or even to question the order that controls, its logic is very perceptibly warped. And it is a specious argument, based upon the false premiss that the working class was actually intent on anarchy and disorder; for the 1867 Reform Act had already made it clear that the great majority of workers would vote for the ruling class parties. But above all it is an argument that refuses to recognize the obvious fact that the social order could not have been maintained at all without the working classes; that it was *they* who produced the wealth that gave such licence to its administrators; and that without that wealth there could have been no civilizing process and hence no pursuit of harmonious perfection.

But this is not the point as far as Arnold is concerned. He seems indifferent both to the logic and the injustice of it. He comes down on the side of the manipulators because he fears 'the playful giant' (Arnold 1932: 81) in his midst. And though he has uncomplimentary things to say about barbarians, philistines, non-conformists and liberals alike, he nevertheless accepts the part they play in maintaining the 'sacred framework' – assuming that, however bankrupt the order of the administrators, it is the only kind of order possible because it is the order that controls.

These are the actual conditions on which Arnold's plea for cultural enlightenment turns out to be based. On the one hand, you have culture as the 'pursuit of our total perfection by means of getting to know, on all matters which most concern us, the best which has been thought and said in the world' (1932: 6), and on the other, 'anarchy' as the enemy of this great aim. The juxtaposition is not very subtle, for it ought to have been obvious that the enemy of any sort of culture worth having is not anarchy but the oppressive conditions imposed upon millions of people by a system which condemns them to poverty and cultural deprivation. But Arnold sticks fondly to it. And because for him culture is ideologically dependent on the state as 'the organ of our collective best self, of our national right reason', and anarchy synonymous with 'whatever brings risk of tumult and disorder' (1932: 97) to the state, all unrest must be kept under rigorous control. Of this he has no doubt. To protect the order of society, all 'monster processions in the streets and forcible eruptions into the parks ought to be unflinchingly forbidden and repressed' (1932: 203–4).

It is difficult to read this as anything other than an affirmation of reactionary power. In giving his undivided support to a framework of order based upon repression, class inequality and exploitation, Arnold clearly puts the aims of culture above the needs of people, and naively provides the ruling class with ideological instruments to justify and make respectable its activities. To assert that the framework of the state is sacred is to affirm the machinery of government, the class-divided structure of society, *as it stands*. And to suggest that this framework, this machinery, this structure, can be transformed from within by 'the elements and helps of perfection' – so 'to fashion its internal composition and all its laws and institutions conformably to them, and to make the State more and more the expression, as we say, of our best self' (1932: 204) – is to put forward a prescription so distant from the actual conditions that prevailed as to incite and thoroughly to deserve the derisory comments it received from the literalists. It is as if Arnold were appealing to everyone – except of course the populace, not to mention women of all classes – to pack themselves voluntarily off to the cloistered repose of Oxford, and there (in sublime inaction) to submit to 'the beauty and sweetness of that beautiful place' (1932: 61); from the experience of which they would emerge imbued with the inwardness and light of right reason required of them in the outside world.

No doubt this is a travesty of Arnold's intentions. But Oxford was, after all, a stronghold for the privileged (and exclusively male) few; and as part of the sacred framework of things and as a source of sweetness and light – which the barbarian and philistine men it existed for seemed capable only of transforming into clap-trap – it was not a place for the working class, 'raw and half-developed . . . half hidden amidst its poverty and squalor' (1932: 105), its sterner self addicted to 'bawling, hustling, and smashing', its 'lighter self [to] beer' (1932: 108). There could be no place in Oxford for such people, even the best. Their place was outside in the dark, where they would have to remain until such time as the light of culture could be filtered down to them from the enlightened organs of the state. As for women, not once does Arnold consider why there was no place for *them* at the universities. From his silence, one can only assume acceptance of the prevailing religious view, very much Arnoldian in tone, that 'desire for learning in women was against the will of God' (Woolf 1986: 29, 172).

Such deficiencies are fundamentally damaging to the whole thesis of *Culture and Anarchy*. They demonstrate a failure to think connectedly or to face up to the contradictions of nineteenth-century industrial society, the ugliness behind the ideological façade. Arnold's culture thus becomes, in John Goode's words, 'both a way of condemning the actual world and all attempts to participate in it by social action as illusory, and an escape from its intractability' (Lucas 1971: 56) into a world apart, 'beyond human history and human relationship' (1971: 57).

It is not surprising, therefore, that Arnold should have wished to avoid all direct reference to the great revolutionary thinkers of his time, though Marx and Darwin were both active, and average men of intelligence (whose normal education as yet included no element of natural science) had been forced by the strident controversy about Darwinism to realize that the patient investigations of the men of science were changing the whole aspect of the universe. They had to be left out, because their ideas would have raised too many awkward questions. Including Hegel, Marx and Darwin among 'the best that has been thought and known in the world' would have meant having to deal with their ideas. Besides, 'best' for Arnold means 'most beautiful', and his pantheon seems to have been made up of people whose souls were filled with sweetness and light. The bitterness and the uncompromising intensity of Marx would never have fitted; he was too Hebraic, too 'severely preoccupied with an awful sense of the impossibility of being at ease in Zion' (Arnold 1932: 135), and, above all, too penetrating. Arnold, flinching away from such unaccommodating truths about his world, puts his faith instead in an ahistorical wisdom beyond the reach of time, and refuses to recognize the material grounds of the unyielding struggle that was being fought out between the forces of reactionary privilege and the dispossessed majority. 'Only so sore and angry a spirit' as that of Marx, 'so ill at ease in the world', as Wilson (1972: 321), observes, 'could have recognized and seen into the causes of the wholesale mutilation of humanity, the grim collisions, the uncomprehended convulsions, to which the age of great profits was doomed'.

Not that Arnold was unaware of what was going on. But he looked upon the collisions and convulsions as dangerous and destabilizing. His response to the proofs of mutilation in the East End of London, for instance, was to appeal to the liberals to stop trying to answer it with their inadequate Hebraic methods and adopt instead a Hellenic view – the accumulation of an adequate stock of light – while at the same time insisting that those who continued to suffer mutilation should be prevented from organizing against it.

It is a feeble argument, and cannot have been taken seriously by anyone with any grasp of the issues that were at stake. It proceeds upon the groundless assumption that there is a special area in which culture can operate on its own, independent of conditions, above the storm, unaffected by dispute, and capable (as a power derived from sojourn at such beautiful places as Oxford) of ennobling the ignoble and breaking down the barriers of class. Envisaging his strictly non-political vision of a 'free play of consciousness, an increased desire for sweetness and light, and all the bent we call Hellenising' as 'the master-impulse . . . of the life of our nation and of humanity', he sees the true workers for a better world as 'docile echoes of the eternal voice, pliant organs of the infinite will . . . going along with the essential movement of the world' (Arnold 1932: 212).

It is difficult to credit that Arnold can have meant what he is saying here. For one thing is certain: that such workers as these – more like passive signifiers, the tranquillized agents of eternity, than human beings – are unlikely to find themselves going along with the essential movement of anything other than those who control the material organs of power. In the world of capitalist competition, the social order is impelled and dominated not by the docile or the pliant but by the perverse, the devious and the cunning, by aggression and self-interest. Nor can we allow ourselves to be deceived into thinking otherwise. Putting one's faith in the occult laws of the infinite will is no answer. Those who want a 'better world' will need to know precisely where they stand and what they are up against and how to act in the world of material reality.

But with Arnold materiality seems hardly to count. In his refusal to recognize that spiritual values have a material base, he is continually drifting off into the ideal. It is as if he were convinced that we only have to take a few steps in the right direction to find some sort of Arcadia waiting for us. He himself may have found it, free to walk the quads and corridors of Oxford or the gardens of great country houses in pursuit of the best. But it is dishonest to suggest that such privileged conditions can magically be made available to everyone; or, to put it another way, that the world at large might in fact be some kind of Arcadian Oxford in disguise, which docility and pliancy and a diligent study of perfection will open up to us.

For, of course, the world is not that sort of place. Though rich in splendour and Arcadian beauty and in so many respects a kind of terrestrial paradise, it is also harsh and complex, rife with contradictions, the historical struggles of people and societies caught up in conflicting stages of development; and as such resistant to the beautifying visions of the cultivated few. Not that this is to suggest that the great cultural achievements of civilization do not have a significant part to play in the process; but only to stress that these achievements are products of material conditions, and derive whatever significance they have from being firmly rooted in the real world of human needs and from the ways in which they reflect and embody the complexities of that world as imaginative extensions of reality.

Arnold's vision of culture, on the contrary, puts the real world – the world of social and political action, where men and women are engaged in a constant struggle for personal and communal solvency – at a distance, as a structure to be stood away from, held at arm's length, while we submit to 'right reason and the will of God', the eternal and the infinite, the forms of perfection. And presumably what happens to those who work the machinery to enable us to indulge in this felicitous activity is unimportant. Beyond ensuring that they are kept under control by the functionaries of law and order – for, as we have seen, the forms of perfection cannot be sought without repression – they are not our concern. Our concern is with 'enlightening ourselves and qualifying ourselves to act less at random' (Arnold 1932: 73), according to 'an instinct prompting [the mind] to try to know the best that is known and thought in the world, irrespectively of practice, politics, and everything of the kind', and 'to value knowledge as they approach this best, without the intrusion of any other consideration whatever' (Arnold 1949: 247).

This is a view of culture which assumes the right of a privileged minority to dissociate themselves from politics and practice and all problems connected with the machinery of living, and turn their minds to the contemplation of more palatable issues, while the rest of us continue to provide them with the means to go on doing so without disturbance. It is a view of culture symptomatic of the dislocations of a class-divided world. And Arnold's mystifying principles of cultural excellence conveniently provided that world with a respectable façade for its activities – helping to justify a system of exploitation, 'of folly, fraud and tyranny' (Morris 1973: 90), by which, millions of people were reduced to dispensable instruments of profit, and everything (including art and culture, for all the 'goods' they gestured to) was calculated according to the commodity values of the marketplace, and reduced to the level of a reified product, a thing.

This is a view of culture that survives today, in spite of all the upheavals the twentieth century has witnessed, to colour our world and keep the Arnoldian vision of disinterested contemplation alive in high and influential places. The system is dead. Long live the system.

8

William Morris:
the change beyond the change

The significance of William Morris's achievement, in forty years of diverse activity as artist and thinker, is to be measured in terms of the passion and commitment with which, through his grasp of history and his visionary concept of socialism, he argued the necessity of the interconnections between one activity and another across the class barriers of a divided society. In this sense, the contribution he made to the contentious debate about the place and function of art and culture in the capitalist order of Victorian England still has much to offer us today. For what distinguishes him is what he did with his fertile inventiveness, the generosity of spirit, the industry and conviction with which he addressed the problems of his time – what he *made* of the privileges he enjoyed as a member of the affluent middle classes of mid-nineteenth-century England.

It may be that his poetry was, as Henry James observed, 'only his sub-trade', and that he himself came to regard his facility as a poet, the narrative ease which enabled him to produce long poems without effort, as a 'form of pleasurable creation and relaxation . . . rather than his central place of encounter with his age' (Thompson 1977: 188), even though he did tell his daughter May that he considered *Sigurd the Volsung* an achievement 'he wished to be remembered by' (Henderson 1967: 206). At any rate, however harshly we judge such work, it is the part his poetry plays in the context of his activity as a whole that matters; what it revealed to him in self-discovery and discovery of the great aims he was moving towards. As a poet, Morris was (like most of his contemporaries) dominated by the Romantic movement, having been born in the aftermath of the great period of social radicalism. And in the two decades following the Reform Act, the years of his boyhood and youth leading up to and succeeding the crisis point of 1848, the revolutionary energy and urgency that had shaped the work of Wordsworth, Shelley and Byron had been transformed into the vatic assumptions of Tennyson and Browning, the irrational idealism of Carlyle and the pessimism of Arnold, in a world which had brought about irreversible changes in the economic and social organization of Britain – a world defined by the fundamental rifts and divisions that were so dramatically opened up between the possessing classes and the great mass of the working class beyond the defeats of the Chartists and the triumph of *laissez-faire* capitalism.

It was Morris's deepening awareness of these rifts and divisions, the contradictory pressures and constraints of his world, that turned his romantic idealism and its cult of passive suffering, its melancholy sense of impotence, its escapist fantasy, into active defiance of the system, and made him a socialist.

The transformation was not sudden. It started from Ruskinian distress and generalized revulsion, and came in stages, step by step, out of the challenge of immediate experience, heralded by the impact of a journey to Iceland, his study of the Norse sagas, the launching of the campaign for the protection of ancient buildings, and his involvement in the controversies over the Eastern Question which brought him into open collision with the forces of ruling-class prejudice and jingoism. But when it came, it brought about a profound and radical change of outlook, which 'broke through the narrowing charmed circle of defeatism of bourgeois culture' (Thompson 1977: 243) – and in this sense represents an essential key to any understanding of the imaginative and exploratory nature of Morris's work from the 1880s onward. To read *A Dream of John Ball, The Pilgrims of Hope, News from Nowhere* and the more directly political writing that forms the groundwork out of which these books were conceived is to register the extraordinary focus of Morris's achievement – his passionate sense of the beauty of the world and its artistic heritage, on the one hand, colliding with the impact upon him of the ugliness imposed upon it as a consequence of the capitalist pursuit of profit, on the other, and the explosive sense of indignation and of disgust this generated in him. But it was his reading of Marx that provided the connections, set the fuse burning, channelled the energy, and committed Morris to the Utopian perspectives of his vision of the future; which made him, in Thompson's words, at once 'a Marxist and a Utopian' (1977: 791), 'a Communist Utopian, with the full force of the transformed Romantic tradition behind him' (1977: 792). For what distinguished the work of the last 13 years of his life, at all levels, is the insistent and unsatisfied quest, 'its open, speculative quality, and its detachment of the imagination from the demands of conceptual precision' (1977: 790); its 'leap out of the kingdom of necessity into an imagined kingdom of freedom in which desire may actually indicate choices or impose itself as need' (1977: 798–9). Indeed, it is the insistence of this quest for the fulfilment of Utopian desire, as generated by 'the tensions of the revolutionary mind' in action (Lucas 1971: 278) towards the transformation of the whole social order, that drives Morris into the endless involvements of these years. It may have been, as May Morris observes, 'a long story of lecturing, travelling, office and editorial work, and that most difficult of all tasks, keeping the peace among people of different temperaments' (Henderson 1967: 325). But then that was all part of what Morris called 'making Socialists'. And though he loved words and the art that could be made from them, he was very much aware that 'if you do not act, you do nothing'. Which was why he spent so much of his time out on the streets, speaking at open-air meetings, selling *The Commonweal*, marching with others, travelling up and down the country. And at this level, words were to be used to incite action, as weapons of criticism and implements of imaginative awareness, as a means of wakening people to the need for action or encouraging those already active to further resistance. But at the same time most of his work of this period, even his late romances and his translation of the *Odyssey*, the designs he continued to busy himself with, the books he printed, has its part to play in pursuit of the aims he had committed himself to in 1883.

Few among his friends and literary acquaintances felt able to move with him when he called upon them to join the Federation. Rossetti had, of course, died in

1882; but if he had lived he would have declined to help – he was 'too extreme an individualist to take an interest in political matters', and, in Morris's view, lacked 'the grain of humility which makes a great man one of the people' (Thompson 1977: 766). Swinburne offered sympathy but nothing more; Edward Burne-Jones, perhaps his closest friend, stepped quietly out of range; Ruskin excused himself as having no strength left for the fight ('It is better that you should be in a cleft stick', he said, 'than make one out of me' (1977: 274)). As for the young W. B. Yeats, he also soon withdrew, though he was among those who met Morris at the height of his activity, in 1887 – after *A Dream of John Ball* had begun to appear in the pages of *The Commonweal*– when Morris opened his lecture room at Hammersmith to speakers of widely differing views, including Shaw, Andreas Scheu, Sidney Webb, Walter Crane, Annie Besant and Ernest Rhys (Henderson 1967: 355); and he has his own generous but strangely ambiguous impressions of Morris:

> I took to him first because of some little tricks of speech and body that reminded me of my old grandfather in Sligo, but soon discovered his spontaneity and joy and made him my chief of men. Today I do not set his poetry very high, but for an odd altogether wonderful line, or thought; and yet, if some angel offered me the choice, I would choose to live his life, poetry and all, rather than my own or any other man's. A reproduction of his portrait by Watts hangs over my mantelpiece with Henly's, and those of other friends. Its grave wide-open eyes, like the eyes of some dreaming beast, remind me of the open eyes of Titian's *Ariosto*, while the broad vigorous body suggests a mind that has no need of the intellect to remain sane, though it give itself to every fantasy: the dreamer of the Middle Ages (Yeats 1955: 141).

It seemed to Yeats (1955: 142) that this

> dream world of Morris was as much the antithesis of daily life as with other men of genius, but he was never conscious of the antithesis and so knew nothing of intellectual suffering. His intellect, unexhausted by speculation or casuistry, was wholly at the service of hand and eye, and whatever he pleased he did with an unheard-of ease and simplicity, and if style and vocabulary were at times monotonous, he could not have made them otherwise without ceasing to be himself.

The strange thing about this is that Yeats should have failed to recognize that Morris – unlike Ruskin, Rossetti and others of his contemporaries, dreaming of an idealized natural past – had made it his business to involve himself in the concerns of daily life; and that, far from knowing nothing about intellectual suffering, he was acutely conscious of the antithesis between dream and actuality, between 'what life might be for the majority of people and what it actually was' (Henderson 1967: 356). In fact, his vision of revolutionary transformation, of 'the change beyond the change', is, as John Goode writes, an 'affirmation of the *responsibility* of dream in a world in which consciousness has become ineradicably dislocated from the field of its existence' (Lucas 1971: 239); and as such his dream world becomes a central feature of all his socialist writings.

But then Yeats did not want to move along the path Morris had taken. He was already in the process of choosing or of having chosen for him paths which were to take him in quite other directions. It is indeed symptomatic that he should record getting angry about an attack upon religion at the last of the

Hammersmith meetings he went to. If there was to be any change of heart, Yeats (1955: 148–9) had argued,

> only religion could make it. What was the use of talking about some new revolution putting all things right, when the change must come, if come it did, with astronomical slowness, like the cooling of the sun, or it may be like the drying of the moon? Morris rang his chairman's bell, but I was too angry to listen, and he had to ring it a second time before I sat down. He said that night at supper, 'Of course I know there must be a change of heart, but it will not come as slowly as all that'.

The difference between the two of them is that, while Yeats 'gradually gave up thinking of and planning for some sudden change for the better' to put on the mask of tragic prophecy and pessimism, Morris knew that he had no right to give up. His socialism was founded not on youthful experiment or on irrational romanticism but on a 'longing for freedom and equality' and on a dialectic vision of the future rooted in 'the study of history and the love and practice of art' (Morris 1973: 245). It was sharpened on a hatred of capitalism, and motivated by the belief that men and women would one day rise up and sweep this noxious system aside to create a civilization *worth* living in. He may have described himself as a practical socialist, and he was that; but it is the vision that counts. And in thinking ahead towards 'the change beyond the change' (Morris 1968: 103), he was able to grasp the necessary logic of connection between the actual conditions of the life around him and the unrealized possibilities of social experience implicit in the concept of socialism.

Today, the kinds of questions Morris asked about the destructive conditions of his time have not lost their urgency. However changed the particular circumstances that govern our lives in the late twentieth century, we still live under the domination of a capitalist economy which functions by feeding off the common wealth of the people and by imposing restrictive and stunting conditions upon them. There is even much talk these days of a return to Victorian values, to 'free market' forces, to the sort of individualism that flourished in the 1880s. And it is perhaps no accident that this new crude emphasis on individual rights should, at the same time as it puts the rights of millions at risk, include a new assertion of the primacy of aesthetics – the aesthetics of art, the universalizing autonomy of 'literary consciousness' – over the ethical; or that such intellectual assumptions should involve the principle of 'critical non-interference' and the apolitical freedom of the (literary) text; and that all this should be taking place in the context of an ideological process which in the capitalist democracies has established a thoroughgoing policy aimed at the privatization of social life and the undermining of all organizations built upon co-operative communal principles.

This reversion to *laissez-faire* liberalism, with its brutalist reliance on the market, the priority of the play of capital – the aesthetics of buying and selling, the philosophy of 'wealth-creation' – over the ethics of social responsibility, is a phenomenon of the 1980s. But what it reverts to William Morris saw happening all around him in the 1880s – the struggle between 'masters and workers', the bargaining for interests, the collisions, the compromises, the destructive process of commercial war bludgeoning people into acquiescence. So it is not difficult to imagine him responding to the conditions we are faced with today. He would have had the harshest questions to ask about a system in which even the central

institutions of the welfare state are little more than palliatives whose effect has
been to weaken the struggle for the socialist transformation of society, since even
while they were being extended the forces of the competitive market were all the
time at work undermining the fabric of the social structure and the will of the
people to protect their rights – an ideology organizing for control, creating
networks of vested interest which are now being actively directed against all
forms of public sector wealth.

This kind of attack Morris would have defined as a direct challenge to the
death. For the system that dictated *his* world, like that which dominates ours, he
describes as

> distinctly a system of war; that is, of waste and destruction; or you might call it
> gambling if you will, the point of it being that under it whatever a man gains he gains
> at the expense of some other man's loss (Morris 1973: 123).

And he did not doubt that the impact of this system, which reduces everything,
however 'intrinsic' its value, to the level of the commodity,

> is of its very nature destructive of Art, that is to say of the happiness of life. Whatever
> consideration is shown for the life of the people in these days, whatever is done which
> is worth doing, is done in spite of the system and in the teeth of its maxims; and most
> true it is that we do, all of us, tacitly at least, admit that it is opposed to all the highest
> aspirations of mankind.
>
>   Do we not know, for instance, how those men of genius work who are the salt of the
> earth, without whom the corruption of society would long ago have become
> unendurable? The poet, the artist, the man of science, is it not true that in their fresh
> and glorious days, when they are in the heyday of their faith and enthusiam, they are
> thwarted at every turn by Commercial War, with its sneering question 'Will it pay?' Is
> it not true that when they begin to win worldly success, in spite of themselves they
> seem to us tainted by the contact with the commercial world?
>
>   Need I speak of great schemes that hang about neglected; of things most necessary
> to be done . . . that no one can seriously set a hand to because of the lack of money?
> While if it be a question of creating or stimulating some foolish whim in the public
> mind, the satisfaction of which will breed a profit, the money will come in by the ton?
> Nay, you know what an old story it is of the wars bred by commerce in search of new
> markets – an old story and still it seems for ever new, and now become a kind of grim
> joke, at which I would rather not laugh if I could help it, but am even forced to laugh
> from a soul laden with anger (Morris 1973: 123–4).

The problem, as he saw it, commenting on the rapid transformations brought
about by the industrial and technological developments of his age, was how to
overcome such conditions; how to counteract the divisiveness, the insecurity,
fear and ignorance the system encouraged; how to generate resistance, the will
and confidence to think alternatives. And this, as Morris believed, was a cultural
problem, a problem of education – not of education as conceived by the ruling
establishment, which considered most people as mere instruments to be fitted
for their menial place in the system, but of education for change, directed to
freeing the working class to think openly and connectedly, in political and social
(and cultural) terms; or, as Morris himself puts it, 'of educating people to a sense
of their real capacities as men (and women) so that they may be able to use to
their own good the political power which is rapidly being thrust upon them'. And
this, for Morris, would lead inevitably to people claiming 'changes in society . . .
which indirectly will help to break up our rotten sham society' and bring to the

foreground that need for 'equality of condition' without which civilization must remain a sham (1973: 158). On this subject Morris was unequivocal: 'I do not want art for a few, any more than I want education for a few, or freedom for a few' (1973: 54). He insisted that everyone has an equal right to these things. And since 'all art, even the highest', as he says, 'is influenced by the conditions of labour of the mass of mankind', it must follow 'that any pretensions which may be made for even the highest intellectual art to be independent of these general conditions are futile and vain' (1973: 67).

Morris was early influenced by the ideas and teachings of Ruskin, and particularly by the ways in which Ruskin's thinking about art and its cultural and ethical implications led him to investigate the social and political assumptions of the Victorian world. But though Morris found much to admire and to emulate in Ruskin's work, especially in its criticism of the devastating impact of *laissez-faire* economics on the living standards of people's lives, he had little in common with Ruskin's authoritarian emphasis upon a hierarchy of classes – that 'organic conception' of society which 'everywhere illuminates his theory and his practical constructive policy', imposing order upon 'his conception of the different industrial classes' and compelling him 'to develop an orderly system of interdependence sustained by authority and obedience' (Williams 1963: 146; Hobson 1889: 82).

This comes very close to what Matthew Arnold was to advocate in *Culture and Anarchy*. Both Ruskin and Arnold conceived of art, literature and culture as products of a 'universal grand design' generated by the operative social order. For them both, the only kind of economy that was acceptable was that which led men to 'the joyful and right exertion of perfect life' (Williams 1963: 148). And though Ruskin himself goes much further than Arnold in criticizing the injustices and aberrations of the economic system that governed British society, he nevertheless remains (like Arnold) a supporter of the established order, advocating a rigid class structure not much different in essence from that of Arnold. It may be that those who governed – their business being to produce, accumulate and distribute wealth – were to be guided by the principles of 'intrinsic value' rather than those of 'exchange value', the 'cash nexus'; but democracy was to be rejected because its conception of equality was 'a disabling denial of order and "function"' (Williams 1963: 151). In his view there must always be a ruling class recruited from the aristocracy, and the function of this class 'is to keep order among [its] inferiors, and raise them always to the nearest level with themselves of which these inferiors are capable' (1963: 151), with its authority and legitimacy rooted 'upon a foundation of eternal law, which nothing can alter nor overthrow' (1963: 152).

The fundamental distinction between the Arnold and Ruskin view of society and that of William Morris lies in the attitude towards class and the interconnections between history and class struggle. Of course, Morris had first to overcome the assumptions and prejudices of his own class and the powerful influence of such men as Ruskin, Rossetti and Burne-Jones, the great mid-century aesthetic-cultural movement, its aversion to and its pessimism about the explosive energies of the capitalist market. As Ruskin himself admirably puts it:

> The great cry that rises from all our manufacturing cities, louder than their furnace blast, is all in very deed for this – that we manufacture everything there except men; we blanch cotton, and strengthen steel, and refine sugar, and shape pottery; but to

brighten, to strengthen, to refine or to form a single living spirit never enters into our estimate of advantages (Clark 1967: 283).

But though Ruskin calls for 'a right understanding of what kinds of labour are good for men, raising them, and making them happy' (Clark 1967: 283), he sees no way of resolving the contradictions between the discourse of the cultural process he and his class were part of and the dynamic of the market economy that governed and contained it. He and others, despite their appalled awareness of the misery and squalor created by the exploitative nature of the system, remained trapped in their class conditioning and impotent to reach across the barriers set up by the system.

True, Ruskin takes his own courageous stand in *Unto this Last* (1860) and *Fors Clavigera* (1871–84), writing bitterly against *laissez-faire* capitalism for condemning four-fifths of the population to poverty and hopelessness. But though he believed that his generation would 'be remembered in history as the most cruel, and therefore the most unwise, generation of men that ever yet troubled the earth' – since 'no people, understanding pain, ever inflicted so much: no people, understanding facts, ever acted on them so little' (Clark 1967: 307) – he could think of no better form of government than that of a paternalistic state run by enlightened landowners, businessmen and artists, properly trained to ensure social justice and regulate production. For he had no more faith in the democratic aspirations of the people than in the concept of freedom – which seemed to him like that of the fly, 'a black incarnation of caprice' (Clark 1967: 302). His idealist vision of reality, that is, left him unable to reconcile the antithesis between his own position as an alienated intellectual on one side of the divide and that of the working class on the other.

Morris was as deeply involved in this alienating process as his friends and mentors. Under the conditions of capitalist production, what Marx (1973c: 452) describes in the *Grundrisse* as the 'absolute separation between property and labour, between living labour capacity and the conditions of its realisation, between objectified and living labour, between value and value-creating activity', it could not have been otherwise. Of this time in his life, looking back on it from 1894, Morris (1973: 244–5) writes:

> What shall I say concerning its mastery of and its waste of mechanical power, its commonwealth so poor, its enemies of the commonwealth so rich, its stupendous organization for the misery of life! Its contempt of simple pleasures which everyone could enjoy but for its folly? Its eyeless vulgarity which has destroyed art, the one certain solace of labour? All this I felt then as now, but I did not know why it was so. The hope of the past times was gone, the struggle of mankind for many ages had produced nothing but this sordid, aimless, ugly confusion; the immediate future seemed to me likely to intensify all the present evils by sweeping away the last survivals of the days before the dull squalor of civilization had settled down on the world . . . So there I was in for a fine pessimistic end of life, if it had not somehow dawned on me that amidst all this filth . . . the seeds of a great change, what we others call Social-Revolution, were beginning to germinate.

For a long time the seemingly unanswerable contradictions, the exploitation and greed that dominated his world, left him struggling against a sense of hopelessness and despair, such as we find again and again mirrored in the 'pervasive melancholy of Morris's poetry in the 1860s and early 1870s' (Thompson 1977: 90). Not that he was not as active and industrious during this period as he was to be later; for indeed 'whatever chanced to be Morris's goal of the moment', as a friend wrote in 1871, 'was pursued by him with as much intensity as though the universe contained no other possible goal' (Thompson 1977: 172). But the path that led from Pre-Raphaelite admiration for the anonymous artisans and craftsmen of the Middle Ages and the culture of an idealized past – from the practice and criticism of art to social criticism, and from social criticism to political action – was fraught with doubts and confusions from which it seemed there was no escape. 'O how I long to keep the world from narrowing on me', writes Morris in 1872 (Thompson 1977: 164).

What saved him, gave him strength to break out of the insulated circle of his own class position, was his grasp of the perspectives of history, his recognition of the economic material conditions that determined the structure of his world, his intuitive sense of fellow-feeling with the oppressed majority. To put it in Morris's own words:

> the study of history and the love and practice of art forced me into a hatred of the civilization which, if things were to stop as they are, would turn history into inconsequent nonsense, and make art a collection of the curiosities of the past, which would have no serious relation to the life of the present (1973: 245).

It was this awareness and his increasing discontent with any sort of detached commentary on the 'rotten sham society' he lived in, that took him across the barriers of class and made him a socialist. He had begun to see for himself how deeply the alienating divisiveness of the capitalist system had estranged people from each other, and reduced society to a mere 'caricature of a true community', since

> all the while its whole energy, its whole organized precision, is employed in one thing, the wrenching of the means of living from others; while outside that everything must do as it may, whoever is the worse or the better for it; as in the war of fire and steel, all other aims must be crushed out before that one object (Morris 1973: 80).

In other words, it was the shock of his reaction to the material conditions determined by a rapacious economic system at work, and its devastating consequences for the people of his world, that drove him towards commitment. What became in the end unacceptable was what Marx (1975: 266) had long before made harshly apparent; that under the conditions of capitalist exploitation the worker's activity becomes

> a torment to him, his own creation confronts him as an alien power, his wealth appears as poverty, the essential bond joining him to other men appears inessential . . . his production is the production of nothing, his power over objects . . . the power of objects over him.

It is symptomatic of the disjunct conditions of the cultural life of mid-nineteenth-century England that Marx's revolutionary theory of society should have had so little impact upon the thinking of writers like Ruskin, Arnold, Carlyle, Browning, George Eliot and Dickens, and that Morris should have been almost alone among them in responding seriously and with any sort of commitment to the challenge of his work. Most were in the grip of a powerful ideology, carried along by it, supported by it; and what Marx had to say was altogether too extreme, too disorientating, too disruptive, too painful. His challenge would have demanded from them not only a recognition of the underlying contradictions of material reality but also a questioning of their own class position, together with the privileges and cultural benefits that went with it. And that was, after all, too much to expect of them. However critical of the injustices and negatives of their world, they remained part of it, on the right side of the class barriers, maintained by the system, respected by the affluent, enriched by the market conditions that prevailed, speaking from within that world, defining and describing its conflicts and limitations, its moral and ethical dilemmas. And the values their work embodied reflected the historical forces that were at work on English society – the ways in which the utilitarianism of the industrial process had shaped and coloured and modified the idealism of the Romantic movement to produce the characteristic forms of Victorian realism. In other words, the discourse of the market had become a fundamental impulse in facilitating and transforming the discourse of culture; and it was only to be expected that such a powerful discourse would tend to confirm and justify the system that maintained it. As Marx himself points out in the *Grundrisse*: 'The bourgeois viewpoint has never advanced beyond the antithesis between itself and the romantic viewpoint, and the latter will accompany it as its legitimate antithesis up to its blessed end' (1973c: 162).

This holds true as much for Dickens and Ruskin, despite their shocked sense of a rampantly exploitative social order, as for George Eliot and Matthew Arnold, for Meredith and Henry James. The Romantic antithesis, reacting to the extant property values it was nourished on, generates the kind of idealism which either ends up in a mystifying (falsifying) affirmation of human potentiality, or shades off into disillusionment or a consolatory individual happiness. It is the metaphysical hazard of even the best Victorian novelists – their vision of an amended world coming up against the brutal conditions of material reality, even when these conditions lay just beyond the boundaries of middle-class comfort and could there be justified.

But Morris faced up to this. For him, no man could exist in society and be neutral, nobody could be a mere looker-on. It may be, in Marx's words, that 'individuals *seem* independent . . . free to collide with one another and to engage in exchange within this freedom'; but 'they appear thus only for someone who abstracts from the *conditions*, the *conditions of existence* within which these individuals enter into contact' (1973c: 163–4). Morris saw this clearly, and set out to argue the necessity of the interaction. Whereas in terms of post-Romantic doctrines emerging as an antithesis of utilitarianism – later to take the kind of reactionary form that is apparent in the work of critics like T. S. Eliot and F. R Leavis – abstraction from these conditions remains a central principle, 'a spontaneous, natural attribute inherent in individuals and inseparable from their nature' (Marx 1973c: 162).

In this sense, Morris's development is unlike that of any of his contemporaries and peers. His reading of Marx changed him, transformed his thinking about his world, set up the necessary interconnections, made him question the central assumptions of his class, brought together the disparate parts he had been so deeply engaged in trying to make sense of, enabled him to break out of the insulating circles within which the terms of cultural (and political) discourse were being defined. And 'the crucial confluence' of interests and conditions he achieved, almost alone among his contemporaries, meant, of course, that he was faced with the actual presence of the class divide and with the necessity of crossing it, of plunging into what he dauntingly describes as a 'river of fire' (Thompson 1977: 244).

He had already begun to move in this direction seven years before with his involvement in the Eastern Question – impelled into action by the shock he felt at the news that England was on the verge of war with Russia in support of Turkey. For in fact the long letter of protest he wrote to the *Liberal Daily News* was his first serious involvement in the politics of his time. His appeal was for 'No war on behalf of Turkey: no war on behalf of the thieves and murderers'.

> I am writing this as one of a large class of men – quiet men who usually go about their business, heeding public matters less than they ought, and afraid to speak in such a huge concourse as the English nation, however much they may feel, but who are now stung into bitterness by thinking how helpless they are in a public matter that touches them so closely (Henderson 1967: 210).

By December, perhaps spurred on by the work he had been engaged on earlier in the year, his epic romance *Sigurd the Volsung*, and the spirit of endurance and courage embodied in the Icelandic sagas, he had been elected Treasurer of the Eastern Question Association, and committed himself to the campaign, which included meetings all over the country in a sort of liberal opposition. And it was after war had broken out between Russia and Turkey in April 1877 that Morris wrote his famous manifesto, 'To the Working-Men of England', which is unequivocal in its condemnation of 'the bitterness of hatred against freedom and progress that lies at the hearts of a certain part of the richer classes in this country'. For these men, he warns the working people of England,

> cannot speak of your order, of its aims, of its leaders without a sneer or an insult: these men, if they had the power (may England perish rather) would thwart your just aspirations, would silence you, would deliver you bound hand and foot for ever to irresponsible capital – and these men, I say it deliberately, are the heart and soul of the party that is driving us to an unjust war (Thompson 1977: 193).

It was this campaign, combined with his involvement in the controversies connected with his secretaryship of the Society for the Protection of Ancient Buildings ('Anti-Scrape'), the problems he was having with his own firm – both bringing him into conflict with the sacrosanct property values of capitalist society – and his disillusionment with Gladstonian liberalism, which drove him to the point of thinking in terms of the 'river of fire' – a river (as he envisaged it in 1881) 'alive and devouring', which would 'put all that tries to swim across to a hard proof indeed, and scare from the plunge every soul that is not made fearless by desire of truth and insight of the happy days to come beyond' (Thompson 1977: 244).

From that moment on, a great deal that he had been working towards began to fall into place, to acquire a new urgency and sense of purpose. Not that this was any sort of sudden Pauline conversion, dramatic and absolute. It was an uphill struggle, against the domination of a system under which 'all of us', as he wrote in 1881, in a commentary that has ominous bearing on the Britain of the 1980s,

> are drilled to the service of Commercial War; if our individual aspirations or capacities do not fit in with it, so much the worse for them; the iron service of the capitalist will not bear the loss, the individual must; everything must give way to them; nothing can be done if a profit cannot be made of it; it is for this that we are overworked, are made to fear starvation, live in hovels, are herded . . . into foul places

called towns; . . . it is for this that we let our money, our name, our power, be used to drag off poor wretches from our pinched fields and our dreadful slums, to kill and be killed in a cause they know nothing of (Thompson 1977: 272).

And when in January 1883 Morris joined the Democratic Federation as a revolutionary socialist, he knew there could be no immediate resolution to the struggle; that 'the battle of grief and hope' against 'riches and folly and wrong' would have to be fought every inch of the way under the greatest odds. As he was to put it in July 1884, any fundamental change involved

first, educating people into desiring it, next organising them into claiming it effectually. Whatever happens in the course of this education and organisation must be accepted coolly and as a necessary incident . . . I mean that we must not say, 'We must drop our purpose rather than carry it across this river of violence'. To say that means casting the whole thing into the hands of chance, and we can't do that: we *can't* say, if this is the evolution of history, let it evolve itself, we won't help. The evolution will force us to help: it will breed in us passionate desire for action, which will quench the dread of consequences (Thompson 1977: 325–6).

By the time he had set up the Socialist League in December 1884, having lost patience with Hyndman's opportunist manipulation of the Federation, there was no question of compromise – of thinking towards

the creation of a new middle class to act as a buffer between the proletariat and their direct and obvious masters; the only hope of the bourgeois for retarding the advance of socialism lies in this device . . . It is a new Society that we are working to realise, not a cleaning up of our present tyrannical muddle into an improved smoothly-working form of that same 'order', a mass of dull and useless people organised into classes, amidst which the antagonism should be moderated and veiled so that they should act as checks on each other for the insurance of the stability of the system . . . The work that lies before us at present is to *make Socialists*, to cover the country with a network of associations composed of men who feel their antagonism to the dominant classes, and have no temptation to waste their time in the thousand follies of party politics (Thompson 1977: 381–2).

Making socialists meant making a different *kind* of culture. But how was that to be made possible? What *is* it that gives people 'the day-spring of a new hope'? It can be nothing less, Morris believed, than 'general revolt against the tyranny of Commercial War'. For

the palliatives over which so many worthy people are busying themselves now are useless: because they are but unorganised partial revolts against a vast widespreading grasping organisation which will, with the unconscious instinct of a plant, meet every attempt at bettering the condition of the people with an attack on a fresh side; new machines, new markets, wholesale emigration, the revival of grovelling superstitions, preachments of thrift to lack-alls, of temperance to the wretched; such things as these will baffle at every turn all partial revolts against the monster we of the middle classes have created for our undoing (Morris 1973: 126–7).

So much has happened since Morris wrote this that it might be legitimate to ask whether there is any common ground between the perspectives he provided in 1884 and the situation we are faced with in the aftermath of the 1980s. In the light of the revolutionary transformations that have occurred, it would seem that the world has moved a long way beyond these perspectives. So how far *have* we gone beyond them? Where, it might be asked, have we got to? How much closer are we now than we were then to creating the kind of conditions Morris considered indispensable for human society? Well, it might be said, in the words Morris himself used to describe the situation in 1883:

> thus much nearer to a great change, perhaps, that there is a chink in the armour of self-satisfaction; a suspicion that it is perhaps not the accidents of the system of competitive commerce which have to be abolished, but the system itself; but as to approaching the ideal of that system reformed into humanity and decency, they are about so much nearer to it as a man is nearer to the moon when he stands on a hayrick (1973: 76–7).

To set such a statement against the present is to achieve a strangely focused perspective, in terms of which it becomes clear not only that the man on the hayrick is no closer now to the moon than he was, even though technology has actually *taken* him to the moon, but also that the system of competitive commerce has still not been abolished, in spite of crisis after crisis and the revolutionary challenge of Russia and China. Difficult as it may be to credit, we have to accept that this is so. Not only has capitalism survived; it has emerged strengthened out of the crisis of two world wars to re-establish its control of the Western world in the form of the economic imperialism of the United States, sharpening its powers against the hostile presence of the Soviet Union through the cold war build-up of the military-industrial complex and the monopolies of the transnational companies to exploit the newest modes of material wealth, and setting itself up as the great defender of democracy and freedom in an ideological onslaught on everything in its path, at immense cost to the socially productive economies of those nations it has subjected to its parasitic demands in the quest for new world markets.

No doubt Morris would have found such aggressive resilience dismaying. But though he believed that, with

> intelligence enough to conceive of a life of equality and co-operation; courage enough to accept it and to bring the necessary skill to bear on working it; and power enough to force its acceptance on the stupid and the interested, the war of the classes would speedily end in the victory of the useful class, which would then become the New Society of Equality (Morris 1973: 229),

he would not have deceived himself that the formidable obstacles standing in the way of that new society were to be easily removed. After all, his own experience of capitalism had proved to him how ruthless its methods were from the ways in which it had gutted and defiled whole continents in the nineteenth century.

Is it any cause for surprise that under these conditions, thinking as he did and living in a world so deeply compromised and dehumanized, with men and women reduced to the level of the instruments they used, Morris should have come to believe that the question of the survival of art and culture was secondary to the overriding question of the need for social change? He was even prepared to countenance doing without art for a while if the shock of its absence and of so many other cultural inducements to inaction could help to bring an end to conditions so barbaric and debasing, so indifferent to human needs:

> I do not believe in the possibility of keeping art vigorously alive by the action, however energetic, of a few groups of specially gifted men and their small circle of admirers amidst a general public incapable of understanding and enjoying their work. I hold

firmly to the opinion that all worthy schools of art must be in the future, as they have been in the past, the outcome of the aspirations of the people towards the beauty and the true pleasure of life [which] can only be born from a condition of practical equality (Thompson 1977: 664–5).

What Morris was wanting to make clear is that there are no issues – not even the issue of artistic autonomy or of individual freedom – more important than the issues of social and economic justice. This, of course, has ominous overtones, especially in the light of Stalinist perversion and the Zhdanov decrees. But in so far as the divisive issues of class crucially affect the quality of people's lives, they are *more* important than art as Morris saw it, for they are the conditioning context out of which art is shaped and upon which the health and quality of culture and civilization depend.

Of course, his preoccupations were such as to leave him with little inclination to theorize about literature or to pursue the craft of the literary critic. In fact, he never discusses at any length any of the great fictional masterpieces of his time, and hardly ever mentions them – though when he does, he is characteristically blunt about their work. Henry James, for instance – who believed that 'it is art that *makes* life, *makes* interest' (Pound 1954: 306) in its subtle probing of psychology – he dismisses with impatience as 'the clever historian of the deadliest corruption in society, the laureate of the flirts, sneaks, and empty fools of which that society is mostly composed'; and he accuses James of insensitivity and indifference towards those 'millions of men, women, and children who are living in misery' (Thompson 1977: 660).

This iconoclastic refusal to be impressed by the great achievements of bourgeois realism indicates a kind of blindness in him to the art of the novel. It is the negative (some would say disabling) consequence of his hostility to the individualistic ethic of capitalist society. Because for Morris the emphasis lies elsewhere. He believes, as Thomas Mann puts it in *Doctor Faustus*, that art needs to be set free 'from being alone with an educated elite called the public'; and he looks towards a future when art could once again, as in the Middle Ages, become 'the servant of a community, a community welded together by far more than education, a community that would not *have* culture but would perhaps *be* one . . . an art on intimate terms with mankind' (Fischer 1963: 206). But it is a fundamental principle of his political concept of the struggle for revolutionary change that this art of the future can only come into being when we have given 'the death-blow to the vulgarity of life that enwraps us all now'; for only then will the worker 'once more begin to have a share in art' and 'to see his aim clear before him . . . of a share of real life for all men' (Thompson 1977: 666).

He defines art everywhere in terms of the labour of ordinary people and the economic and social conditions under which they are obliged to work. For him there is no escape from these conditions, and the work of art itself is, like every other form of work, a material product, a product of human labour. And this in turn has its context in a particular economic and social system, as determined by history. 'Nothing', he says, 'should be made by man's labour which is not worth making, or which must be made by labour degrading to the makers' (Morris 1973: 123). And in his view, art being 'man's expression of his joy in labour' (1973: 67), the only healthy art is 'an art which is to be made by the people and for the people, as a happiness to the maker and the user' (Thompson 1977: 647). In this sense, the art produced by the anonymous medieval craftsman was a healthy art. For though at that time men and women lived under an oppressive system which denied them basic rights, and 'the robbery of the workers, thought necessary then as now to the very existence of the State, was carried out quite crudely, without any concealment or excuse, by arbitrary taxation or open violence' (Morris 1973: 161), people nevertheless 'worked shorter hours than we do' and 'all their work depended on their own skill of hand and invention, and never failed to show signs of that in its beauty and fitness' (Thompson 1977: 644).

Morris distinguishes two kinds of art: the 'highest intellectual art', which 'was meant to please the eye . . . as well as to excite the emotions and train the intellect', and 'appealed to all men, and to all the faculties'; and 'the humblest of the ornamental art', which 'shared in the meaning and emotion of the intellectual'. And when the arts were at their most creative 'there was an intimate connexion between the two . . . a connexion so close that . . . the higher and the lower kind were divided by no hard and fast lines'. For Morris (1973: 59), that is, 'the best artist was a worker still, the humblest workman was an artist'.

But capitalism destroyed that interaction by imposing upon society a crippling division of labour which deprived most people of any right to the benefits of culture, though it was their labour which produced the wealth to create ease for the leisured pursuits of the cultivated few. And it was the disgrace of this system of privilege and inequality that so angered Morris, for the ways in which it encouraged and maintained the gulf between art and the people, to the impoverishment of both. This left artists isolated, having little choice 'save to do their own personal individual work unhelped by the present, stimulated by the past, but shamed by it, and even in a way hampered by it', feeling that 'they must stand apart as possessors of some sacred mystery which, whatever happens, they must at least do their best to guard'. Under which conditions, 'it is not to be doubted', as he says,

> that both their own lives and their works are injured by this isolation. But the loss of the people, how are we to measure that? That they should have great men living and working amongst them, and be ignorant of the very existence of their work, and incapable of knowing what it means if they could see it? (Morris 1973: 61).

Morris's vision of culture and of art requires a different kind of world:

> a society which does not know the meaning of the words rich and poor, or the rights of property, or law or legality, or nationality: a society which has no consciousness of being governed; in which equality of condition is a matter of course, and in which no man is rewarded for having served the community by having the power given him to injure it (1973: 201).

But even to outline such terms for society is to move so far beyond any conceivable idea of the world as we know it, whatever its ideology, as to invite ridicule. Yes, we might say, such a vision of reality would certainly require a different kind of world – some sort of unattainable and faintly absurd, if not frankly dangerous, Utopia. And if this is what Morris calls 'dreaming ahead', we might then ask whether, confronted by the evidence of the world as it is, there is any *point* in dreaming ahead.

Morris would probably have answered that the world is as it is because powerful minorities have made it what it is to serve their interests, and that

without the power to create a blueprint for what it could be, we should be unable
to see beyond the alienating conditions that *define* the world as it is, and hence
powerless to transform them. In order to be able to bring into being any of the
unrealized conditions for a free and fulfilling life for human beings, we need first
of all to be able to imagine them as conceivable alternatives. And it goes without
saying that such conditions can only be *enacted* as alternatives so long as they *are*
conceivable in terms of the underlying contradictions of progress, the multiple
references which make up the contexts of reality, and which define the historical
perspectives on which to proceed.

   In this respect, and as a commentary on the problems connected with the
renewal of socialism in Britain, the value of Morris's work lies in the sharpness of
the perspectives, the temporal and historical parallels, it has to offer. For the
nature of these perspectives and parallels is determined by the manner in which
Morris's vision of the historical and social conditions of his own time comes into
conjunction with the present to reflect and illuminate the historical and social
conditions of late-twentieth-century Western culture. And it is from his dialectic
awareness of alienation, his 'sense of the radical dislocation of consciousness
from historical reality (with its potential for change)', that he conceives the tasks
of art. Art has 'to create a new consciousness that moves away from the
immediate towards the possible'. And in order to give art the power to see 'the
future in the present . . . realism has to be transcended'. Which is not to say that
art can escape the alienating conditions that determine the life of the citizen.
What it has to do is to transform these conditions 'into revolutionary consciousness by the recognition of the collective possibilities of the mind's curve away
from actuality'. In other words, 'for Morris, in dreams begins responsibility'
(Goode 1971: 238–9).

   It is the insistence of responsibility and of a whole structure of values
concerning the place of literature in a world in which the survival of people
matters at least as much as the survival of art that gives such cogency and force to
so much of Morris's writing. As he put it in 1882:

> In these days the issue between art, that is the godlike part of man, and mere
> bestiality, is so momentous, and the surroundings of life so stern and unplayful, that
> nothing can take serious hold of people, or should do so, but that which is rooted
> deepest in reality and is quite at first hand: there is no room for anything which is not
> forced out of a man's deepest feeling because of its innate strength and vision
> (Thompson 1977: 667).

9

Dislocation and despair:
Eliot's view of history

After such knowledge, what forgiveness? Think now
History has many cunning passages, contrived corridors
And issues, deceives with whispering ambitions,
Guides us by vanities. Think now
She gives when our attention is distracted
And what she gives, gives with such supple confusions
That the giving famishes the craving. Gives too late
What's not believed in, or if still believed,
In memory only, reconsidered passion. Gives too soon
Into weak hands, what's thought can be dispensed with
Till the refusal propagates a fear. Think
Neither fear nor courage saves us. Unnatural vices
Are fathered by our heroism. Virtues
Are forced upon us by our impudent crimes.

The view of history defined by T. S. Eliot (1969: 38) in these fourteen lines from his dramatic monologue 'Gerontion' is not to be judged by the objective rational standards of the historian. It reflects a psychological, subjective, emotional response to a deranged world, the despair of a man – 'an old man in a dry month' incapacitated by some sort of psychic disaster – whose belief in the very *concept* of history as a record of the civilizing human process has been shattered. For on one level, of course, the poem is a response to the trauma of war. 'After such knowledge, what forgiveness?' Gerontion cries – to which there can be no rational answer. Set apart, an alienated and impotent spectator, bypassed by the positives of life, this man waits without hope, or almost without hope, for release from the torment of nothingness he feels. In his crippled view of things, the future is no more than an empty dream and the struggle for the great aims and ends of life a derisive echo of the past, because for him the real world of people's lived and living histories has receded to a shadowy vaporous abstract. Lost in the 'dark wood' of the psyche in the aftermath of private catastrophe – 'I that was near your heart was removed therefrom / To lose beauty in terror, terror in inquisition' (Eliot 1969: 38) – he is unable to find any answering affirmative in his contact with the outer world that will give him the confidence or the will to stir himself from apathy and seek the way out.

I have lost my passion; why should I need to keep it
Since what is kept must be adulterated?
I have lost my sight, smell, hearing, taste and touch:
How should I use them for your closer contact? (1969: 38).

Nothing is left to such a man, it seems – possessed, like the Gerontius of Cardinal Newman's poem, by a sense of 'ruin which is worse than pain . . . a masterful negation and collapse' – but withdrawal, resignation, surrender, renunciation, the death of the body: 'an old man driven by the Trades / To a sleepy corner' (1969: 39).

Whether he is ever to experience the mystical transformation that is the theme of Newman's poem, he is at any rate too far gone ever to be part again of the world where histories are made and the struggle for life continues, as it does and as it must, in both subjective and objective terms, beyond ruin, beyond loss, beyond adulteration. He has sunk too deep into the labyrinth of disabled being, 'drunk among whispers', to be of any use to others. All he can hope for, as Eliot implies, is some form of salvation from the world beyond this world. But here, while he lives, he is doomed to endure a lingering sense of the nothingness of being, of emotional death.

This nightmare glimpse of catastrophe, of a man trapped with the wreckage of his life in a limbo of vacancy, of desiccated feeling, has its own strange fascination as a case history of breakdown. It is symbolic in the general sense of the breakdown of European civilization in the aftermath of the 1914 war, and in particular terms of what could be described as a condition of violent primary shock. But since the voice that speaks is the voice of a sensibility crippled by disaster, of a man who has no ghosts, it can have little to say to those who live beyond disaster in the world of human events and actions, of history in the making, where people are engaged (with other people and their living needs) in the necessary struggle for solvency and survival and social change. It might perhaps serve as a warning against giving in to the aberrations and neuroses of subjective being while there may still be other ways of dealing with them. But what can these 'Thoughts of a dry brain in a dry season' (Eliot 1969: 39), this 'chilled delirium' (1969: 38), have to offer as an incentive to those faced with problems of social injustice and social deprivation? That way leads, however imperceptibly, to dislocation, subsidence, apathy, social collapse, a living death. And most people are too poor and too exposed to be able to afford to give in. Demands are made upon them, the demands of others, of material survival, of work, of social action, of the historical struggle they are involved in as makers, as producers, as men and women trying to live in a society not of their making.

In objective terms, however deceptive and confusing, history is a process – a material conditioning process which determines the lives of people in society independently of the individual will. For if, at a certain level, it can be said (as Engels puts it) that 'we make our history ourselves', we do so 'under very definite assumptions and conditions'; because 'history is made in such a way that the final result always arises from conflicts between many individual wills, of which each in turn has been made what it is by a host of particular conditions of life' (Marx and Engels 1968: 682–3). But at the same time our consciousness of this process, as embodied memory of the struggles of men and women in society, gives perspective and context to the world we live in and to our understanding of the nature of our *place* in that world. For even by the ways in which it extends and sharpens our awareness of the actualities of the past, so it extends and sharpens our awareness of ourselves in the present and of our possible actions in the future. Indeed, in a certain sense, as Berger (1973: 64) writes in his novel *G*, all history is contemporary history: not in the ordinary sense of the word, where contemporary history means the history of the comparatively recent past, but in the strict sense: the consciousness of one's own activity as one actually performs it. History is thus the self-knowledge of the living mind. For even when the events which the historian studies are events that happened in the distant past, the condition of their being historically known is that they should vibrate in the historian's mind.

This is what one may define as a constructive, exploratory view of history – history as discovery or as rediscovered consciousness of the social (class) conditions which determine the relative power of men and women to act upon their environment and fulfil their essential needs. And this is at the opposite pole to the view defined in 'Gerontion': history as a form of derangement, as knowledge dislocated, generalized, loosed from its contexts, the conditions of social practice. But then in 'Gerontion' Eliot is already on his way to shaping for himself 'that negating path to God which is one of the classic forms of religious mysticism . . . to seek the absolute through guilt, sin, and despair' (Jameson 1974: 134). And this is not the path history takes. History is a process. And the function of historical analysis is to penetrate the confused interactions of the changing world, its bewildering complexities, the hard skins that form upon the surface, the accumulation of undifferentiated facts. It is an attempt to grasp the relevance, the logic, the underlying pattern and the actuality of events. And one thing is certain: that we cannot get at the pattern by abstracting ourselves from the historical process, or (as Eliot has done) by attempting to 'fix the religious sentiment as something by itself and to pre-suppose an abstract, isolated human individual' (Marx 1975: 423); which is what his renunciatory view of reality postulates – an individual who, in search of God, is thus essentially isolated not only from the historical process but also from the conditions and complexities of the world he actually inhabits.

But how do we keep ourselves open to the influence of this process and the things it has to teach us? How do we defend ourselves against confusions that deceive and alienate? No doubt first of all by adopting, if we can, a cool and rational attitude towards the outer world; by constructing for ourselves an intellectual framework which will take into account its contradictions and permit us freely to observe and record the complex interplay of the forces and impulses at work around us; by keeping a sceptical and distanced eye upon the unfolding pattern as it changes and develops; by refusing to make facile judgements about the continuing questions and dilemmas that confront us; and by resisting the temptation to build around our fundamental predilections a fortress of dogmatic opinion.

Thus, to abstract from the historical process is to abstract from the material conditions that do so much to make us what we are. So that when (for a man like Eliot) the world is made to seem devoid of meaning – when, as his despair defines it, differences are eroded, polarities dissolve, and the 'supernal life', ineffable and outside time, becomes the one sure refuge for the self – such a view of things is unlikely to be of much benefit to those who are trying to face up to the threat and the challenge of reality and to come to terms with the conditions that determine their existence. And when, in the same spirit, Eliot (1953: 212) takes it upon himself to conclude 'that whatever reform or revolution we carry out, the result will always be a sordid travesty of what human society should be', one is no more encouraged to believe that he has any solutions to offer the oppressed peoples of the world which might serve to answer their urgent social needs. For *his* solution is to exhort us all to 'become Christians' (1953: 210) and to revert to the questionable standards defined by the Christianity of Europe, thus inviting us to continue to submit to the oppressive institutions of the past. One wonders, indeed, whether he has anything to say to his world and its needs that is not coloured by the bitterness and the ache of his own sense of alienation and disillusionment. 'We are the hollow men', he writes in the anguish of shocked dismay at the horror and the hypocrisy of the Western democracies in action. 'We are the stuffed men . . . / Shape without form, shade without colour, / Paralysed force, gesture without motion' (Eliot 1969: 83). It is an indictment, this vision of the 'dead land', the 'cactus land', where 'Lips that would kiss / Form prayers to broken stone' (1969: 84). It is a vision of a bankrupt world, which holds out no hope except for that of 'death's twilight kingdom'. As Eliot sees it in the despair of his yearning for a smashed past, it is an indictment of the world of post-war Europe, collapsed, subsiding; of the bankrupt irrationalities of the imperialist West, whose institutions and elitist orders had dragged humanity into the obscene mockery of the war. But registering its horror – 'In this valley of dying stars / In this hollow valley / This broken jaw of our lost kingdom' (1969: 84) – is this all life has to offer? The epigraph to 'The Hollow Men' (1969: 83–6), from Conrad's novel, *Heart of Darkness*, refers to the white man's murderous exploitation of the Congo, the expansion of a capitalist Christian culture in its most degrading form. In other words, the poem seems a bleak refutation of the civilization that permitted and condoned such enormities. But to what end? Is there any escape from the trap of that civilization and its bankrupt hypocrisies? Not apparently by seeking answers in the historical struggle, the human struggle for renewal. For if the poem refutes the literalist materialism attacked in *The Waste Land*, it makes its implicit appeal to what Eliot later (in 'Ash Wednesday' and elsewhere) prescribes as his answer to the evils of his time: a return to the discipline and the authority of a static and absolute order, submission to a state of being in which 'the lost heart stiffens and rejoices', where, in 'the Garden / Where all love ends' we shall 'have our inheritance' (1969: 92). But this submission, in concrete social terms, is a submission to the institution of the Church, which, as the embodiment of spiritual power, was inseparable from the hypocritical system that had imposed its imperialist policies upon Africa, and, by specious methods remote from the ethics of Christianity, justified and stood behind those who had betrayed into war the peoples of Europe.

Of course, the significance of Eliot's poetry is its embodiment of the bankruptcy, the inhuman abstractness, the impotence and dislocation of the civilization of his world – the world, that is, of the cultivated elites who, controlling all the institutions and organs of the state, legislated and manipulated the issues of his age. And Eliot is a representative figure of his time – in the sense in which, as he says, the great writer writes his time – to this extent at least: that it forced him to write the way he did, or that its bankruptcy, impotence and dislocation so deeply affected and disabled him that it inevitably *became* his theme and his dilemma, and in the end the trap from which he could only escape by some sort of regressive retreat from life and the hurt it had caused him into the fortress of Christian orthodoxy that was to colour and to determine the drift of all his subsequent work.

But it is debatable whether he was a writer representative of the larger, wider historical currents of his time. Against the context of the revolutionary changes, the massive upheavals and contortions, the complex record of the struggles of human beings in this century – not only in resistance to evil but also in the selfless pursuit of liberation and dignity, the emancipation of the oppressed and the defenceless – he takes his place as the representative of a restricted and disdainful elite. For Eliot is among the cultivated few speaking to the cultivated few, lamenting the past and prescribing a return to the values of the past, in spite of the fact that history had exposed these values as destructive and thus unacceptable because utilized to the detriment of the health of the very structure of society itself.

The problem here – at least for those who have a grasp of historical perspective, the potentialities of the present, and the struggle for the future – is not with Eliot's formal, innovatory, linguistic techniques, which are the manifest sign of his distinction as an artist, but with his attitudes, the content of his work, its regressive, renunciatory themes. Though Pound (1954: 420) was not alone in praising the work 'for its fine tone, its humanity, and its realism', it is precisely on this level that it is most ambiguous, most open to criticism. Fine the tone may be in rhythmic, musical, aesthetic terms (and it is often very moving in the transparency and spareness of its verbal patterns and in its representation of religious despair and hope); but in terms of the vision of *humanity* it registers (its attitude towards people) and the realism it reflects, it is at once negative, disdainful and reactionary. For what it registers is the stages of the poet's personal retreat, his withdrawal, from participation in the crucial political and social issues of his time, even a refutation of the *validity* of these issues ('not here the darkness, in this twittering world' (Eliot 1969: 172)); and with that refutation an assertion of the essential isolation of the individual in 'the world of perpetual solitude', as a man alone with God. It registers, in fact, a rejection of the struggle for community in the world of men as a sordid travesty. For him:

There is no help in parties, none in interests,
There is no help in those whose souls are choked & swaddled
In the old winding-sheets of place and power
Or the new winding-sheets of mass-made thought.

The only help, it seems, though it cannot be so in fact, is in God. Hence the reality it reflects it turns against the world to reject and condemn reality, the objective reality of the external social order – envisaged as 'devising the perfect refrigerator', or 'working out a rational morality', or 'printing as many books as possible', or 'plotting happiness and flinging empty bottles', or turning from 'vacancy to fevered enthusiasm / For nation or race or what you call humanity' (Eliot 1969: 155–6). The fine tone, that is, has a derisive edge to it that denies the achievements of humanity, presumably because (as Eliot clearly designates in 'The Rock') humanity appears to have denied God; and it is therefore both ungenerous and inhumane. It represents, moreover, a wildly irrational attack upon the social and historical concerns of humanity, even in the associations it sets up, by linking such things as refrigerators and rational morality, happiness and empty bottles, as if they were inherently connected, and thus implying the utter futility of all social activity. It may *be* that a fevered enthusiasm for 'what you call humanity' is deplorable, but the ungenerous assumption that people turn from *vacancy* to enthusiasm as if these were their only habitual states is even more to be deplored.

Views of this sort, rooted in distaste and mistrust of the mass of the people, reflect the assumptions of many Western intellectuals in the 1920s and 1930s – that 'the people, the mass, represented the principle of irrationality, of the merely instinctive, as opposed to the superior powers of reason' (Lukács 1969: 321). With such a conception, the Western democracies undermined their strongest defence against the spread of fascist power, which was built upon a ruthless appeal to the irrational, the psychology of mass hysteria. By treating the common people with ill-disguised condescension and putting their trust in divisive and persistently devious policies, they only succeeded in weakening resistance to the irrational appeal of Nazism. According to Namier (1962: 216), it would appear that 'intellectuals who had seen themselves as the rational leaders of mankind . . . were to find that the disintegration of spiritual values . . . had released demoniac forces, beyond control by reason'. But if this was so, the blame was not to be laid upon those who had spent their lives fighting for a world in which the rights and needs of the millions might be answered. It was so because too many of the so-called rational leaders of Europe – the Baldwins, the Chamberlains, the Hoares, the Lavals, the Daladiers, belonged to a hypocritical elite whose muddled thinking and fear of the Left gave support to specious and inhumane spiritual values – values that paid little more than lip-service to the needs and rights of the millions. It was so, that is, because, whatever the intentions of these men, their policies at best failed to oppose and at worst condoned (and even secretly admired) the arrogant assertiveness of fascist power.

In such a context as this, the writer has a very special part to play, both intellectually and artistically, as a witness to the underlying human values of his time. Thus, in seeking to define the character of Eliot's work and the nature of its response to the objective historical concerns of the world it is part of, it is important for us to know where it stands and what it represents, who it speaks for, and why; because, in terms of the struggle for clarity and rationality against the forces of mystical irrationality that threatened Europe in the 1930s, this matters crucially. As Lukács (1963: 54) has written: 'Talent and character may be innate; but the manner in which they develop, or fail to develop, depends on the writer's interaction with his environment, on his relationships with other human beings'. And the manner in which Eliot's talent and character developed was clearly determined by, among other things, his consistent personal opposition to socialism, liberalism, democracy, and all the implications of 'the threat which mass society poses to the ruling elite' (1963: 62). What one is concerned with here, as Lukács (1963: 63) points out in his essay 'Franz Kafka or Thomas Mann', is not the

> directly political attitudes, but rather with the ideology underlying [the writer's] presentation of reality. The practical political conclusions drawn by the individual writer are of secondary interest. What matters is whether his view of the world, as expressed in his writings, connives at that modern nihilism from which both Fascism and Cold War ideology draw their strength.

On these terms at least, I do not think it can be denied that Eliot's view of the world – in its constant appeal to a regressive Christian orthodoxy, its metaphysical pursuit of a timeless condition of being which advocates escape from the determining condition of time, its rejection of the struggle for democracy and the aspirations of the masses, its refutation of the logic and justice of such a struggle in favour of the intangible mystical laws of God's logic and justice – does in fact encourage such connivance, even as it led him in the 1930s to fraternize in print, however ambiguously and diffidently, with the ideas (if not the politics) of fascism.

The point is that Eliot, having early suffered some kind of profound psychological disorientation, of personal disablement – brought about perhaps by the alienating, inhibiting pressures of the world he grew up in – writes from the very beginning in terms of damage and of loss and deepening despair, as a man for whom the things of this world seem increasingly futile and meaningless. Even in *Prufrock*, for instance, a deep sense of weariness and of negation prevails. Prufrock says: 'I should have been a pair of ragged claws / Scuttling across the floors of silent seas' (Eliot 1969: 15). And with the shock of the War, this condition is at its most extreme: 'I can connect / Nothing with nothing. / The broken fingernails of dirty hands' (1969: 70); for *The Waste Land* creates that vision of disaster and of breakdown from which no escape seems possible except perhaps into the remote promise of the words from the Upanishads at the end, and the fragments from Isaiah, Dante, Arnaut Daniel, the anonymous Latin, and de Nerval (1969: 75), which – suggesting the disciplines of a lost order – point forward to a mystical 'other' world beyond this world's perplexing waste.

It is hardly surprising, therefore, that Eliot should have rejected the influence of anything that hinted at a secular social ethic as a solution to the problems of survival and of solvency. He had set his course (or had had it set for him) in an opposite direction, mystical, religious, which – finally crystallizing in his acceptance of an institutional right-wing Christian orthodoxy – was to determine the nature of his reaction to the fundamental issues of social and ideological crisis. For him the future is 'a faded song', 'the way up is the way down, the way forward is the way back' (1969: 187); and, sickened by the actual present, he turns away from it to a contemplation of its metaphysical equivalent, the timeless moment of death, the moment *between* time, 'at the still point of the turning world' (1969: 173). In the end, neither reason nor faith can reconcile him to the rooted actualities of the human world. 'Here is a place of disaffection . . . Tumid apathy with no concentration / Men and bits of paper', the 'eructation of unhealthy souls / Into the faded air, the torpid / Driven on the wind . . . in this twittering world' (1969: 173–4). Trapped in the seemingly insoluble contradictions posed for him by his innate predilections, he sees everything reduced to a condition of futility, distorted and distorting, for which the only salvation appears to be his conception of a resolutely Christian society. Or, to put it in other terms, salvation lies in the metaphysical quest for God:

> We must be still and still moving
> Into another intensity
> For a further union, a deeper communion
> Through the dark cold and the empty desolation,
> The wave cry, the wind cry, the vast waters
> Of the petrel & the porpoise. In my end is my beginning (1969: 183).

As a personal attempt to resolve a subjective dilemma, this is a moving and impressive utterance. And, up to a point, one can appreciate the force and drift of Eliot's argument for a Christian community. But the fact that he could have thought it even credible that a *merely* Christian society – least of all one organized on the hierarchic lines he prescribed – could answer the complex conflicting needs of the great mass of the peoples of the modern world, is a measure of his remoteness from and his inability to cope with, or even to envisage, the nature of the problems that are there to be dealt with.

It may be that for Eliot (1953: 193), writing about Baudelaire,

> the recognition of the reality of Sin is a New Life; and the possibility of damnation is so immense a relief in a world of electoral reform, plebiscites, sex reform and dress reform, that damnation itself is an immediate form of salvation – of salvation from the *ennui* of modern life, because it at last gives some significance to living.

But what possible incentive or consolation could this give to anyone seeking positive conditions on which to build his life, and faced with the massive social injustices of the modern world, that condemn so many to a life of poverty and deprivation? Sin, it seems to me, is not the issue. The very perversity of the conjunction – of damnation as salvation, of damnation as release from the boredoms of reality – suggests a view of humanity similar to that which juxtaposes the 'plotting of happiness' with the 'throwing of empty bottles'. It expresses an ill-disguised contempt for the concerns and interests of ordinary people, and has nothing to contribute to the crucial issues of the human (that is, the extra-Christian) community but a gesture of weary dismissal. Indeed, on the subject of people's beliefs, Eliot is not inclined to flatter. In his Commentary to *Criterion* no. 12 (in April 1933) he turns his attention to communism and its appeal to 'those young people who would like to grow up and believe in something': 'Stupidity is no doubt the best solution of the difficulty of thinking'. And, as if this were not condescending enough, he cannot resist adding that 'it is far better to be stupid in a faith, even in a stupid faith, than to be stupid and believe nothing . . . I would even say that, as it is the faith of the day, [!] there are only a small number of people living who have achieved the right not to be communists'.

The tone is unmistakably contemptuous, the attitude austerely superior, the mood one of impotent irritation, 'paralysed force'. The despicable majority seems, at any rate, to belong to an order of being incapable of intelligence, and if capable of faith (even of a stupid faith) more likely to commit some kind of unspeakable vulgarity. What is one to make of such an unpalatable and ungenerous view of humanity, so devoid of compassion or of common human feeling? Nothing *can* be made of it, for it offers no way forward towards any position – Christian or otherwise – that involves caring for people. It is too insensitive; and, in relegating people to some nether region one has no intention whatsoever of visiting, it deserves to be dismissed with indignation. Better on any count, however 'soiled by error', the unrepentant humanism of a Victor Serge (1963: 374): 'It is worse to live for oneself, caught within traditions soiled by inhumanity'. But Eliot's own answer, in *After Strange Gods*, is that 'in a society like ours, wormeaten with liberalism, the only thing possible for a man with strong convictions is to state his point of view and leave it at that' (1934: 12).

The trouble is that people are rarely content to state their point of view and leave it at that. Nor will the dynamic changing structure of the human world and the essentially inquisitive nature of human responsiveness permit a point of view to be left at that. Life leaves nothing at that; and no man of responsibility can possibly proceed on the basis that the effect of what he says or does is not (partly at least) his responsibility. To 'leave it at that' is to abdicate responsibility, just as to profess to be 'interested in political ideas, but not in politics' ('The Literature of Fascism', *Criterion* 8, December 1928), is to indicate some sort of congenital failure to see the connection between (and the significance of) theory and practice. But such equivocation is deeply symptomatic of Eliot's habitual attitude toward the outer world. It is all of a piece with his plea for a contemplative, static, Christian concept of the social process – which, like Burke's, is anti-liberal, authoritarian, closed – and with his equivocal attraction towards fascism in the late 1920s and early 1930s. It represents a wilful reluctance to take a responsible position or to think ideas through to some constructive and positive conclusion, however unpopular. One may not find it palatable to hear him state: 'I confess to a preference for fascism in practice, which I dare say most of my readers share' (*Criterion* 9, 1929); but such a confession seems at least to sound a note of conviction, even if it does presume too much from his readers. But what are we to make of it against his dismissal the year before (*Criterion* 8) of both fascism and communism, because they 'seem to me to have died as political ideas, in becoming political facts'? Apparently, his preference for fascism in practice is a preference for dead political ideas; and there is little to be made of that sort of equation. It simply confirms the equivocal stance of the alienated conservative intelligentsia of Western democracy towards those barbaric defenders of privilege and power who were so soon to be dictating the rules and bullying Europe into pusillanimous retreat.

These enemies of reason built their triumphs upon the equivocal and the confused, in Abyssinia, Spain, the Rhineland, Austria, and at Munich. They knew what they wanted, and set out to achieve it. In face of *their* convictions it could never have been enough to state a point of view and leave it at that. But then few of Eliot's political and social views suggest that he was a man of strong conviction. Rather, they give the impression that he was possessed by a sense of weariness and distaste for the concerns of society. 'The world,' he writes in 'Thoughts After Lambeth' in 1931, 'is trying the experiment of attempting to form a civilised but non-Christian mentality'. And at once comes the response, delivered with abrupt Olympian disdain, to a world no more than a quarter Christian: 'The experiment will fail' (Eliot 1951: 387). There is no equivocation, it seems, about this. It will fail, full stop. Eliot is clear. His mind is made up. It will be 'a sordid travesty of what a human society should be'.

This last statement comes from Eliot's essay 'The Idea of a Christian Society', which, written eight years on from 'Thoughts After Lambeth', puts forward a more considered view of the place of Christianity in a non-Christian world. But still it is assumed that the only alternative to the 'regimentation and conformity' of a totalitarian democracy 'is a religious control and balance; that the only hopeful course for a society which would thrive and continue its creative activity in the arts of civilisation, is to become Christian' (Eliot 1953: 210). And this is the context in which he defines what he sees as 'the fundamental objection to fascism, the one which we conceal from ourselves because it might condemn ourselves as well . . . that it is pagan' (1953: 217–18). All other objections, whether 'in the political and economic sphere' or 'to the oppression and violence and cruelty' (1953: 218) by which fascism had prospered, are apparently of secondary importance. The crucial fact for Eliot is that fascism rejects Christianity. But then he levels the same charge against the Western democracies. Having deceived ourselves, as he says, 'that *we* have a Christian civilisation', we merely 'disguise the fact that our aims, like Germany's, are materialistic' (1953: 218). Which is as much as to say that there is no *fundamental* distinction to be made between fascist and non-fascist societies, and that the only hope for civilization from either (irrespective of their politics, since politics remains a subsidiary issue) is to become Christian – though this is a hope that Eliot seems to have little faith in, since he himself sets against it the perverse fact that in 'all civilised countries . . . the masses of the people have become increasingly alienated from Christianity' (1953: 215).

Not everyone, fortunately, thinks in such vague (and vaguely dislocated) terms. Fortunately, there are many who consider it necessary and desirable to attempt the experiment of forming 'a civilised but non-Christian mentality', and to do what they can to help it to succeed, whatever the odds, rather than dogmatically (or gloomily) to assume its failure. But then Eliot, by his own 'transcendent lassitude', as Chace (1972: 205) has written,

> is absorbed into a class of people that wills no change, sees all progress as hostile, and would return to a state of affairs (usually imaginary) in which the restless motion of men and of their minds towards greater awareness and liberation would be stilled. Thus the reactionary impulse, whether or not he so desires, everywhere guides his arguments to their final forbidding implications.

Of course, there is much more to Eliot than his negativity, disdain and gloom. With his innovatory skill as a poet (stylistically the most revolutionary poet of his time) he involved himself in the struggle as he knew it for solvency and equilibrium, and pursued it through public crisis and psychic disability with scrupulous concern for what he most believed in, even though his firmest convictions ran counter to the creative ideas and needs of his age. One can only accept that he sincerely believed that to put himself on the side of the authoritarian institutions in the struggle against liberalism (let alone *socialism*!) was to plead for the ideas and needs his age required for its sanity and health. And if history has proved him wrong and his prescriptions misplaced, it may be that we have as much to learn from his example, and from the anguish of his attempt to understand the world he suffered, as from anyone.

It is pointless, at any rate, to wish that Eliot had been another kind of writer. He was what he was. He acted as he felt himself able to act. He wrote what he felt he had to write. And if we are aware of the inadequacies and defects of his response to the complex issues of the living world, we are at the same time poignantly aware of his dilemmas as a man who had had his path chosen for him – and nowhere more intensely than in the lucid embodiment of the quest for being and place, for reconciliation and redemption, for the 'impossible union' of love, itself unmoving, at 'the point of intersection of the timeless / With time' (Eliot 1969: 189–90), that marks the achievement of the *Four Quartets*.

But ultimately the nature of one's response to a writer of Eliot's distinction depends upon the nature of one's response to the world, and the nature of one's convictions and beliefs concerning the functions of literature and the part it plays in the life of its time, the ways it reflects and registers the conditions and complexities of that life and the people – those 'older creatures and more real' –

who are its substance, the makers of its history. And it seems to me that, though Eliot's contribution to the life of his time is not invalidated by the illiberal stance he took toward the outer world, it is lessened by this and by the psychic disaffection that colours it, his inability to respond to so much that is central to the continuing challenge of the present and the future, to the needs of the oppressed millions, and to each one of those millions (however inarticulate) as a contributor to the historical process.

His contribution is lessened, one would stress, not invalidated. Eliot has too great an influence to be ignored. As Leavis (1978: 228) has observed:

> The defeated genius *is* a genius, and the creative power is inseparable from the significance of the defeat. Eliot was a victim of our civilization. We all suffer from the malady that afflicts it, and the power with which he makes us recognize the malady and feel it ('Cry what shall I cry?') for what it is, establishes him as a great poet of our time, one whose work has the closest relevance to our basic problems. This is not to say that his diagnosis, in so far as he offers one, is acceptable. But it is not to be dismissed as merely unacceptable.

Indeed, it would be absurd to do so; for the work demands attention, and has been given it in abundance. Nevertheless, Eliot's recoil from human responsibility, his negative concept of time and change, his denial of history as a rational process, his dismissal of the struggle for creative change in society, and his substitution of religious mysticism for the proofs of historical progress, represent a divisive and distorted vision of reality, a dislocation between personal subjective truth and the social material contexts in which truth is rooted, or between the individual and his world, and thus an alienation from the concerns of human history and human relationships.

This is apparent even in such an attractive work as *Four Quartets*, with its seemingly reconciliatory themes. For the metaphorical intent of these poems is grounded on an ideological apparatus which – claiming the autonomy of aesthetic form and obscuring the paths traced by history and time and the demands of materiality – functions through a metaphysics of mystical transcendence. Its metaphors serve, that is, as 'bridges thrown out towards an unseen shore' (Jung 1983), bypassing or passing over the complex changing conditions of historical reality; drawing us seductively away from the 'this-sidedness' (Marx and Engels 1968: 29) of things to where another world beckons; offering us an aesthetics of renunciation in place of the difficult logic of temporal reality

But if, as Eliot (1969: 174) puts it, 'the world moves / In appetency', it matters that it moves, and what it moves towards as people make their history and are changed by what moves *them*. To 'put off / Sense and notion' (1969: 192) is to deny that the making of history can ever be material to build upon (since 'the future is a faded song . . . And the way up is the way down' (1969: 187). In these terms, what we are as instruments of change does not count – for where the world moves 'on its metalled ways / Of time past and time future' is 'a place of disaffection', of 'Tumid apathy . . . Men and bits of paper . . . Eructation of unhealthy souls' (1969: 173–4). What counts, at least for those who have been reduced to a 'cold friction of expiring sense / Without enchantment' ('bitter tastelessness of shadow fruit') (1969: 194), is 'liberation / From the future as well as the past', a 'constitution of silence' (1969: 195–6), a place beyond materiality 'where prayer has been valid', where 'the communication / Of the dead is tongued with fire beyond the language of the living' (1969: 192), and 'At the still point of the turning world' (1969: 173) time and change and history can be what you want them to be: 'nowhere. Never and always' (1969: 192).

Eliot invites us to define his work as the record of a man's attempt to work out his own salvation, to free himself from

> the final desolation
> Of solitude in the phantasmal world
> Of imagination, shuffling memories and desires,

as Sir Henry Harcourt-Reilly puts it in *The Cocktail Party* (1969: 419). And in his quest for a pattern of values, a reconciliatory order that could make sense of a devastated world, it is hopelessness and despair, an irrational sense of the nothingness to which he is reduced, paradoxically, that enable him to rejoice 'that things are as they are', 'having to construct something / Upon which to rejoice'. Thus, as he says in 'Ash Wednesday', taking the step that is already implicit in *The Waste Land* and 'The Hollow Men':

> Because I do not hope to turn again
> Because I do not hope
> Because I do not hope to turn
> Desiring this man's gift and that man's scope
> I no longer strive to strive towards such things
> (Why should the aged eagle spread its wings?)
> Why should I mourn
> The vanished power of the usual reign? (1969: 89).

In this way he chooses, or seems to choose – dismissing (or seeming to dismiss) the vital proofs and the rooted conditions of the actual world of human aspirations ('the infirm glory of the positive hour') – in favour of a mystical (and metaphysical) alternative, beyond hope. But in making that choice, or in having it made for him, Eliot's crippling experience (the air become 'thoroughly small and dry' (1969: 90)) places him (the alienated victim) on the side of the illiberal institutions above the world of common human interests and common human needs. And it is in this respect that his work has its gravest limitations. It speaks, that is, a language of disaffection, and holds too narrow a view of the richly varied patterns of human life to stand comparison with the work of the greatest writers – writers such as Shakespeare, Tolstoy or Dickens – whose art stays close to, and draws its strength and resilience direct as it were from, the material-social world it is a product of.

The distinctions one is here concerned to make are not with the purely aesthetic or the purely literary qualities of a writer's work; but, taking these as an integral part of the artistic process, with what that work has to tell us about the world the writer lives in, and the historical-social struggle that defines the human situation *in* that world, which cannot be ignored without falsifying the record of history. As Lukács (1971: 77) has said: 'To gaze down arrogantly upon the petty struggles of the world and to despise them is indefensible'. And this is what the great work never does. Its significance is its power to celebrate, to embody and to involve the pleasures and sufferings of men and women in terms of the diverse conditions that shape their lives. And the greater the work, the deeper its insight and grasp of these conditions, the less likely it is to lose touch with the primary sources of creative energy or to betray them by making of an idea or a concept a thing superior to them.

This would seem an obvious point to make. But unfortunately the divorce of theory from practice, of form from content, of culture from its roots, of the aesthetic experience from what gives it substance, the machinery from what it is supposed to serve, society from people, continues to infect, to damage and diminish not only the integrity, scope and significance of the work of art, but also (and more destructively) the integrity and coherence of the structure of reality itself, the rational framework within which people live their lives. And therefore it needs to be continually stressed. For the dislocating pressures of the modern world – of a world which has become increasingly dominated by the abstract falsifying dogmas of ideology – are such that, if we do not keep a constant and watchful eye upon the dangers that threaten us, we shall find ourselves effectively isolated, estranged (as Eliot was) from the objective driving forces of society. In fact, if we accept Marx's view that 'no individual and no society divided into classes is what it thinks it is' (Timpanaro 1980: 195), we are all the more obliged, as Kolakowski (1971: 174) puts it, 'to know everything that argues against us', and to adopt an attitude of rigorous scepticism as much to the bigotry of fact as to that of the dogmatist. But not only this. In a world that, for the artist, seems often to reduce itself to a hostile inhuman chaos, distorted and distorting, it is essential (a moral duty even) to be always seeking those links and connections, those rational binding principles, which encourage perspective and community, and which will enable the writer, as Lukács (1963: 61) has it, 'to portray the present age truthfully without giving way to despair'.

10

Literature and appeasement

Pre-1939: the other side of history –
An age of nightmare endings
Which the poets could not change
Because they too were of that world,
Its walls of language forged
From the rules of the arrogant few
That in the aristocracy of art
Too many failed to recognize
Served dislocation and betrayal. (Hampton 1980: 53).

The debate about literature in the 1930s is not yet over. As part of the crisis of contemporary culture, it is involved in the continuing debate about the struggle for progress and the nature of the relationships between literature and politics, the use of language and its manipulation, the clash of opposing ideas and creeds at a time of economic breakdown, social instability and world change. And the challenge of this debate, as we see it now, looking back at the 1930s from beyond the 1980s – a decade in which the Western democracies seemed caught in the grip of a brutalist ideology in many ways similar to that which ushered in the decade of Hitler's rise to power – is that literature cannot be adequately defined or put into any sort of proper focus unless it is treated in terms of the complex changing conditions it emerges from; and that this remains true even if the writer, the intellectual, the literary critic, chooses to ignore these conditions. Which is to say that, whether we like it or not, we are *all* involved in the complex running battle of the ideological process – its confusions, its distortions, its lies and deviations – and that the writer is as intimately involved in that process, and has as great a responsibility as a participant in the battle for people's minds, as anyone. In Ezra Pound's words – and we have to accept the fact that Pound was himself among those who put their talents at the disposal of Mussolini in the 1930s – it is

> in proportion as [the writer's work] is exact, i.e. true to human consciousness and to the nature of man [that it is] durable and so . . . useful, [maintaining] the precision and clarity of thought, not merely for the benefit of a few dilettantes and lovers of literature, but . . . [for] the health of thought outside literary circles and in non-literary existence, in general individual and communal life (1954: 22).

Of course, it could be argued that such terms as 'truth to human consciousness', 'the nature of man' – themselves peculiarly ambiguous in their abstractness and therefore open to abuse – are part of the problem; and that if we are to accept any such thing as 'the precision and clarity of thought', we shall need to move beyond the hollowness and rhetoric of liberal-humanist assumptions and begin to grapple with the underlying contradictions they conceal. Indeed, this was a fundamental necessity for the writers of the 1930s, faced as they were with the deadly imperatives of the struggle that confronted Europe from the moment fascism began to challenge the hypocrisies of the democratic process. The unprecedented social crisis forced many of them, however reluctantly, to question their assumptions about the independence of literature and to re-examine the interrelations between art and politics, history, culture and society.

In such a context, there could have been no more startling transformation than that of the great German critical realist, Thomas Mann, who had declared himself at the outbreak of the First World War 'profoundly convinced . . . that all historic justice, all real modernity, future, certainty of victory, lie with Germany' (Mann 1975: xvii); and who, in a bitter response to his republican-socialist brother, Heinrich, was to write in his 1918 *Reflections of a Non-Political Man* 'a last great rearguard action of the romantic middle-class mentality in face of advancing modernity' (1975: xvii). Having defended in this book his own reactionary conservative nationalism, and his belief that 'before too long the conservatives will again have the greatest say in Germany' (1975: 92), by 1923 he was to find himself (the great ironist, the 'apolitical humanist' (1975: 113)) painfully and inexorably drawn to the left. This shift of position might never have gone much further than a vaguely Goethean internationalism, in spite of his 1925 recognition that 'the racially German world . . . is always but three steps from barbarism' (1975: 123), since (as he confesses to Ernst Fischer in 1926) his roots 'lie in the cultural world of Goethe's Autobiography, in the bourgeois atmosphere, in romanticism' (1975: 137). But the Nazi seizure of power, the shock of exile and the confiscation of his property – not to mention his 'Jewish' Joseph trilogy, finished in 1936 – forced him to confront the fundamental issues of politics and art, and to write his denunciatory Open Letter to Eduard Korrodi (Mann 1975: 205–10), which deprived him of his citizenship, followed by his famous Bonn Letter condemning 'the rulers of Germany as robbers and murderers' (1975: xxix), which made him a leading voice of public resistance not only to the Nazis but also to the forces of conservative Europe that had condoned and affirmed Hitler's triumph. As he was to write in his 1936 *Defence of the Spanish People*, by now putting all the weight of his reputation into an effort to arouse the conscience of 'civilized' Europe:

> Democracy is a realised and intrinsic fact today to the extent that politics is everybody's business. Nobody can deny this; it stares us in the face with an immediacy never before known. Sometimes we hear people say: 'I take no interest in politics'. The words strike me as absurd . . . But they are more; they betray an ignorance at once intellectual and ethical . . . For the political-social field is an undeniable and inalienable part of human society . . . And today the problems of the human conscience are put to us essentially in the form of politics – today perhaps more than in any other epoch in history . . . with a final life-and-death seriousness. Then shall the artist – he who by nature and destiny seems to occupy man's furthest outposts – shall he alone be allowed to shirk a decision? (Mann 1942: 84–5).

This declaration, in its recognition of the need to take an unequivocal stand 'against the stultifying, all-embracing confusion between politics and villainy from which we suffer in our time' (1942: 83), may have come too late to make much difference to the outcome, even as it reminds us ironically that Mann had once considered *himself* superior to politics. But it remains a telling plea for intellectual responsibility and for the logic of connectedness in a world profoundly and violently divided – a world in which the capitalist division of labour and its ruling-class ethics, its ruthless exploitation of people and resources, had so deeply infected the integrity of the consciousness as to threaten the very structures of European society, the rational framework within which people lived their lives.

Yes of course, as Orwell (1961: 316) puts it: 'There is no such thing as a non-political literature, least of all in an age like our own, when fears, hatreds and loyalties of a directly political kind are near to the surface of everyone's consciousness'. But many would have liked to pretend otherwise. And what matters anyway is what that literature functions in terms of – what it accepts, what it condones, what it chooses to ignore, what it speaks for, what it stands as a witness against, when 'every idea, every conviction, every doctrine or conception of the world we live in' can be made 'to serve as a screen, a pretext, a technique of trickery in the pursuit of a goal voided of all moral content' or used as 'a bulwark and shelter against disruption' (Mann 1942: 234). And in the 1930s the struggle for basic rights and liberties, for economic and cultural freedom and the survival of the creative imagination, took on a 'life-and-death seriousness' precisely *because* people were faced with such lethal manipulation at every level of their lives – not only from the fascists themselves in their contempt for democracy but also from the ruling minorities of the conservative democracies in their crusade against socialism and its incitement to fascist reaction.

Unfortunately, despite constantly reiterated warnings from people as variously motivated as Trotsky, Churchill, Brecht, Mann and Einstein, and the unequivocal response of those who volunteered for the International Brigades in Spain, too few had a clear enough sense of what was happening or were powerful enough to break through the ideological conditioning that kept people passive. Such was the divisiveness and confusion of the social process, so deeply had the people been worked upon by the distortions and lies of the public institutions, and so obtusely impressed were the ruling classes of Britain by Hitlerian 'strength' and 'sincerity', that no one seemed able to lift a finger to stop Europe from drifting towards war.

But what was it, we have to ask, that had so corrupted the awareness and the moral integrity of the European consciousness as to make it incapable of acting against the forces of irrationality and barbarism that held the whole continent hostage? What was it that had brought about this apparent collapse of the will, this humiliating acquiescence in face of a philosophy of violence, this pusillanimous spirit of compromise which, culminating in the crisis of Munich and the betrayal of Czechoslovakia, was, in Mann's bitter conclusion, to 'finally appease the bad consciences of the democracies over the peace of Versailles' and 'to have undone, down to the very last shred, their victory of 1918' (1942: 183)?

When we talk of the barbarism from which the nations of Europe have in the twentieth-century suffered so grievously, and of that barbarism as linked to the breakdown of rational interaction, the falsification of history, the triumph of tribal emotion, of the myth of racial superiority and the mystical entity of the Nation, we have to include not only Germany, Italy and the Spain of Franco but also the whole of what we are accustomed to think of as civilized Europe. The barbaric outbreak of fascism is not an isolated phenomenon, to be blamed upon those countries directly exposed to its evils; its roots are embedded in the very foundations upon which European capitalism had developed throughout the nineteenth-century – the divisive double standards it had long functioned in terms of, the dehumanizing process by which, alienated in a world dominated by money and the commodity, men and women are reduced to objects among objects. As Auden (1950: 74) was to write in 1939 at the edge of the new abyss:

> Accurate scholarship can
> Unearth the whole offence
> From Luther until now
> That has driven a culture mad.

For its symptoms lie deep in the psychic disorders and derangements of nationalism and the destructive greed of the capitalist order. It is as if, in Nietzsche's comment on the rise of nihilism, 'the whole of our European culture has been moving, for a long time past, with a tortured tension that increases from decade to decade, towards something like a catastrophe' (Fischer 1963: 87). And if there is any kind of scholarship that is capable of tracing this process to its roots, it can only do so in the aftermath, and not even then without some extraordinary act of insight or of psychological penetration, a sort of descent into hell – that hell which is 'the being of the lie / That we become if we deny / The laws of consciousness and claim / Becoming and Being are the same' (Auden 1941: 48). For it is in this denial – in the liberal cult of the inner life, the pursuit of metaphysical pure spirit in the dark of the self, its withdrawal from the crudities of the external world – that the betrayal begins. Having retreated to an apolitical defence of 'culture', the liberal idealist invokes the transcendent, the unseen, the invisible spiritual essence, indefinable and thus irrational – what, in Marcuse's words, 'must be acknowledged absolutely, against all that is first to be known critically; as the essentially dark against all that derives its substance from the clarity of light; as the indestructible, against everything subject to historical change' (1972b: 6); bringing about, through a nebulous appeal to 'Nature', the 'privatisation of reason' (1972b: 18), 'the devaluation of time in favour of space, the elevation of the static over the dynamic and the conservative over the revolutionary, the rejection of all dialectic, the glorification of tradition for its own sake' (1972b: 24).

To Auden (1941: 64), looking back at this process of betrayal from the darkness of 1940, it seemed

> The flood of tyranny and force
> Arises at a double source;
> In Plato's lie of intellect
> That all are weak but the elect
> Philosophers, who must be strong.
> For knowing Good, they will no Wrong,
> United in the abstract Word
> Above the low anarchic herd;
> Or Rousseau's falsehood of the flesh
> That stimulates our pride afresh
> To think all men identical
> And strong in the irrational.

And to D. H. Lawrence in 1922, thinking of the First World War and the incubus-like power of the state and its leaders battening upon the people, inducing in them 'the dream helplessness of the mass psyche' (Lawrence 1950: 145): 'We'll *never* get anywhere till we stand up man to man and face everything out, and break the old forms' (1950: 146–7). For it was obvious that the old forms had not been broken. As Churchill (1964: 13) declares in *The Gathering Storm*: 'Apart from the excesses of the Russian Revolution, the main fabric of European civilization remained erect at the close of the struggle'. It was the generals, the statesmen, the diplomats, the makers of the war who, ignoring the disillusionment and the stunned silence of the millions, 'preserved the semblance of civilized states' (1964: 13), at the same time reasserting the aggressive unregenerate spirit of capitalism. And so, with the 'indifference', as Read (1938a: 43) comments, 'which people in power felt for the opinions of the men who had fought', the nations settled exhaustedly back behind the 'erect' façades of their fractured worlds, and the peace was left with nothing but 'trophies of hatred and greed, of national passion and commercial profiteering, of political reaction and social retrenchment'.

How could such a concept of society, embodying such profoundly divisive inequalities in its class-bound contempt for the democratic process, have summoned up sufficient moral strength to stand firm against the fascist principle of contempt or the brutality of its methods, its irrational appeal to the masses? If the leaders of Britain and France had really wanted, as Lukács (1969: 321–2) put it, 'to unmask the hostility of fascism towards the people', they would have needed to 'concentrate on the fallaciousness and mendacity of this appeal', and used their power to *protect* and *strengthen* the creative energies of the people from its slanders. Instead, ignoring all the danger signals, industrialists, businessmen, financiers, diplomats, politicians, liberal, conservative or apolitical representatives of monopoly power, helped to create the *ground* for fascism even if they did not literally offer it their moral or financial support, which many of them did.

What they would have argued in doing so was not that they considered fascism a good thing but that they were trying to make Europe safe against communism – because, of course, the 1917 Revolution and the threat of it in central Europe had deeply shocked the Western powers, calling forth economic and military blockades against the risings of a starving continent, which were applied with particular ruthlessness against Germany, Austria, Hungary and Russia. It could even be said that it was this determined attempt of the ruling forces of the West to strangle communism at birth which (from 1918 onward) encouraged the forces of reaction to organize against the Left and to cripple the growth of democratic socialism, thus fertilizing the seeds of fascism. At any rate, by the mid-1920s Germany had become the explosive nerve centre of Europe's predatory system, left in a state of torpid exposure to those insecurities and fears and crises which lead people to surrender their rights and destinies to the mercy and protection of the so-called strong. With Hitler already active in 1920, beginning to build a mass party out of mass humiliation, 'the German Messiah', as General von Lossow contemptuously described him at their Munich trial, had arrived (Bullock 1952: 105). There could have been no more disastrous consequence of the destructive policies which the institutions of state power and the men of blinded conscience who had driven the people into war had unleashed upon Europe. 'The past has deceived us', Yeats was to write of the disillusionment of 1918; 'let us accept the worthless present' (O'Brien 1972: 169). And that present was to continue to deceive not only writers but whole societies into acquiescence and appeasement. The prediction of Wilfred Owen (1931: 116) in the very last poem he wrote seems almost literally applicable to the depressing submissiveness of the times: 'None shall break ranks though nations trek from progress'. The 1930s defined the direction of that backward march, by the combination of weakness and aggression with which the disciplined strength of the Third Reich was conjured into being, and which the coming war determined. To the envy and admiration of competitors, in three years Hitler had virtually solved the problem of unemployment, stabilized prices, and welded Germany into an aggressive and dominating military power. He could not have done so, of course, without the support of the leaders of finance, business and industry, and help from abroad. But in the end such total submission to an enflamed cause, such mass euphoria as that displayed by the organized crowds at the great public rallies, can only be explained as a surrender of the will, a resignation of rational social conscience to the concept of force. It was a moral resignation in the face of absolute confidence – particularly among the middle classes, governed by fear and insecurity; a resignation even of the power to resist, a blind submission to the will of the strong, to the intoxication of the unknown, the ecstasies of the mystical, the irrational spirit of ritual sacrifice, the Valhalla-call of the dark.

This was the direction Europe had been moving in, as we see it now with the useless clarity of hindsight, for a hundred years or more. In the 1930s the Western democracies, with their continual attempt to placate and to accommodate the forces of reaction they had done so much to create in their fear of communism, were undermining the credibility of morality, reason and sanity, and the power of democracy to act against its enemies. Thus Manchuria, Abyssinia, the Rhineland, Spain, China, Austria, Munich, Czechoslovakia. Such a sequence of defeats, so shaming and so destructive to the spirit of international co-operation embodied in the League of Nations and the Popular Front, could not have occurred at all except in a Europe already 'psychologically prepared for the infiltration of fascist ideas into her political, intellectual and moral life' (Mann 1942: 170).

By 1938, it was clear to Thomas Mann (1942: 175–6), as, in his view, it ought to have been clear to everybody, that

there prevailed in the capitalist democracies of the west a sentiment stronger than any antipathy for Nazi Germany's mob rule and gangsterdom, for its debasement of moral standards, its shattering effect on cultural values; a sentiment stronger even than its fear of the anarchistic theory of nationalism, so perilous to the security of all established states. I mean the nightmare of bolshevism, the dread of socialism and of Russia. This it was that brought about the capitulation of democracy as a political and intellectual concept, and drove it to affirm the Hitler thesis, the division of the world into two camps, fascist and communist. This it was that made conservative Europe take refuge behind the fascist bulwark. Nobody would have deemed it possible that what had happened in Germany would repeat itself with such exactness and detail in the rest of Europe. It is uncanny to see how the wretched figure of von Papen, the conservative who delivered up Germany to Hitler, recurs again in the English Chamberlain. Everything is the same: the treachery, the underlying motives, above all the fundamental self-deception . . . It is hard to imagine the mentality of these British statesmen, conscientious only in the service of their own class and their own interests, passing their days in their clubs and their government offices, their weekends in the country – and wholly undisturbed by thoughts of the thousandfold cases of individual tragedy which were willy-nilly the accompaniment of their astute calculations.

This would have seemed an impossible consequence a few short years before. But with the *anschluss* and the betrayal of Czechoslovakia – so brilliantly evoked by Sartre in *Le Sursis* and by Rex Warner in *The Professor*, and described by Mann (1942: 183) as 'one of the foulest pages in history' – there was no doubting the nightmare fact that the forces of European capitalism had driven its people to the edge of war – blindly, obtusely, it would seem, by 'imbecility of will and weakness of intellect, . . . a defective sense of responsibility, and a feeble and sometimes inoperative regard for the truth' (Collingwood 1939: 164); but also in contempt for the people's real needs, against what was called then (and is today still called) 'the creeping disease of socialism'. Again it is the anger of the exiled Thomas Mann (1942: 167), writing in the immediate aftermath of Munich, that strikes home:

> The events of the past few weeks have plunged a large part of the world . . . into profound disillusionment, discouragement, and even despair. We have been shocked . . . and cruelly bewildered spectators at proceedings of far-reaching significance; proceedings too positive . . . rooted too deep in the collective will of Europe, employing as its instrument the classic hypocrisy of English statesmanship, not to be regarded as decisive for many decades to come.

And what of the peace which meant life to uncountable millions? In the despair of a man like Stefan Zweig (1943: 323) – who had personally witnessed 'the sickly unclean fantasies of hate' at work in the streets of Vienna – this peace had been put into the hands of perhaps a dozen men of questionable integrity who 'made decisions in which we had no part and the details of which we knew nothing, and yet made final dispositions about my own life and every other life in Europe'. In Brecht's words:

> The chiefs of state
> Have gathered in a room.
> Man in the street:
> Give up all hope.
>
> The governments
> Write non-aggression pacts.
> Little man:
> Write your testament (Ewen 1970: 314–15).

This puts the issues before us bluntly and with biting precision, drawing attention to the disastrous consequences of decisions over which ordinary people seemed to have no control. And as it does so, speaking on behalf of the 'man in the street', it brings us back to Mann's question about the artist's right to *shirk* decisions, and forces us to consider whether in fact the situation in the 1930s may have been, in part at least, the consequence of decisions shirked by artists and writers as by others all along the line. Certainly Zweig may have recognized this in himself. But if so, after the fall of Vienna, as an *émigré* anti-fascist liberal, he despaired of doing anything about it. For him the situation had become intolerable; and in the end suicide was to be the only way out. But for Brecht the subjective, individualist response to reality would have seemed a dead end, a betrayal. Defiance and refusal to surrender to the irrational forces that had seized control of Europe were essential, not only to sanity and the survival of the self, but above all to the survival of other people and of literature as a voice for their concerns and the freeing of the consciousness. As for those who thought of literature as concerned exclusively with 'ordinary, non-political, non-moral, passive man' (Orwell 1961: 128) in the world of broken marriages and work and crying children and private dying and shoes that needed repairing and the undogmatic beauty of the world, Brecht's answer is direct: 'All roads led into the mire'. And in such dark times, as he writes,

> The guileless word is folly. A smooth forehead
> Suggests insensitivity. The man who laughs
> Has simply not yet heard
> The terrible news (Brecht 1976a: 318–19).

Literature, that is, was no mere background pattern to the game of life, but a social act inseparably involved in the world of other people's lives, their struggles and dilemmas, the conflicts and confusions of the historical process. And no writer could afford to ignore the murderous contradictions Europe was faced with at that time without risking the betrayal of culture and intellectual freedom into the hands of its unscrupulous manipulators.

It was an intolerable situation. For what could the isolated individual do? The collective conscience of Europe had been stunned and bludgeoned into submission. Muddled thinking and a devious morality, together with an attitude towards the principles of social justice and the rights of workers – which was, at a time of mass unemployment, to say the least, grudging and minimal – had radically weakened the resistance of democracy to the intolerant positives of fascism. Though there were organized working-class protests against what was happening in Germany, many people in England, particularly among the middle and upper classes, even applauded Hitler's success in disciplining the people, in curbing the 'unruly' by outlawing strikes, and maintaining a healthy control of the young by appealing to co-ordination and the 'dignity of labour'. Perhaps it could be argued that these people, with their corrupted pragmatism, knew no better. Their eyes and ears were shut to the irrationality and violence of the appeal, which was turning the nation into a war machine and creating those repressive conditions which were so soon to translate the concept of dignity into the unspeakable slogan of Auschwitz: *Arbeit macht frei*.

But writers are witnesses. And it is their task, in defence of truth and intellectual freedom, to stand firm against the dehumanizing falsifications of ideology and, in attempting to register the actual conditions of the struggle for connectedness and community, to counteract the public lies and misrepresentations of all those 'hirelings in the Camp, the Court, and the University, who would, if they could, for ever depress Mental, and prolong Corporeal war', as Blake (1974: 480) wrote of another intolerance. If, that is, what their work celebrates is worth celebrating, it is worth preserving; and if it is worth preserving it is worth fighting for and has to be fought for when threatened, even to the bitterest end, for the sake of the survival of the *right* to celebrate.

Not that writers and intellectuals are to be excused on these grounds. And whether they are willing to take their stand when put to the test depends upon many factors – nationality, class, background, social awareness, psychological conditioning, depth of commitment. And among the writers of the Munich decade, there were some whose attitudes it is difficult to be charitable about – who in aloofness and superiority, as proponents of the aristocracy of culture and art, chose to stand apart from the struggle, or above it, or even to take their place on the side of the reactionary powers in support of anti-democratic concepts of society. For different reasons, and with different motives, men like Eliot, Yeats, Pound, Gottfried Benn, Stefan Georg, Charles Maurras, Jean Cocteau and Roy Campbell, found themselves either actively supporting or arguing for or refusing to speak out against fascism. And though it may be that in the long run their acquiescence made little or no *practical* difference to the outcome of events, it is one more disquieting symptom of the general malaise of the time, the mood of undemocratic superiority, of 'paralysed force', prevailing among the conservative ruling minority which, treating the common people with ill-disguised condescension and contempt, helped to ease the way for the irrationalists who were taking over Europe.

W. B. Yeats, for instance, professed at times a perhaps justifiable 'horror of modern politics', seeing in the manoeuvrings of opposing nation-states 'nothing but the manipulation of popular enthusiasm by false news' (O'Brien 1972: 188). But at other times his Anglophobe Irish nationalism and authoritarianism led him (particularly from 1933 onward) to make political pronouncements demonstrating a clear preference for the fascist powers and their victory in war. Like Gottfried Benn, who at one time believed the Nazis were the only hope for civilized Europe, he favoured German efficiency against what he called the 'bed-hot' harlotry (O'Brien 1972; 192) of the English mind and the threat of communism. 'What is equality? muck in the yard' (1972: 177), he had written when helping to launch the Irish fascist movement in 1933. And in 1938, during the Munich crisis, thinking towards a fascist-dominated Europe: 'The danger is that there will be no war, that the skilled will attempt nothing, that the European civilization, like those older civilizations that saw the triumph of their gangrel stocks, will accept decay' (1972: 192). The only solution, for him, was an age at once 'hierarchical, masculine, harsh, surgical', with 'wealth everywhere in a few men's hands' and 'an inequality made law' (1972: 196). This may have been an edifying prospect for the minority; but it has ominous implications for the rest of us.

It is difficult to reconcile such savage contempt for people, such meanness of vision, such an ugly politics, with the great poems of these years, which in their tragic purity and integrity seem to thrust aside all calculated intent or partisan politics to become a telling human witness. To attempt to do so is to find oneself having to deal with the aesthetics of disgust which characterized (and fuelled) Yeats's assumptions about the aristocracy of art, and with the hatreds that purged his style to bring into being (at the very time when his ideas were at their most sinister) the last and most impressive of his poems. And in this context one has to take into account the dislocating upheavals, the 'telepathic streams of violence and cruelty' (O'Brien 1972: 194), as Yeats puts it, set loose upon European culture by the butcheries of the First World War and its 'blood-dimmed tide', 'vexed to nightmare by a rocking cradle'. And perhaps it is true that, being an Irishman, with 'great hatred, little room', he *was* 'maimed from the start' (1972: 195) by what had happened, crippled by it, by the 'vague hatred' he felt, which he hoped would one day (intensified by 'minds strong enough to lead others') have 'issued in violence and imposed some kind of rule of kindred' (1972: 196).

This is a bleak and nihilistic view of the future; and one is therefore not surprised to find the poet possessed at the end by a ravaging pessimism and self-disgust, left stranded ('Now that my ladder's gone') in the trap of the self, his 'masterful images' issuing from nothing, it seems, but 'A mound of refuse or the sweepings of a street, . . . that raving slut / Who keeps the till' (Yeats 1950: 392). Is this desolating verdict, matched against the 'base-born products of base beds', what class contempt and class alienation come down to in the end? If so, there can be no way forward. Though the voice compels, and casts its spell, the intensity consumes because it speaks only for the subjective self, and therefore leaves the objective contradictions of reality and its dislocations unresolved.

Fortunately, many of the writers of this period were free of such problems, and could take their stand as convinced anti-fascists against the tide of irrationality and violence that was flooding Europe. They saw what was happening. They knew that the fragile structures of democracy, already so vulnerable from within, would need to be strengthened and fought for at every level across the spectrum of the Left – as liberals, militant humanists, socialists, communists. Indeed, writers like Gide, Romain Rolland, Jules Romain, Malraux, Eluard, Aragon, Sartre, Thomas and Heinrich Mann, Brecht, Arnold and Stefan Zweig, Koestler, Silone, Serge, Auden, Spender, Orwell, John Cornford, Ralph Fox, among many others, used every opportunity they could. They spoke and wrote with increasing urgency against the approaching disaster; some stopped writing and went to Spain with the workers and died there fighting. But even those who fought hardest began in the end to yield to the inevitable and to register the deepening sense of gloom and impotence and betrayal that infected so many thinking people. They could not make their voices heard across the barriers. In a class-fractured world it was too late to speak for values that were being systematically obliterated. As Bertolt Brecht (1976a: 320) puts it in one of his later Svendborg Poems (1938):

We know too well,
Hatred of evil
Can distort the features,
Rage at injustice
Makes the voice hoarse. Alas, we
Who wished to make room for friendliness
Could not ourselves be friendly.

Brecht was among those forced to watch the noose of barbarism being gradually tightened. And even from exile he could see how little was being done to resist. For by the mid-1930s, when the First Writers' Congress for the Defence of Culture took place, the Left Book Club was launched, and the Popular Front against Fascism organized, the Left was everywhere having to fight for survival against the institutionalized powers and interests of capitalism, an ideological process that made it increasingly difficult to organize and co-ordinate any common policy of resistance to fascism. The fact that in Germany the Socialist and Communist Parties had been outlawed or that Gramsci was languishing in an Italian gaol did not seem to matter much. And it was one of the myths of the 1930s that this was a time for the Left of unparalleled political involvement.

Though Cambridge University students might have made it seem so, the record tells quite a different story – a story of small groups of people struggling to make themselves heard and to generate action in a divided and apathetic world. In England, for instance, a deadly blow had been struck against the morale of the socialist movement with the failure of the 1926 General Strike, which left the working class stunned and betrayed by the sell-out of their leaders; and hard on the heels of this came the devastating effects of the depression and of mass unemployment, which successive National Governments did little to alleviate. And it was under these conditions that the Conservatives reasserted their control over the country; and under these conditions (on the Continent as in England) that socialism was effectively prevented from organizing any sort of coherent mass resistance to what was happening.

True, the Popular Front did make its belated attempt to mobilize against the forces of reactionary power in Europe. And with the outbreak of the Spanish Civil War, the Left made its final desperate bid to stem the tide and awaken the conscience of the people. For they knew, as Orwell (1961: 201) points out, that 'in essence this was a class war' and that it had to be won to strengthen 'the cause of the common people everywhere'. But, of course, the odds were too heavily stacked against such a win, for the Great Powers remained implacably opposed to the spread of socialism; and so Franco was permitted to win. According to Orwell (1961: 202).

> In 1936 it was clear to everyone that if Britain would only help the Spanish Government, even to the extent of a few million pounds worth of arms, Franco would collapse and German strategy would be severely dislocated . . . Yet in the most mean, cowardly, hypocritical way the British ruling class did all they could to hand Spain over to Franco and the Nazis.

In other words, by their adoption of a seemingly neutral policy of 'non-intervention', the British made it more or less impossible for the Republicans to win the war. Though many British people, mostly working-class and a few middle-class radicals, fought and died in Spain, knowing that democracy had to take its stand there because if fascism was not stopped at that point there would be no stopping Hitler from bringing Europe to its knees, they got no official support at all. For these people were not to be trusted. They were socialists, fellow-travellers, communists, and such misfits did not count. The fact that it was left to a few thousand individuals – among them men like Esmond Romilly, Ralph Fox, Christopher Caudwell, Julian Bell and John Cornford – to speak for the conscience of Britain and to defend democracy against its enemies is the real disgrace of the time. For they knew that the war in Spain was a war being fought for Britain, too. As John Cornford has it in 'Full Moon at Tierz', not long before he was killed, linking the conditions:

> England is silent under the same moon,
> From the Clydeside to the gutted pits of Wales.
> The innocent mask conceals that soon
> Here, too, our freedom's swaying in the scales.
> O understand before too late
> Freedom was never held without a fight (Skelton 1964: 139).

For him, and for others like him, there was no question of holding back, whatever the consequences. This was a time for action, not words; for embodying the dialectic of thought and action; putting theory into practice. 'Tomorrow, perhaps, the future' (Skelton 1964: 135), as Auden was to write in 1937; 'but today the struggle' (1964: 136). Not that this was the *only* way of standing up to the irrationalist violence that was threatening Europe; there were those, for instance, who felt it was more important to expose the cultural assumptions of the class order that condoned such violence. But for men like John Cornford there seemed no alternative. It was too late for anything else. They *had* to take their stand – against passivity, against the apathy and acquiescence, the demoralization of the depression years, the ideological undermining of resistance, that ominous conditioning of the public which played upon complacency and prejudice and even the good intentions of the pacifists to paralyse the will and leave democracy fatally weakened and exposed. Of course, men like Cornford – justifiably impatient of 'the talkers and verbal professors of freedom' (Hampton 1984: 232) – acted in the belief that the freedoms they were fighting for could still be won if only others could be persuaded to fight with them.

Unfortunately, the disabling passivity and divisiveness of the system had gone too deep. And everywhere socialism was being beaten and betrayed; so that when in the midst of the battle for Spain the Stalinist purge trials started coming through they struck at the heart of the opposition and gave added plausibility to the arguments of pro-fascist policy-makers. It may be, as Lukács (1969: 315) believed, that 'with the advance of Fascism, in the struggle against it, the humanism of the democratic opposition was becoming ever more broadly political and social', and that 'the main effect of the popular front, ideologically and politically, [was] one of fermentation', a rekindling of 'the spirit of revolutionary democracy . . . among a number of important writers'. But the triumphs of reactionary force had a very different impact upon others, driving many of them (particularly among the radicals of the English middle class) into disillusioned retreat – resigned by 1938 to the degradation and the nightmare of the 'coming war':

International betrayals, public murder,
   The devil quoting scripture, the traitor, the coward, the thug
Eating dinner in the name of peace and progress,
   The doped public sucking a dry dug;
Official recognition of rape, revival of the ghetto
   And free speech gagged and free
Energy scrapped and dropped like surplus herring
   Back into the barren sea;
Brains and beauty festering in exile,
   The shadow of bars
Falling across each page, each field, each raddled sunset (MacNeice 1966: 138).

For MacNeice, as for so many of his contemporaries, fighting their rearguard action against the killers, 1938 (Vienna and Munich) was the last squalid straw. After the anschluss no one could any longer pretend that there was any will to resist Hitler. This brutal event virtually signalled the end of the resistance of the Popular Front. And it had long been glaringly apparent, from the equivocal attitudes of the British ruling class, with their pro-German anti-French policies, that Hitler would be permitted to do almost anything he liked. Had not Lloyd George, in an article in the *Daily Express* (16 September 1936) called him 'the greatest living German . . . a born leader . . . a magnetic, dynamic personality' (Seton-Watson 1939: 39)? Had not Thomas Jones, Deputy Secretary to the Cabinet, written in his record of discussions with Baldwin (23 May 1936): 'We do not mean to fight for Austria any more than for Abyssinia. We are not going to impose sanctions against Germany under any formula of collective security. Has this been made clear to France?' (Seton-Watson 1939: 47). With pro-Germans like Hoare-Belisha, Neville Henderson, Kingsley Wood, Londonderry, Lothian, Halifax and Horace Wilson prominent in support of Chamberlain, and the Foreign Office ruthlessly purged of its pro-French 'bias', the scene was perfectly set for the sell-out of Czechoslovakia.

In such an atmosphere, there was little the mere writer could hope to do to counter such obscenities; for by then it was too late. Catching the mood, MacNeice (1966: 139) writes:

> No wonder many would renounce their birthright,
>   The responsibility of moral choice,
> And sit with a mess of pottage taking orders
>   Out of a square box from a mad voice –
> Lies in the air endlessly repeated
>   Turning the air to fog,
> Blanket on blanket of lie, no room to breathe or fidget
>   And nobody to jog
> Your elbow and say 'Up there the sun is rising;
>   Take it on trust, the sun will always shine'.
> The sun may shine no doubt, but how many people
>   Will see it with their eyes in Nineteen-Thirty-Nine?

Churchill was blunt enough, speaking in the House of Commons on Munich. 'We have sustained a total and unmitigated defeat' (Churchill 1964: 287), he said. But the storm of rejection that greeted his words was decisive, and no one could compete with that. The 'clever hopes' of 'a low dishonest decade' were expiring. Thus Brecht (1976a: 228) defines it in his 'Dying Poet's Address to the Young':

> I must ask you
> To say everything that was not said
> To do everything that was not done, and quickly
> To forget me, please, so that
> My bad example does not lead you astray.
>
> Ah why did I
> Sit down at table with those who produced nothing
> And share the meal which they had not prepared?
>
> Ah why did I mix
> My best sayings with their
> Idle chatter? While outside
> Unschooled people were walking around
> Thirsty for instruction?
>
> Ah why
> Do my songs not rise from the places where
> The cities are nourished, where they build ships, why
> Do they not rise from the fast moving

Locomotives like smoke which
Stays behind in the sky?

Because for people who create and are useful
My talk
Is like ashes in the mouth and a drunken mumbling.

Or so it must have seemed. With the groundwork of common values being continually eroded and the power of literature to communicate narrowly defined by the language of a privileged minority, there was little chance of the writer reaching through to people, least of all in England, where they were most often reduced to writing for each other or for university students or for those in high positions addicted to reading, whose activities did little but confirm the conservative status quo. Socialist poets as harsh and uncompromising as Hugh MacDiarmid and writers like Lewis Grassic Gibbon – whose trilogy *A Scots Quair* (an epic narrative of peasant smallholders defying poverty and dispossession against a predatory system) uniquely catches the feel of twentieth-century Scotland, and in the transition from country to city the active presence of the labour movement of the 1930s – were virtually ignored. They did not *belong* or fit in, perhaps because they wrote from the viewpoint of the working class itself. As Ewan Tavendale puts it defiantly in *Grey Granite* (the last in the trilogy), speaking of his revolutionary aims, one has to *be* history – 'not a student, a historian, a tinkling reformer, but LIVING HISTORY ITSELF, being it, making it, eyes for the eyeless, hands for the maimed' (Grassic Gibbon 1973: 161). Nor is his mother's rejection of 'creeds' – 'Yours is just another dark cloud to me, or a great rock you're trying to push up a hill' (1973: 194) – a denial of this; for her sense of the land enduring complements his in confirming the need to make the rhythms of the earth work for its anonymous producers. As for MacDiarmid (1970: 110), he was clearly not impressed by his middle-class contemporaries:

Michael Roberts and All Angels! Auden, Spender, those bhoyos,
All yellow twicers: not one of them
With a tithe of Carlile's courage and integrity.
Unlike these pseudos I am *of* – not *for* – the working class
And like Carlile know nothing of the so-called higher classes
Save only that they are cheats and murderers,
Battening like vampires on the masses.

Crude and excessive as this may be, it makes its point. Even Orwell's attempt in *The Road to Wigan Pier* to set up links with the working class merely emphasizes the gulf that separated ordinary people from the ruling minorities, and ends up confusing the issues. Brecht (1976a: 225), writing for 'all the non-conquerors of the world', recognized the nature of the problem. 'Solely because of the increasing disorder', he declares,

Some of us have now decided . . .
To speak in future only about the disorder
And so become one-sided, reduced, enmeshed in the business
Of politics and the dry, indecorous vocabulary
Of dialectical economics
So that this awful cramped coexistence
Of exploitation, etcetera, should not engender
Approval of a world so many-sided: delight in
The contradictions of so bloodstained a life.

And if, as Morris (1973: 223) had written of socialism in the 1890s, *'staying* power is what we want', it was never more needed than in the England of the late 1930s. But there did not seem to be much of it around by then, perhaps because too many of those who had earlier shown such will to fight were of the insulated middle class and themselves the privileged beneficiaries of a system which had thrived upon separation, dislocation, class division, the assumptions of minority culture – a structure everywhere built to discourage the breaking of the mould.

In the mid-1930s it had seemed evident to Auden (1950: 35) that the function of the writer 'in this hour of crisis and dismay' was to 'Make action urgent and its nature clear'. But by 1939, in face of the overwhelming odds, he had abandoned the more active emphasis, that emphasis which narrows the gap between literature as art and literature as propaganda (the Brechtian mode) to come closer to the Yeatsian view – a vision of tragic pronouncement. What in 'Spain' (1937) had appeared to urge the necessity of active struggle and the poet as an agent in history, for the sake of 'tomorrow' and 'the enlarging of consciousness', had become by 1939 an outlook based upon tragic acceptance, the impersonal moral view, Christian rather than Marxist in its emphasis. If, as the ending of 'Spain' tells us, 'the time is short and / History to the defeated / May say Alas but cannot help or pardon' (Skelton 1964: 136), by early 1939 a devastating shift has occurred; for now, in face of the triumph of reactionary force, it seems 'poetry makes nothing happen'; it is only 'a way of happening, a mouth'. For now

> In the nightmare of the dark
> All the dogs of Europe bark,
> And the living nations wait,
> Each sequestered in its hate;

and all the poet can do is to register and to accept the suffering, where 'intellectual disgrace / Stares from every human face, / And the seas of pity lie / Locked and frozen in each eye' (Auden 1950: 66–7).

This defines the nature of the shift that took place in the 1930s from positive commitment to increasing disaffection and uncertainty, from affirmation of the historical process to resignation and defeat. And it cannot be an accident that Auden should here so closely echo the mood of Yeats's 1920 prophecy:

> The ceremony of innocence is drowned;
> The best lack all conviction, while the worst
> Are full of passionate intensity (1950: 211)

on the assumption of which retreat is inevitable; for it seems that the struggle for the survival of civilizing values can only be carried on from a neutral distance – metaphysically, so to speak. Though Rickword (1978: 105), in his criticism of Auden, tried to insist that the great issue was not 'social struggle *versus* inner struggle' but 'the reintegration of the poet into the body of society', only the Utopian or the poet as man of action (like John Cornford) could argue the possibility of bridging the gap. For the Auden of *In Memory of W. B. Yeats* onward (and even of *Journey to a War*, his and Isherwood's report of the Sino-Japanese conflict) responded increasingly to the sense of crisis in terms of individual morality. Active commitment had been displaced by impersonal compassion, the power to 'forgive' and to 'bless'. And there was no longer any question of actually confronting fascism. For by 1938, with pro-German politicians in control, retreat and non-resistance had taken too deep a hold.

In other words, it was too late – the end-product of an ideological process that had long been at work in England, embodied in the inequalities and injustices of a class-divided society which encouraged acceptance among the privileged and assumptions about the ahistorical 'nature of man' and his 'rights' that left millions out of the reckoning on the wrong side of the tracks. No wonder, then, that with so little thoroughgoing commitment to the enactment of democracy and so little real contact with the exploited working class, the alienated middle-class intellectual should find himself drawing back from the battle-ground in disillusionment. As E. P. Thompson sees it, looking back from 1960 on the 'cultural fault' that had opened up, this disillusionment

> went through two stages. In the first stage, responsible minds recoiled from a social reality which they found inexplicable or unbearable. The characteristic form of recoil was disillusion in Communism, so that by the mid-forties this disenchantment had become a central *motif* within Western culture. The resultant withdrawal has been reminiscent of the disillusion among the radical intelligentsia in Britain in the aftermath of the French Revolution . . . In the second stage, withdrawal leads on to capitulation to the *status quo*; it is proper to speak of a cultural *default*. Disenchantment ceases to be a recoil of the responsible in the face of difficult social experience; it becomes an abdication of intellectual responsibility in the face of all social experience (Thompson 1978: 3–4).

This seems precisely to describe the process of the retreat from commitment in the 1930s, taking a parallel course to that of the so-called leaders of democracy in their capitulation to the pressures of the fascist creed. It is not just that conviction seems to have been undermined; but that, abdicating the grounds on which theory and practice can interact, writers like Auden, Roberts, Isherwood, Spender find themselves reverting to a kind of abstract, inner-directed world defined in terms of pity, grief, compassion, the metaphysics of liberalism. In *Trial of a Judge* (1938) Stephen Spender presents the issues characteristically through the sufferings of his liberal Judge, who wavers under pressure after sentencing five fascists to death for the murder of a Jew, is persuaded to reverse the decision and is himself destroyed by the power of fascism. This dilemma, and the play itself, illustrated not only the failure of liberalism and its compromising institutions, but the ways in which the economic process itself undermined the will of those who had stood out against the values it enshrined. By 1939, Spender himself (like Auden) had withdrawn 'to a defensive position from which he felt that poetry at least could be defended'. 'The duty of the artist', he writes in May 1939, 'is to remain true to standards which he can discover only within himself' (Hynes 1976: 362). In other words, there is no longer any external social standard by which the poet's personal values are to be measured, no interconnecting fabric of history linking art with society – the writer has (honestly enough) acknowledged the *failure* of connectedness and the inability of the artist to change anything. 'The violence of the times we are living in, the necessity of sweeping and general and immediate action', he writes, to justify the drift from involvement, 'tend to dwarf the experience of the individual' (Hynes 1976: 364); which is, in effect, to signal his retreat from left-wing politics. And perhaps this was inevitable; for after all, in the 20 years since 1918, liberal-conservative democracy (maintained and directed largely by the products of the public school) had persistently failed to do anything to transform the divisive structure of society, and that melancholy history had now borne its poisonous fruit. 'We cannot choose our world, / Our time, our class', is Auden's comment at the end of *On the Frontier* (1938), about the devastation of war.

> None are innocent, none.
> Causes of violence lie so deep in all our lives
> It touches every act.
> Certain it is for all we do
> We shall pay dearly. Blood
> Will mine for vengeance in our children's happiness,
> Distort our truth like an arthritis,
> Yet we must kill and suffer and know why (Hynes 1976: 309).

This is a language beyond political struggle, of defeat and resignation and of universal guilt. And if it is not yet quite the language of the later Auden, for whom 'all societies and epochs are transient details' it is on the way to becoming so. With the journey to America and the humanist summing up of *New Year Letter* ahead, what it settled for was the religious humanism of the middle ground, not all that far from the ground inhabited by a writer like E. M. Forster. And Forster's response to the dilemma of the time, as a liberal justifying his rejection of communism in a review of Caudwell's *Studies in a Dying Culture*, is: 'Do good, and possibly good may come from it. Be soft even if you stand to get squashed. Beware of the long run. Seek understanding dispassionately, and not in accordance with a theory' (Hynes 1976: 339). It is characteristically unheroic advice; but such counsel could hardly have been enough to fight the harsh and rigorous battle that was going to have to be fought against fascism. For how can goodness and understanding be defended by dispensing with all theory? Yet this was exactly what was being argued at about the same time by Orwell in his strangely ambiguous support for socialism in the second part of *Wigan Pier*. Ideas were suspect – Marxism is a mere 'pin-and-thimble trick' (Orwell 1962: 155), and socialists are defined as 'intellectuals', wanting to pour 'European civilization down the sink at the command of Marxist prigs' (1962: 186). It was sentiment and common sense that counted. It did not seem to matter whether you had laid the proper foundations of theory if your intentions were good. But unfortunately good intentions are not enough. Goodwill hemmed in goes bad. Witness what it did to Orwell in *1984*. Witness the *surrender* of the will that had already taken place, collapsing into pessimism. Or the placatory mildness with which Czechoslovakia was handed over to the Nazis. Sartre (1963: 367) provides an epitaph to that in his description of Mastny reading the terms of the Munich agreement in *Le Sursis*:

> The monotonous voice rose up into the silence of that somnolent town. It stumbled, stopped, then quavered on; millions of Germans, as far as the eye could reach, lay asleep, as it described how a historic murder was to be committed.

But 'Peace in our time' – or, as MacNeice (1966: 117) has it:

> Save my skin and damn my conscience.
> And negotiation wins,
>   If you can call it winning,
> And here we are – just as before – safe in our skins;

Glory to God for Munich.
And stocks go up and wrecks
   Are salved and politicians' reputations
Go up like Jack-on-the Beanstalk; only the Czechs
   Go down and without fighting.

And in the long run, as Europe was shortly to discover, fascism could only be
defeated by the directest possible means. To be anti-war, Julian Bell concluded
(he was killed in Spain), 'means to submit to fascism; to be anti-fascist means to be
prepared for war' (Hynes 1976: 195).

Many writers had risked themselves and taken a stand, raising their voices in
the midst of a divided world; but the cultivated minorities who controlled the
fate of millions did not listen. So that 'even the best', as Auden (1941: 26) writes
in *New Year Letter*, 'Les Hommes de bon volonté, feel / Their politics perhaps
unreal / And all they have believed untrue'. How could it have been otherwise in
the England of 1939–40, the England of the middle classes? If 'the social virtues
of a real democracy are brotherhood and intelligence, and the parallel linguistic
virtues are strength and clarity' (Hynes 1976: 352), as Auden declared in an
obituary article on Yeats, arguing the aesthetics of the poet against the ideas of
the man, the poetry against the politics, what in fact could such general attributes
amount to on their own beyond justifying the metaphysics of retreat? For now it
had become clear that the survival of such humane values depended upon the
support of a militant humanism and the existence of more direct and lethal
means of defence – weapons of violence and of war, and the determination of
the despised and democratic working class to act against enemies encouraged
and strengthened by the culpable vacillation of their own leaders and the
passivity of the literate minorities who defined the cultural and political climate.

The crisis of the 1930s cannot be explained merely as a failure of conviction, of
the democratic will to act. In what European society condoned and what it
betrayed, it demonstrated its own cultural poverty and bankruptcy and the ways
in which its divisive social system had undermined the foundations of democracy
and created those very fears and insecurities upon which fascism prospered.

Things might have been very different if socialism had been allowed to
develop. But the governing classes of Europe, and of England in particular, had
made sure that it could not succeed. And, whether by ineptitude, imbecility of
will, or sheer reactionary obtuseness, they had sought to appease and to
accommodate the Nazis as, in Thomas Mann's words, 'the breakwater which was
to hold back the unacceptable forces of socialism' (1942: 169) in the Soviet Union
dragging Europe step by step, in retreat after retreat, from Manchuria to
Munich, from the fall of Czechoslovakia and the victory of Franco in Spain to the
brink of war and over the edge.

In the darkness of that time it must have seemed to many who cared that the
struggle for the decent life was nothing but a hollow dream. To have lived
through such sustained abuse of what progressive thinking meant, it was no
wonder that the liberal writer, on his 'melting iceberg', should have concluded,
as Orwell (1961: 157–8) concluded, that people had been swindled by both
'progress and reaction' and were better off 'inside the whale' – quietist and
non-political, non-moral, passive, unconcerned, indifferent. Not that this was
the people's view. For them the abuse had been long-term, the swindle had gone
back many generations. They could not afford to indulge in metaphors. Nor were

they to be dismissed as unconcerned or indifferent. They were the ones, after all, who were going to have to be called upon to form the armies. Once again it was up to them. As Brecht (1976b: 334) has it, the moment of reckoning comes 'when the downtrodden and despondent raise their heads and / Stop believing in the strength / Of their oppressors'. With the war upon them, they responded in their millions to salvage the values of democracy from the irreversible damage done to their world by those who had led them into it from that other war.

And today the legacies of that struggle and its horrors are with us still. In the language of the complacent, we say:

> Ah, but all that's over –
> obsolete insanity, the European fit –
> for more than forty years now, cleansed.
> Today the opportunities accumulate,
> we have the secrets at our fingertips,
> the beasts are being slowly tamed,
> we're not to be so easily deceived.
> Or so it seems.
> Community, communion, the social heritage, a better future!
> All the clichés trotted out (Hampton 1980: 23).

With the mass slaughter and the mass betrayals of this century behind us, 130 wars on and the nuclear arms race continuing on its genocidal course, the realities behind the clichés remain. And these realities are as much a challenge to writers and to the literary culture they work in terms of as to anyone else. In Sakharov's words:

> The division of mankind threatens it with destruction. Civilization is imperilled by: a universal thermonuclear war, catastrophic hunger for most of mankind, stupe-faction from the narcotic of 'mass culture', . . . bureaucratised dogmatism, . . . and destruction or degeneration from the foreseeable consequences of swift changes in the conditions of life on our planet. In the face of these perils, any action increasing the division of mankind, any preaching of the incompatibility of world ideologies and nations is madness and a crime. Only universal cooperation under conditions of intellectual freedom and the lofty moral ideals of socialism and labour, accompanied by the elimination of dogmatism and pressures of the concealed interests of ruling classes, will preserve civilization (1974: 58).

Part Three

11

Raymond Williams: towards cultural materialism

In the light of the fact that cultural and intellectual activity in Britain since 1945 has continued to be dominated by the assumptions of a liberal-capitalist ideology, despite the persistent challenge mounted by such socialist critics as Edward Thompson and Raymond Williams, it is important to recognize the nature of the conditioning that is at work upon us all, and the problems we are likely to find ourselves confronted with in any attempt to break through the barriers of that conditioning. This is related in turn to the problem of understanding the ways in which ideas are manipulated and transformed in the act of passing from one historical-ideological situation to another, and as changing conditions interact upon them; which is crucial to an understanding of the cultural process. It involves a recognition of the challenge of ideological conflict and ideological resistance, and of the manner in which the forces governing historical change influence and modify the formulation of ideas – which, as Marx long ago pointed out, can only 'be explained from the contradictions of material life, from the existing conflict between the social forces of production and the relations of production' (Marx and Engels 1968: 182).

The difficulty of communicating the logic and momentum of those radical ideas which are capable of breaking through the barriers that contain them is nowhere more clearly indicated than in the unevenness and incompleteness with which Marx's own thinking has come through to us. Since works like the *Economic-Philosophical Manuscripts* of 1844 were not available (even in German) till the 1930s, and the *Grundrisse* of 1857–8 – a sourcebook indispensable to an understanding of Marx's dialectic methods – did not appear for the first time till 1939 and was not published in English till 1973, it is hardly surprising that in the England of the 1930s those who considered themselves Marxists should have approached Marx with an inadequate understanding of the philosophical and theoretical groundwork that had gone into the making of *Capital*. Added to this, the decade was dominated by the 'vulgar Marxism' imposed upon the Soviet Union by 'the sheer rigidity of official doctrine, the *rigor mortis* which [had] already gripped Marxism under Stalin' (Colletti 1975: 15), perverted by the concept of 'socialism in one country'; and English Marxists knew very few of the works of the major European Marxists of their time. Neither Lukács nor the theorists of the Frankfurt School nor Gramsci were to become generally known in translation until after the Second World War, and even then not widely until the 1960s.

All of which could explain why we had to wait so long for any sort of significant body of Marxist theory to establish itself in Britain. And this, too, might serve to explain the insecurity and lack of confidence, the theoretical confusion, the uncertainty, the brittleness, of so much socialist thinking in the 1930s. One can, of course, point to people like A. L. Morton, Alick West, Edgell Rickword, Jack Lindsay, Ralph Fox and Christopher Cauldwell, who provided invaluable arguments to counteract the prevailing modes of critical debate led by Richards, Leavis and Eliot. But theorists like Maurice Dobb, whose *Political Economy and Capitalism* was published in 1937, remained isolated, for the rise of fascism and a climate dominated by the obtuse forces of European conservatism and the Stalinist purge trials, made a wider dialogue impossible. And the disaffection, the political disenchantment, that darkened the end of the decade and the beginning of the war itself must further have frustrated socialist debate and resistance to conformity. Edward Thompson (1978: 21) even claims that, since 'the shape of cultural history is decided by minorities . . . it was the default of the disenchanted' – that minority of intellectuals and writers of the 1930s who started by being 'actively associated with Communism' and 'followed through the whole declension from disenchantment to acquiescent quietism' – 'which gave to Natopolitan ideology its form'. In other words, 'the flight from humanism did not take place in some vacant plot but inside the whale of Western capitalism', creating 'an accommodation between the disenchanted intellectuals and the establishment of power' (1978: 25).

Nevertheless, there *were* minorities at work during the war that refused accommodation, even though this meant they could have very little direct influence upon the establishment. And the experience of war brought about a significant radicalization in British politics, which resulted not only in the early reforming achievements of the 1945 Labour government, but also in a renewal of the Marxist challenge. For many intellectuals identifying with the aims of revolutionary socialism joined the Communist party and were active within it, particularly after the onset of the cold war, against the resurgent forces of monopoly capitalism – which (as we all now know) were to regain the initiative and realign the course of European politics from the 1950s onward. And the work begun then by the seminal Communist Party Historians' Group – among them A. L. Morton, John Saville, Christopher Hill, Eric Hobsbawm, George Rudé, Rodney Hilton, Victor Kiernan and Edward Thompson – was to have a profound influence on the study of the past and to produce in the 1960s and 1970s 'a canon of commanding weight well beyond their own formal discipline' (Anderson 1983: 25) with books which opened up the whole spectrum of history to Marxist analysis.

But it was only in the late 1950s (when many Marxist intellectuals left the Communist Party because of the Soviet invasion of Hungary and founded the dissident *New Left Review*) and the early 1960s (after Perry Anderson became editor of the *NLR*) that the great seminal works of European Marxist theory – of Lukács, Gramsci, Marcuse, Horkheimer, Benjamin, Goldmann, Althusser – were made available, and issues central to the revolutionary critique of capitalism could cross the boundaries and be applied to the literary and cultural debate. By the mid-1970s they had generated a range of critical and theoretical responses which was to bring controversial and salutary issues to the forefront of the debate about culture and the conditions of the literary process, even a radical rethinking of the terms of debate, as Edward Thompson's (1978) challenge to Louis Althusser's structuralist Marxism demonstrates, in its insistence on the necessary interaction of the theory and practice of history. So that it could be said, as Callinicos (1982: 21) was to claim, that there 'now exist[ed] in Britain a socialist intelligentsia pledged to Marxism', both in the socialist parties of the Left and in certain of the academic institutions.

This, however, did not lead to any real breakthrough for socialist ideas, any significant strengthening of the links between theory and popular practice. On the contrary, despite the successes of the late 1970s, socialists found themselves entering into a period of peculiar retrenchment and reaction, during which the New Right was beginning to move aggressively onto the attack and to seize the initiative against a confused and equivocal opposition. And what has now become clear is that even the grounds of intellectual discourse have begun dramatically to shift, partly as a result of the brutalist economic-social policies of Britain and the United States, but at a deeper level through the influence of French structuralism and the reactions of the New Philosophers, with their post-structuralist, post-Marxist, post-modernist views upon the 'post-industrial' New Times we are assumed to be living through. In this volatile situation, which has suddenly confronted the Left with harsh and difficult problems, it has become all the more important to be clear about the fundamental issues that are at stake. And I do not think we can anywhere more usefully chart the terms of the struggle for these issues than by looking at the work of Raymond Williams and attempting to define his intellectual development over the whole period from the late 1940s to the late 1980s – from the proto-liberal-humanist assumptions of *Culture and Society* (written in 1958) to the cultural materialism of *Marxism and Literature* (1977), *Towards 2000* (1983), *Writing and Society* (1983), and the posthumous *Resources of Hope* (1989).

For Williams firmly resisted or refused to be diverted from his path towards socialism and the concept of cultural materialism that became central to his work by the blandishments and fashionable adjustments of theorists like Foucault, Derrida, Lacan and Baudrillard. From the start, indeed, he never permitted himself to lose sight of the fact that politics, history, the forces of production and the relations of production were rooted in the concrete material conditions (and contradictions) out of which all cultural activity is generated. And in developing his theoretical grasp of 'the inescapable materiality of works of art' (Williams 1977: 162), he comes to argue the closest links between history, culture and language in the articulation of the material development of societies, even as he argues that culture and all forms of communication are central to the historical process. It is his insistent probing of the complex interplay of such conditions and forms of practice – at once contingent and determined by deep (if often obscure) continuities kept alive by tradition and by historical memory – that distinguishes his discourse. To have accepted the dispersal of meaning, the 'randomisation of history' (Anderson 1983: 48), the post-structuralist contention that language has become a process in which 'every signified is also in the position of a signifier' (Derrida 1981: 20) – that is, 'a system of floating signifiers pure and simple, with no determinate relations to any extra-linguistic referents at all' (Anderson 1983: 46) – would have seemed to him (as to Bakhtin) an absurdity, a severing of the dialogic roots of language and all its antecedent material referents, the conditions it emerges from and reflects. As Anderson (1983: 46) puts it, 'the necessary consequence of such a contraction of language into itself is, of course, to sever any possibility of truth as a correspondence of propositions to reality'.

Williams's emphasis, however difficult to keep sight of or to prove, is always upon the pre-existent material conditions that determine even the most abstract intellectual activity, since that activity is intimately a product of its surrounding social context. For him, as he puts it in a late work,

> the literature is there from the beginning as a practice in the society. Indeed, until it and all other practices are present the society cannot be seen as fully formed. A society is not yet fully available for analysis until each of its practices is included. But if we make that emphasis we must make a corresponding emphasis: that we cannot separate literature and art from other kinds of social practice (Williams 1980: 45).

And his concept of cultural materialism insists upon 'the analysis of all forms of signification, including quite centrally writing, within the actual means and conditions of production' (Williams 1983: 210). It is, as he said in *The Guardian* (11 October 1984),

> from the experience of real communities, and now also from ecology [that] we can learn to see living systems and relationships as primary. They begin before and not after 'individuals'. Thus 'individual freedoms' are not primarily to be justified by proprietorial assertions of 'rights', but from the absolute need of all living systems and relationships to communicate as well and freely as they can.

And so it is that 'the contemporary effort to reshape ideas of socialism . . . rests on this wholly alternative premise: that it is in relationships that both individuals and values begin'.

In the determined sense with which he has pursued this path and sought to open it up and to define his grounds, Williams is a kind of phenomenon. For his work is not only extensive in scope and penetrating in its analysis of the conditions that have governed the culture of capitalist Britain over the last 200 years; it sets out to challenge and to unmask the ideological assumptions on which this culture has flourished. And in its consistent attempt to absorb and to apply the fundamental challenge of Marxist thinking – historically determined, dialectic, relating the contradictions of material existence to the various manifestations of the superstructure that emerge from these basic conditions – it is a rigorously socialist attempt to measure and to keep abreast of the changing climate of intellectual inquiry and social activity over the last 40 years, in both general, political, cultural and literary terms.

It was, in other words, a very ambitious pattern of work that Williams launched into with his first major book, *Culture and Society*, involving a constant adjustment to the changes that have occurred over the last 30 years in the context, primarily, of their impact upon the culture of the people of Britain. And it proceeds upon the urgent and unapologetic conviction, pitted against the blunt proofs of a market economy at work, that men and women can direct their own lives, by breaking through the pressures and restrictions of older forms of society and by discovering new common institutions.

How, he has insistently asked, is literary and cultural activity to be made sense of, placed, got into focus, except in terms of the shifting currents of the social process and the underlying conditions by which they are determined? This is the context he has made it his purpose to deal with, from Burkeian conservatism and Arnoldian liberalism, the insulated minority assumptions of the bourgeois cultural establishment, to the Marxian challenge of the 1970s – an opening up, a breaking down, a reappraisal at once disturbing and crucial, reorientating and essential.

From the beginning of his conscious intellectual life, his position was defined in terms of what he describes as the 'experience of growing up in a working-class family on the Welsh borders' and his 'first contacts with Marxist literary argument' as a student at Cambridge in 1939 (Williams 1977: 1). The political and economic conditions that shaped his thinking at home were thus extended to the cultural and literary argument pursued in wide-ranging discussion with his fellow students, though this came into collision at the same time with the attitudes of the establishment and the Eng. Lit. requirements of the academic system. The consequences of the interaction between what he learned then from 'the dominant tones of English Marxist argument' and the 'radical popu-lism' of F. R. Leavis which he was for a time to be much influenced by, brought about (as he puts it) a kind of crisis. For he was faced with many difficulties and problems 'in the areas of activity and interest with which [he] was most directly and personally concerned' (Williams 1977: 2), as between the theoretical and the practical, the judging of literature and the making of it, the distances be-tween English literary culture (almost exclusive to the middle class) and the lives of the majority of the people, for whom it hardly, or at most peripherally, existed.

If Williams's early experience at Cambridge clearly had its impact, he was soon to have to cope with an altogether different kind of crisis – the disorientating upheavals of war. As an instrument of the war-fighting machinery in the Tank Corps, he came up against the brutalizing imperatives of a primary struggle for survival – society monopolizing its material and spiritual resources at all levels for the waging of war; and no doubt the chaos and the violence he encountered forced him to rethink a great deal that he might otherwise have taken for granted.

Returning after the war to Cambridge, he found the place completely changed, with the accent now on a kind of Leavisite literary culture rather than politics. And it was then – first through writing about Ibsen, and (when he had left Cambridge) by starting up *Politics and Letters*, which combined left politics with Leavisite literary criticism – that his commitment to 'a new cultural politics' (Williams 1979: 65) began to take shape. It was an attempt, that is, to deal with problems relating to both culture and politics and the social conditions inseparable from the experience of literature as a manifestation of the life of the mind. And this, in its response to the contradictions of material reality, was to become a running commentary of change and development around three distinct levels of approach: pragmatic, radical populist, and Marxist. So that what emerges from the long process of Williams's intellectual struggle for a comprehensive socialist perspective is a clear recognition of the difficulty and complexity of the struggle to maintain focus and to strengthen his socialist roots against the pressures of the cultural establishment and its ideological domination of cultural issues in general, and literature in particular.

It is perhaps difficult for us today to think back to the period of the late 1940s and early 1950s when Williams was beginning to confront these issues and to give shape to his ideas. This was in the aftermath of two or three years of socialist progress, when, as Williams (1979: 70–1) sees it, 'the whole prospect of democratisation . . . with the collapse of the Right at the political level' was compromised as a result of the acceptance of the Marshall Plan, which made 'a Labour adaptation of the American version of the world' and its capitalistic underpinning (what E. P. Thompson calls the 'Natopolitan philosophy') inevitable. And at the same time it was the period (bound up with this acceptance of US capital) which began the regeneration of the Right, when the Labour government itself turned against the working class by exhorting the workers during the fuel crisis of 1946–7 to 'produce to save the Nation'; for this put labour not only into the hands of the finance manipulators behind the scenes but also on that path towards bureaucratization which led to the wholesale disarray of working-class values and the triumph of compromise and accommodation – that process of devious juggling by which Harold Wilson diverted the struggle for new popular community institutions into the dead-end of 'organisational and financial' arrangements.

What also has to be borne in mind is the fact that the late 1940s saw the onset of the cold war. In the wake of the Truman Doctrine, fear of communism and the determination to contain it became a central theme of US foreign policy. Priority was given to a programme of military preparedness, including the further development of nuclear weapons. This programme, together with the NATO Treaty which confirmed it, the Marshall Plan for Europe, and Truman's Four-Point programme of 1950 proposing economic aid to underdeveloped nations throughout the world, were all part of an ideological design: to combat communist aggression everywhere and to strengthen US power. And of course, though the Soviet Union had suffered even greater devastation than Europe, there was no question of co-operation between East and West. The people of the USSR were thus forced to make huge new sacrifices to meet the US challenge. For it was only by imposing new forms of repressive state militarism upon a crippled economy that the Soviets could have exploded their first atomic bomb as early as 1949.

This was the process that led to the beginning of the arms race and the cold logic of superpower competition, fuelled by paranoid mistrust and the fanatical anti-communism of the West, particularly after the communist victory in China and the outbreak of the Korean war. In less than four years – some say even before 1945 – the disastrous course of world politics had been determined: a massive concentration upon the development of weapons technology in both camps, which was to witness over the next thirty years an unprecedented and reckless growth in the armaments industry, the militarization of earth and space, pursued at disabling cost to the socially productive economies of the world.

The inconceivable destructive powers thus brought into play to create the ideology of deterrence, the 'Balance of Terror', were no accident. They were, as Williams (1985: 220) himself puts it, 'a specific climax of a specific social order – its industry and its politics', occurring in a world which consciously sought such powers 'and which had invariably to select and invest in them if they were to become significant'. Indeed, Williams draws conclusions from this in 1983, as he had done in the 1950s. Such developments, he says, have involved an attempt in capitalist societies 'to achieve a symmetry between the external (military) threat – directly identified as the Soviet Union – and the internal threat to the capitalist social order which is primarily constituted by an indigenous working class and its organisations and allies' (1985: 224). Had this not, after all, been the original aim of the Truman Doctrine – 'containment' of the internal threat both at home (in proceeding against 'un-American activities') and abroad (in support of reactionary regimes against the Left)? At any rate, there can be little doubt that the Attlee government in Britain, and Ernest Bevin in particular – himself motivated by fanatical anti-communism – played their part in furthering the US cause, not only in their acceptance of US aid, but also, above all, through the signing of the NATO Treaty and the confirmation of top-secret planning for Britain's own atomic bomb.

These were the conditions that determined the climate of the 1940s. And the issues they raised presented Raymond Williams at the time with certain intractable problems. There was the problem, for instance, of the growing influence at all levels of the liberal-capitalist Right, and the need to counteract a literary establishment (represented by such magazines as *Horizon, Encounter*, the *London Magazine* and the quality weeklies) which aimed at reviving and strengthening the bourgeois, anti-political or anti-socialist drift of literary culture along the paths of aesthetic neutrality taken by so many writers who had at one time been on the Left. And there was, above all, the problem of the Labour government's increasing tendency towards 'reconstruction of the cultural field in capitalist terms', and of getting it to give resolute backing to 'institutions of popular education and popular culture that could have withstood the political campaigns in the bourgeois press that were already gathering momentum' (Williams 1979: 73).

It was inevitable that these attempts to generate support for the widening of popular culture should have failed, given the quickening momentum of market capitalism, so soon to register its booms and slumps and to bolster up the individualist consumerism of the Macmillan years. The fateful decision to accept US capital, which forced the Labour government into disastrous compromises with the forces of the Right, spelt retreat from any sort of real commitment to the working class and its cultural-educational needs. It was because of this, in Williams's view, that the position of the Labour party so quickly disintegrated in the 1950s, even as it faces a similar falling away of support today as a consequence of the failure of the Wilson and Callaghan governments to provide socialist incentives for the seeming advances made in the mid- and late 1960s. And this was the background for the tasks Williams set himself as a critic – in writing *Drama from Ibsen to Eliot* (finished 1948, published 1952), rewriting his novel *Border Country* (begun originally in 1947, published 1960), and formulating the arguments for *Culture and Society* (published 1958) and its sequel *The Long Revolution* (completed 1959, published 1961).

Both *Culture and Society* and *The Long Revolution* had a powerful impact, and gave Williams his place as a critic of the cultural establishment. Breaking new ground in their attempt to widen the conditions of the literary-cultural debate, they dealt with the development of the intellectual process in British society since the 1780s around certain key concepts, such as industry, democracy, class, art and culture, and brought into play those ideas that began to cluster round terms that first became current from 1780 onward, such as ideology, humanitarianism, utilitarianism, romanticism, bureaucracy, capitalism, communism, liberalism, the masses, the working class, socialism, and so on.

What immediately strikes one about these books is their curiously non-Marxist tone. They take their bearings from somewhere between the norms of the pragmatists and the cultural radicalism of F. R. Leavis. And why this is so Williams himself was to explain in 1977. He was, as he says, reading widely from Marx at the time, but he felt 'exceptionally isolated in the changing political and cultural formations of the later 40s and early 50s'; and thus, while 'continuing to share' the 'political and economic positions' of Marxist thinking, he felt obliged to carry on his own 'cultural and literary work and inquiry at a certain conscious distance' (Williams 1977: 2). For it was only in the 1960s and early 1970s that he came into contact with 'the later work of Lukács, the later work of Sartre, the developing work of Goldmann and of Althusser', together with that of the Frankfurt School, of Walter Benjamin and of Gramsci, not to mention the 'newly translated work of Marx and especially the *Grundrisse*' (Williams 1977: 4). By which time the Marxist debate had been or 'was being vigorously and significantly re-opened' as a 'central body of thinking ... seen as active, developing, unfinished, and persistently contentious'; whereas in the 1950s it was confined to small groups of committed socialists, and was simply not available at the time to the socialist student of literature.

So it is in a historical sense that we now have to approach *Culture and Society* and *The Long Revolution*. For though both books are, of course, of more than historical interest, it is important to recognize their function as instruments for opening up the debate about culture. They form a kind of bridge, that is, between the intuitive radicalism of Leavis, the experimental pragmatism of I. A. Richards, and the more integrated social thinking of the Marxist critique at a moment of peculiar difficulty for an emergent socialist thinker steeped in the actual process of English social contradictions. The Conservatives were in power and, with Labour still trying to find its way through the morass of its perverted welfare thinking, were continuing to strengthen the forces of the capitalist market and to encourage those forms of private monopoly control and technological consumerism which have since had such a devastating effect upon our cultural needs and our democratic rights.

In *Culture and Society* Williams tells us that he was feeling his way from book to book into a clarification of his theoretical position, and that the individual figures he chose to focus upon as models of social and cultural thinking were actually chosen because they were the ones he happened to have read, whereas others were left out or dealt with only peripherally. Reading the book in the 1980s and looking in it for an explicit socialist critique – for (in a word) a dialectic which would have the scope and objectivity one associates with a Marxist analysis – one finds oneself continually diverted from the fundamental conditions. For if it 'still remains very close to socialist debate' (Williams 1979: 107) and has its own vigorous terms of reference, one is at once struck by what it does not say or what it fails to get into focus or even to touch upon. For example, it provides no clearly-defined historical framework, and leaves the underlying conditions which determine the logic of the discourse largely unexplored.

This is apparent from the start, even in the decision Williams (1963: 18) makes to examine, 'not a series of abstracted problems, but a series of statements by individuals'. For in choosing to open his account by dealing with the writings of Edmund Burke, and in praising Burke for his eloquence (his 'magnificent affirmation' (1963: 38)), Williams makes no attempt to set that eloquence, as we see it at work in such a book as Burke's *Reflections on the Revolution in France*, in its proper context. Though he is set in some sort of contrast to Cobbett, there is almost no reference to his contemporaries, and none whatsoever to Tom Paine, who, after all, directly challenged the reactionary denunciations of Burke, and delivered his own 'magnificent' and devastating reply to them in the two parts of *The Rights of Man*. It is difficult to understand why Paine should have been ignored, and even more difficult to understand why there should have been so little discussion of the French Revolution and its English supporters, particularly in the light of Burke's fanatical attack upon the principles of equality and democracy, his call for a kind of crusade against Revolutionary France; since the response to the dispute he initiated was the reassertion of counter-revolutionary government in England, which did so much to transform the structure of European society and to lay foundations for the triumph of minority-class rule at the Congress of Vienna in 1815.

Williams does his best to explain these omissions, and others like them, in the course of the series of interviews he gave in 1977 to the editors of the *New Left Review*, recalling the major influences that went into the making of the book – dominated, as he says, by the ideas of Eliot, Leavis, Clive Bell and Matthew Arnold. 'I started work on [*Culture and Society*] in '48', he says, 'at a time when my separation from the possibilities of political action and collaboration was virtually complete. There was a breakdown of any collective project that I could perceive, political, literary or cultural' (Williams 1979: 102) – which is perhaps a way of justifying what the *NLR* calls the 'virtually systematic depreciation of the actual political dimension' of all the figures discussed in the book (Williams 1979: 100). But this is not much of a compensation either for the omissions or for those figures actually chosen – why, for instance, Carlyle and Burke (and later Arnold) should be treated on the whole so admiringly, while the great poets of the Romantic Revolt (and later even William Morris) should be given so comparatively negative a place in the record. If it can be seriously argued that 'the confutation of Burke on the French Revolution is now a one-finger exercise in politics and history', and that 'the quality of Burke is the quality indicated by Matthew Arnold' – to the effect that 'almost alone in England, he brings thought to bear upon politics, he saturates politics with thought' (Williams 1963: 24) – then one must expect to find the terms of one's argument being disputed. It is not enough, after all, to take one line of (largely conservative) thinking and deal with this as though it were an acceptable fact rather than an arbitrary opinion. For what this does is to give such weight to the views of the establishment as to distort the record, leaving the impression that other views did not count. True, Williams (1963: 24–5) immediately qualifies Arnold's judgement by defining Burke's thought as 'a special immediacy of experience, which works itself out, in depth, to a particular embodiment of ideas that become, in themselves, the whole man', or 'a personal experience become a landmark'. But in developing this curiously idealist, Arnoldian view of the man and his 'organic' concept of society, Williams makes no attempt to set against it the kind of thinking represented by the radicals, the Jacobins of the time, and above all by Paine.

Apart from a single reference to Dr Price, they are passed over in silence –
William Godwin, Mary Wollstonecraft, Joseph Priestley, people like Thomas
Hardy, Maurice Margorot and John Thelwall. And if Cobbett is there, and
Owen, Hazlitt is not; nor are men like Richard Carlile or the Chartists
O'Brien and O'Connor even mentioned, though four pages are given over to
Carlyle's reactionary views on Chartism, which reduce such voices for
working-class action (in what Thompson (1968: 914) has described as 'the
most distinguished popular culture England has known' to 'bellowings, in-
articulate cries of a dumb creature in rage and pain' (Williams 1963: 93).

Nor, later on in the book, is any place at all given to the revolutionary upheavals of 1848 which, as a decisive turning point in the history of Europe
and of England, brought about the triumph of industrial capitalism in the
second half of the nineteenth century, and in that sense profoundly influenced the intellectual and cultural assumptions of men like Ruskin, Arnold
and Mill. This perhaps helps to explain the misrepresentations and distortions that occur in the book, which takes its position almost from within the
establishment and argues the relative place of those it selects for analysis without taking into consideration the contradictions, the dialectic interplay of material forces that were at work, the underlying terms of the economic situation
and its determining influence upon the culture.

Such omissions constitute serious and damaging flaws in a book that professes to delineate the terms and conditions of cultural activity in English society. And since it is a work that is still being widely read, it is important to be
wary of many of its assessments – the disorientating pull towards Burke, Carlyle, Arnold, T. E. Hulme, Eliot and Richards at the expense of more radical
forms of thinking, even though we might well agree with Williams (1979: 110)
that 'it permitted a reconnection with a very complex tradition of social
thought and of literature which had been short-circuited by Scrutiny and
indeed by a whole class formation'

To turn from *Culture and Society* to its sequel, *The Long Revolution* – which
was an attempt to register the terms and conditions presented by the 1950s
(described by Williams (1979: 135–6) as 'a very base period, which appeared
to have neutralized and incorporated many of the very institutions of struggle
to which socialists were appealing') – is to come to grips with the sheer difficulty of changing the organizational structure of an intractable social system.
As Williams (1979: 136) observes: 'The truth about a society . . . is to be
found in its actual relations, always exceptionally complicated, between the
system of decision (politics), the system of communication and learning (culture), the system of maintenance (economics) and the system of generation
and nurture (family)'. But in adding that 'it is not a question of looking for
some absolute formula by which the structure of these relations can be invariably determined' and stressing that they 'are never really separable', he
seems clearly to be resisting the Marxist emphasis upon 'the primacy of economic production in the historical process' (1979: 147). In other words, faced
with the complex conditions of British society, there is no straightforward
answer to the problems of determining the conditions of the struggle for
change, since we are involved in a multiple, overlapping process which includes the economic but insists that all cultural manifestations have their influence upon the whole, even though they may seem demonstrably to be the

products of underlying material conditions. Indeed, in this, Williams (1965: 11–12) is unequivocal:

> We cannot understand the process of change in which we are involved, if we limit ourselves to thinking of the democratic, industrial, and cultural revolutions as separate processes. Our whole way of life, from the shape of our communities to the organisation and content of education, and from the structure of the family to the status of art and entertainment, is being profoundly affected by the progress and interaction of democracy and industry, and by the extension of communications.

And this is the emphasis of the book's conclusion, which looks towards British society in the 1960s, and takes the form of an attack upon the assumption that any real socialist advance can be made in association with the conditions of a consumer society or through bureaucratic nationalization.

For what, above all, Williams is concerned about in *The Long Revolution* is the manner in which increasingly in the development of monopoly capitalism 'all the essential needs that could not be co-ordinated by commodity production – health, habitation, family, education, what it calls leisure – have been repressed and specialized' (1979: 151). He is aware, that is, of the disastrous consequences of ignoring the need to transform the structures of society – consequences we are even now having to accept from the brutal pressures of a government which has come out from behind the 'decorous equivocation' of the consensus decades to apply all the economic and political weapons it has at its command to force communal forms of social wealth into subservience to the demands of the market.

Of course, in 1959 Williams was still in basic terms feeling his way through the confusions and uncertainties that afflicted the labour movement throughout the decade as defeat followed defeat. But in this book, as in all his subsequent work, there is a deepening criticism of the strategy of socialist response and (in the light of the Labour Party's failure to put forward any sort of alternative to the forces of a resurgent market economy) an increasing awareness of the need to provide the theoretical terms for such an alternative. Not that *The Long Revolution*, with its call for a new realism, an 'interpenetration of the personal and the social – idea into feeling, person into community, change into settlement' (Williams 1965: 314), goes quite far enough. For, while it may be true to say that 'people are what their world is and their world is a complex changing structure of relationships rooted in the communal process of society, this, however conflicting, however divided' (1965: 315), still one is left with a structure that people can only control if they have control of the structures of power; for otherwise they remain alienated and divided within it by the contradictions of the system that controls. Which is to say that if such a proposition is to be anything more than a fine Utopian gesture, it is necessary to act against the conditions which determine the structures of power, so that the alienating barriers that divide people from each other can be broken through and the human connections made.

Further transformations in the development of Williams's theoretical position were to be achieved between the writing of *The Long Revolution* and the formulation of the narrative themes of *The Country and the City* (written in 1973), and particularly with *Communications* (1962), the novel *Second Generation* (1964), the new dimensions defined by *Drama from Ibsen to Brecht* (1968), which distanced

Williams from the Leavisite concepts that dominated the first edition of that book, and *Orwell* (1971). And it is interesting to note that the first half of the *Country and the City* was written in 1968, at the same time as Williams was undertaking a major revision of *Communications* for its second edition; by which time it had become cruelly apparent that the Labour Party under Wilson, operating on the restrictive terms of the capitalist economy, was pursuing a course diametrically opposed to the strengthening of socialism, and making itself 'an active collaborator in the process of reproducing capitalist society' (Williams 1979: 373). In this context, *The Country and the City* is a sustained and penetrating attempt to make sense of the underlying contradictions of the system in terms of the long struggle of the English people for their rights and freedoms. And it does so by examining the literature of country and city as a social and historical record of the changing pressures imposed upon the people by the forces of economic change, on the assumption that 'the contrast of country and city is one of the major forms in which we become conscious of a central part of our experience and of the crises of our society' (Williams 1975: 347).

Williams sets out from his own roots as a countryman to trace this complex interactive process through its many stages

> within a single literature and society: a literature, English, which is perhaps richer than any other in the full range of its themes of country and city; and a society which went through a process of historical development, in rural and then industrial and urban economies and communities, very early, and very thoroughly; still a particular history but one which has also become . . . a dominant mode of development in many parts of the world (1975: 350).

And in the urgency and eloquence of his narrative, and its characteristically open approach, he develops at once 'a sustained polemic against false attempts to idealize . . . the values of a ruling-class agrarian order of the past' and 'a major plea for the continuity and relevance of the real values of rural life and labour, created by the direct producers themselves, for the socialism of an increasingly industrialized world' (Williams 1979: 313).

But there is more to it than that. As he puts it toward the end of the book: 'In the deepening crisis of modern metropolitan and industrial living, and in the more serious crisis of persistent and intractable poverty in the rest of the world' (Williams 1975: 361), it is necessary to recognize that 'if we are to survive at all, we shall have to develop and extend our working agricultures' (1975: 360–1), and that to give 'any effective shape to our future . . . work on the land will have to become more rather than less important and central' (1975: 361). But here the crucial perception is 'the clear impossibility of continuing as we are' (1975: 360) – that is, by ruthlessly exploiting the natural resources of the world according to the methods of capitalist appropriation. For it is these destructive methods that have brought about the crisis we are living through. Which means we have to 'begin to see, in fact, that the active powers of minority capital, in all its possible forms, are our most active enemies, and that they will have to be not just persuaded but defeated and superseded'. For

> the scale and connection of the necessary decisions require social powers and social resources which capitalism in any of its forms denies, opposes and alienates. The different social consciousness of the dispossessed labourers and of the urban workers, born in protest and despair, has to come through in new ways as a

collectively responsible society. Neither will the city save the country nor the country the city. Rather the long struggle within both will become a general struggle, as in a sense it has always been (1975: 362).

And in the end, as Marx and Engels declared, it is only through socialism that we can 'restore the intimate connection between industrial and agricultural production' (Williams 1975: 365). This, as Williams acknowledges, was the imaginative concept envisaged by William Morris in *News From Nowhere* beyond the destructiveness of the capitalist system; and this 'has been significantly revived, among Western revolutionary socialists, as a response to the crisis of industrial civilization and what is seen as megalopolis' (Williams 1975: 366).

Visiting the country today, it may be fashionable to admire the many beautiful houses of the rich; but Williams (1975: 132) asks us to register the social effect these houses have had in exploitation and enclosure across the centuries as 'visible triumphs over the ruin and labour of others' – to 'think it through as labour and see how long and systematic the exploitation and seizure must have been to rear that many houses, on that scale'. We might then, he thinks, see differently – not only in terms of the 'robbery and fraud' embodied in 'the sites, the façades, the defining avenues and walls, the great iron gates and the guardian lodges' of these estates, but what they signify: the 'mutually competitive but still uniform exposition, at every turn, of an established and commanding class power' (1975: 133). And seeing this, we might then begin to see the ways in which that power developed into 'the social crisis of nineteenth-century England' to become 'a general crisis, because of the intricate interconnections of urban and rural poverty, industrial and agricultural production, and industrial and agricultural labour and settlement'. Indeed, it is Williams's task to demonstrate the many forms this crisis took everywhere:

> the long struggle over rents and leases, between owners and tenants; the long struggle over prices, and the relation of home production to exports, in a developing trade economy; the long struggle between employers and workers, on wages and the right to form unions; the long struggle between the demand for cheap labour and the rights of men, women and children, and specifically the right of education (1975: 227).

But, of course, there is the salient fact that

> by the middle of the nineteenth century the urban population of England exceeded the rural population: the first time in human history that this had ever been so, anywhere. As a mark of the change to a new kind of civilization [this] has unforgettable significance (1975: 261),

not only because it defines the triumphs of industrial capitalism, but because of the emergence of an organized socialist movement.

> Out of the very chaos and misery of the new metropolis, and spreading from it to rejuvenate a national feeling, a civilizing force of a new vision of society had been created in struggle, had gathered up the suffering and the hopes of generations of the oppressed and exploited, and in this unexpected and challenging form was the human reply of the city to the long inhumanity of country and city alike (Williams 1979: 321–2).

As for the image of nineteenth-century London, Williams is as richly graphic and particular in his literary references as he is elsewhere. It is seen through the eyes of many writers, but perhaps above all Blake, Wordsworth, Dickens and Gissing, undergoing the most radical transformations – becoming 'the creation of industrial capitalism' (Williams 1975: 181). This is what Dickens's London was, dramatized in terms of its people, its institutions, its streets, its squalor, 'as at once a social fact and a human landscape' (1975: 195), 'a destructive animal, a monster' (1975: 196), 'a stream, a way of life' (1975: 197), 'as not only an alien and indifferent system but as the unknown, perhaps unknowable, sum of so many lives, jostling, colliding, disrupting, adjusting, recognizing, settling, moving again to new spaces' (1975: 201).

Whatever new spaces the twentieth century has opened up, an increasing sense of isolation, of meaninglessness, of atomized existence, has been the experience of modern city life; and this is registered above all in the sense of a 'profound alteration' that has taken place in the twentieth-century imagination. The fragmentation resulting from the alienating conditions of commodity production seems to have induced, at least in the work of the great modernists, a subjective retreat from the dialectic of interaction with the external world and its objective conditions. In Joyce's *Ulysses*, for instance, it is as if 'the forces of the action have become internal', so that 'the relation between action and consciousness' (1975: 292) ceases to be an objective social experience, a quest for a transformed world. The fragmentation rules, and we are caught up in a web of conditioning, as single individuals reacting helplessly to the bewildering facts of the commodity world that dominates.

Williams recognizes the restrictive nature of the ideological trap. As a socialist with a clear objective grasp of the determining forces of the historical process, he can see where the modernist vision falls short, what it fails to take into account in its subjectivist monologic view of reality. For him the perspectives are by now dialectic, social, concerned with the struggle between men and women and the contradictory material conditions of their world. Considering the terms of his quest, it is no surprise to find him doing justice to the work of a writer like Lewis Grassic Gibbon, so persistently ignored by the literary establishment, and putting him on a level with (and even in some respects superior to) D. H. Lawrence. For Grassic Gibbon uniquely confirms 'what Lawrence again and again rejects, though the fact that he is continually drawn to it is equally significant, . . . the idea and the practice of social agencies of change'. His *Scots Quair* 'is a trilogy which moves through the classical historical process from country to city' (Williams 1975: 321). And

> the strength of *Sunset Song* . . . is the strength of a living people: Chae Strachan, Long Rob, Chris Guthrie. The demands of the war reach in and break the settlement . . . But what is exciting is that in the subsequent move to borough and city the spiritual inheritance is seen as surviving, in the radically altered conditions. A new and predatory system has taken the people for its wars, displaced them from their land, but: 'need we doubt which side of the battle they would range themselves did they live today?' This is a decisively different structure of feeling. The spiritual feeling for the land and for labour, the 'pagan' emphasis which is always latent in the imagery of the earth (very similar, through its different rhythms, to the Lawrence of the beginning of *The Rainbow*), is made available and is stressed in the new struggles: through the General Strike, in the period of *Cloud Howe*, to the time of the hunger marches in the period of *Grey Granite*. Even the legends sustain the transition, for their spiritual emphasis makes it possible to reject a Church that has openly sided with property and oppression. More historically and more convincingly, the radical independence of

the small farmers, the craftsmen and the labourers is seen as transitional to the militancy of the industrial workers. The shape of a whole history is then decisively transformed.

And, 'in a narrative that more clearly than in any other novel embodies the active labour movement of the thirties', what makes this Grassic Gibbon trilogy so important is that it 'speaks for many who never got to speak for themselves in recorded ways' (1975: 323–4).

The Country and the City is an original and important book, not only for the ways in which it adapts and qualifies the Marxist debate, but because it 'breaks through to what are in substance wholly new areas of debate' (Williams 1979: 315). It is this book which makes Williams, as Perry Anderson (1976: 105) wrote of him in 1974 in a note on Gramsci's idea of 'organic intellectuals', 'perhaps the most distinguished socialist thinker to have so far come from the ranks of the Western working class itself'. For even though his work is not considered Marxist in concept, it has 'certain qualities which cannot be found anywhere else in contemporary socialist writing, and which will be part of any future revolutionary culture'.

The distinction being made here between socialism and Marxism is interesting. As Williams himself comments on this book:

The peremptory way in which I mention Marx and Engels is very significant of my particular biographical trajectory . . . I had such a curious entry into a Marxist culture, at a very specific time, . . . that it is only quite recently that I have thought, when I sit down to work on a problem, that I must relate what I am writing in a sustained way to what Marx and Engels or certain other classical Marxist thinkers had to say (1979: 316).

His Marxism has, in other words, tended to function as a parallel and even invisible influence upon his writing. In almost all his books, he points out,

I have been arguing with what I take to be official English culture. I have done that in different ways in different phases, but always the people in my sights . . . have been this other tradition . . . For that kind of attention still seems to me an absolute necessity for contemporary Marxists, working in a specifically national culture.

He sees the need 'to expand, to revalue the Marxist tradition', and to do this without 'renouncing . . . the necessary engagement with the established English culture'. He chooses to discuss a minor eighteenth-century poet in more detail than Marx 'because this is where a really reactionary social consciousness is being continually reproduced'. And though 'there would be a good many people in English cultural circles who would be delighted if I spent the rest of my time clearing up some questions of Marxist literary theory . . . I don't propose to give them the satisfaction' (Williams 1979: 316–17).

Marxism and Literature may not have done quite that; but it certainly addresses itself to the fundamental problems of Marxist literary theory – and it does so in order to define a specifically Marxist response to literature as creative practice and as a form of cultural materialism. It is a difficult book because it deals with these issues theoretically; but the difficulty is inescapable, for it is concerned with the underlying conditions that dictate the forms and relations of material production. To this end, it sets out the historical development of the basic concepts of 'culture', 'language', 'literature' and 'ideology' as the grounds for a theoretical analysis of the materiality of culture and of literature which, rejecting the distinctions between 'base' and 'superstructure', argues that there is 'a single and indissoluble real process' going on which materializes all aspects of the social structure, including 'the material character of a cultural order' (1979: 350–1). Indeed, for Williams the argument which separates the economic conditions of production (as the base) from 'a whole body of activities' – art and ideas, aesthetics, ideology (as the superstructural) – is a falsifying argument. For then 'none of these [activities] can be grasped as they are; as real practices, elements of a whole material social process; not a realm or a world or a superstructure, but many and variable productive practices, with specific conditions and intentions (Williams 1977: 94).

Here there seems to have been some kind of telescoping of the distinctions between primary and secondary forms of material production; for it is demonstrable that art and ideas are products of more fundamental conditions. Nevertheless, *Marxism and Literature* insists on putting 'at the very centre of Marxism . . . an extraordinary emphasis on human creativity and self-creation'. For 'the notion of self-creation, extended to civil society and to language by pre-Marxist thinkers, was radically extended by Marxism to the basic work processes and thence to a deeply [creatively] altered physical world and a self-created humanity' (1977: 206). And, this in turn has its *roots* in language as the

> living evidence of a continuing social process, into which individuals are born and within which they are shaped, but to which they also actively contribute, in a continuing process. This is at once their socialisation and their individuation: the connected aspects of a single process which the alternative theories of 'system' and 'expression' had divided and dissociated. We then find not a reified 'language' and 'society' but an active *social language*;

not 'a simple "reflection" or "expression" of "material reality"', but 'a grasping of this reality through language, which as practical consciousness is saturated by and saturates all social activity' (1977: 37). So that even 'the process of articulation is necessarily . . . a *material* process, and . . . the sign itself becomes part of a (socially created) physical and material world' – 'literally a means of production' rather than 'an operation of and within "consciousness"' (1977: 38); though 'in addition to its social and material existence' it has the capacity 'to become an *inner* sign, . . . part of a verbally constituted consciousness which allows individuals to use signs of their own initiative' (1977: 40).

Such a concept of language, as the location of dynamic social practice, is central to Williams's cultural and social theory. 'It is a decisive theoretical rejection of mechanical, behaviourist, or Saussurean versions of an objective system . . . beyond individual initiative or creative use', and 'of subjectivist theories of language as individual expression' (1977: 40). It insists that the 'fundamental relationship between the "inner" and the "material" sign' is 'always lived as an activity, a practice', since even the 'internalized' sign is involved in the material process of communication. And it stresses that this relationship is 'specifically historical', involved 'in the movement from the production of language by human physical resources alone through the material history of the production of other resources . . . to the active social history of the complex of communicative systems' (1977: 41). Thus, for Williams (1977: 42), in the context of the 'dynamics of social language', both 'sign' and 'system' will need 'to be revalued'. Because, as he sees it, 'the area of signification is not confined to the system itself, but . . . extends to the users of language and to the objects, and relationships about which language speaks' (Williams 1976: 20). And this language has its location everywhere people speak and act, as a material and historical phenomenon, recording and defining in the changing forms of social practice the multiple interactions of history. It may be that at certain levels the meanings of words as signs determine the practice of language. But, more significant, the forms of practice – the social uses of language, the ways in which pressure is put upon the system through the conflicting, changing process of social experience – interact upon and influence meaning. For things are always happening, being lived and therefore changed, between the interstices of ideology, in the *praxis* of living. There are pressures, that is – active historical tensions – continually at work upon the received forms and structures of language. And these pressures and tensions make it impossible to think of any one set of meanings as having permanence, though it is a persistent fact of social history that 'many crucial meanings have been shaped by a dominant class' and ideologically imposed *as* a permanence, a construct to be accepted as if it were the 'truth'. But this, in Williams's view, merely demonstrates the terms of struggle and of conflict involved in the social and cultural process that dominates people's lives. For even while the meanings of the dominant class are being imposed upon them, people go on speaking their own (demotic) language, that cuts across and implicitly questions the terms of the formal system. And in this sense the attempt to break the domination of certain sets of meanings is part of the social struggle between the classes – the struggle of people to create meanings in which 'the sense of edge is accurate', so that language can serve their own complex real needs as 'a vocabulary to use, to find [their] own ways in' (1976: 21).

Language (like history and like the social process which it is inseparable from), functions on many levels, in a multiplicity of ways, reflecting the tensions and conflicts and distinctions of social life, the differing rhythms and registers of social and class experience, often in forms 'for which there is no external counterpart' (Williams 1954: 22), existing 'at the very edge of semantic availability' (1977: 134) – the active, unformulated meeting-point of language and praxis. But, crucially, its vocabulary,

> inherited within precise social and historical conditions . . . has to be made at once conscious and critical – subject to change as well as continuity – if the millions of people in whom it is active are to see it as active: not as a *tradition* to be learned, nor a *consensus* to be accepted; nor a set of meanings which, because it is 'our language', has a natural authority; but as a shaping and re-shaping,

which we change as we use, 'as we go on making our own language and history' (Williams 1976: 21-2).

Williams (1979: 352–3) explains that what he was wanting to do in *Marxism and Literature* was

> something very much against the grain of two traditions, one (the liberal humanist) which has totally spiritualised cultural production, the other (Marxist) which has relegated it to secondary status. My aim was to emphasize that cultural practices are forms of material production, and that until this is understood it is impossible to think about them in their real social relations . . . But, of course, it is true that there are forms of material production which always and everywhere precede all other forms . . . the production of food, the production of shelter, and the production of the means of producing food and shelter – an extended range which is still related to the absolutely

necessary conditions of sustaining life . . . Very often today, however, there is a slide from this pattern of activities to the structure of a late capitalist economy, as if everything which occurred in contemporary industry or agriculture were forms of production self-evidently related to primary need, as opposed for example to writing novels or painting pictures . . . At the same time, . . . a great deal is now produced that has to do with relative social position or indeed with entertainment or leisure. Now this is where it would have been very much better to have argued my case historically. The economy Marx described was much more directly related to satisfying, or rather failing to satisfy, basic human needs than the economy of advanced capitalism.

In *Problems of Materialism and Culture* (1980) and in *Culture* (1981), Williams extends the terms of his argument for cultural materialism both historically and analytically. But important as these books are, I shall not deal with them here. I want instead to conclude this study of Williams's work by looking briefly at two other books. For both *Towards 2000* (1983) and *Writing in Society* (1983) move probingly forward: the first in the broadest historical and social terms, picking up threads Williams had dealt with in *The Long Revolution*, and confronting the threat to world survival posed by the reactionary materialism of advanced capitalism at work in the 1980s; the second dealing with the interactions of intellect and feeling at the specific (and specifying) level of language and writing, where the broader issues of *Towards 2000* have their intellectual and seminal focus – where consciousness of livelihood, of place, condition and potentiality can be precisely defined, and history made culturally and materially manifest.

Towards 2000 represents a determined attempt, after having dealt with cultural and social changes and deformations in Britain since 1959, to provide 'an analysis which can take us beyond both the national and the international forms' of cultural development (Williams 1985: 20). 'Thus there are shifts of gear, in most of the essays, from closely analysed British situations to more general situations and the ideas necessary to interpret them' (1985: 21).

Williams is fully aware, for instance, of the destructive process of advanced capitalism as a system of appropriation and of dispossession moving from place to place, nation to nation, in search of new markets for exploitation – a process which continues to operate as it did in its earlier stages, 'irrespective of the needs and preferences of its inhabitants' (1985: 186), or indeed of the ecological-environmental conditions it threatens with extinction. And what he finds 'really astonishing' about this

> is that it is the inheritors and active promoters, the ideologists and agents, of this continuing world-wide process who speak to the rest of us, at least from one side of their mouths, about the traditional values of settlement, community and loyalty. These, the great disrupters, not only of other people's settlements but of many of those of their own nominal people, have annexed and appropriated, often without challenge, many of the basic human feelings about a necessary and desirable society. They retain this appropriation even while their hands are endlessly busy with old and new schemes in which the priorities are wholly different: schemes through which actual people and communities are depressed or disappear, under the calculations of cost-benefit, profit and advantageous production (1985: 186–7).

To Williams (1985: 187), who speaks for many of us, 'it is an outrage that this has happened and been allowed to happen'. But what we have to face is that it *has* happened, and that the international market system that now dominates our lives as a 'system of mobile-privatised social relations' (1985: 189), remains immune to both its critics and its victims. And if, as Williams (1985: 190) has it, this system 'is an evil system, by all fully human standards', he is quick to stress that it is not to be modified, let alone changed or overthrown, without understanding and analysing how and why it has managed through its rhetoric of 'economic efficiency', its global control of resources, to retain the support and acquiescence of large majorities and to override 'all the real and increasing divisions and conflicts of interest' (1985: 192) within it.

Williams's attempt to answer (and to analyse) such questions in the final chapters of *Towards 2000* inevitably remains at the level of hypothesis and of principle. As he sees it, alternatives are not to be found 'in the mere negation of existing social perceptions'. He suggests that 'two positive and connected initiatives' are necessary – 'first, the cultural struggle for actual social identities; and second, the political definition of effective self-governing societies' (1985: 193). Not that he believes that these initiatives can in themselves break through the barriers the system has set up; for we cannot afford to pretend 'that the capitalist social order has not done its main job of implanting a deep assent to capitalism' (1985: 254). Though significant mass movements linking peace, ecology and feminism have emerged in recent years to challenge the aggressive radical Right, it remains a fact that, 'back in the strongholds of the economic order itself, there are not only the dominant institutions and their shadow subordinates. There are, for most of the time, most of the people' (1985: 254).

And this remains the most intractable problem, the resolution of which must involve at least 'three changes of mind' (1985: 260). First, and most crucial, 'the connection between the forces and the relations of production has to be re-stated', rethought and transformed. Second, beyond the concept of 'society as production', a 'broader concept' of reality has to be developed, involving new 'forms of human relationships within a physical world', a 'new orientation of livelihood: of practical, self-managing, self-renewing societies, in which people care first for each other, in a living world' (1985: 266). And out of this fundamental emphasis the third change follows: a reassertion of the fundamental (and creative) human emotions (or 'structures of feeling' (Williams 1977: 128–35)) as indispensable to the full perception of what is meant by 'a way of life' and to the continuity of human relationships in society. Thus:

> The central element is the shift from 'production' to 'livelihood': from an alienated generality to direct and practical ways of life. These are the real bases from which cooperative relationships can grow, and the rooted forms which are wholly compatible with, rather than contradictory to, other major energies and interests. They are also, at just this historical stage, in the very development of the means of production, the shifts that most people will in any case have to make (Williams 1985: 267).

All this is, of course, pitched at a level of high abstraction from within an alien system, but in the insistent belief that 'inevitabilities' can be challenged, and that, once they are, 'we can begin gathering our resources for a journey of hope' (1985: 268). And though the book was written too early to take into account the unprecedented initiatives that were so soon to be launched by Mikhail Gorbachev, its perspectives now begin to look quite different in the light of the extraordinary changes being brought about in the balance of world power by *perestroika* and *glasnost*, which are forcing not only the Soviet peoples and their allies but also the recalcitrant forces of Western capitalism to rethink and to loosen up their most rigid assumptions. What Williams seems to be suggesting is that we have to reverse our habitual concepts of and relationships with reality (dominated by the destructive aggressions and greeds which threaten our survival) and choose instead to be caring and co-operative not only in our social lives but in our response to the physical world, the environment we live in terms of.

Writing in Society has a different function. Here it is Williams's underlying concern to register the interconnection between forms of writing and social reality; and the ways in which these forms of writing, as products of history, structures of communication, structures of feeling, reflect and influence the changing process of history. He is intent, that is, to demonstrate – against the tendency of industrial societies 'to exclude history', to 'neutralize' writing – that 'the whole series of changing relationships which are evident in the practice of writing' can actually show us 'how . . . people assumed, developed, extended, realized and changed their relationships' (Williams 1983: 2).

In this sense the book complements and provides specific evidence for the more purely theoretical analyses of *Marxism and Literature*, *Culture* and *Towards 2000*. As Williams himself points out, many of the essays and lectures collected here – the earliest published in 1964 and 1969 – 'are the working papers through which the theoretical arguments were directed'. But they also extend and develop ideas dealt with in such books as *The Country and the City*. In terms, that is, of the 'major cultural shift of our period' and of changes brought about or 'newly developed in radio, television and film', these essays define,

> in some new ways, the historically specific relations between writing, print and silent reading which had been taken for granted, and at the same time privileged, in the four centuries in which these relations were dominant and . . . assumed to be universal (1983: 6).

The theoretical implications of the earlier essays are cogently spelt out in the most demanding section of the book, containing the three Cambridge lectures of 1981–3. These take further the question of language as signification, as 'a constitutive element of material social practice' (Williams 1977: 165), and its challenge of the Leavis–Eliot view of literature as a defining canon for 'culture', 'life' and 'thought'. Putting his emphasis upon 'a newly active social sense of writing and reading through the . . . material historical realities of language' and 'the whole set of social practices and relationships which define writers and readers as active human beings', Williams (1983: 189) refutes the idealized view of '"authors" and "trained readers" who are assumed to float . . . above the rough, divisive and diverse world – of which yet, by some alchemy, they possess the essential secret'.

His purpose in *Crisis in English Studies* is to identify and distinguish certain tendencies within Marxism and structuralism, and to determine their impact upon what he calls the dominant paradigm (or canon) of establishment ideology: literature as 'a perceived field of knowledge', indeed as 'an object of knowledge' (1983: 192). After describing seven differing positions within the Marxist tradition and setting them (through the agency of Lucien Goldmann's 'genetic structuralism') into the context of formalist theories that emerged (particularly in Russia) in the 1920s and 1930s, Williams singles out the connections and conflicts between early Marxism and the later formalists – Voloshinov, Bakhtin and Murakowsky – as 'very important', since the work of these formalists (unlike that of their earlier and more influential colleagues) 'transformed the whole argument about the study of literature, and in the end, the status of the paradigm itself' (1983: 203). Voloshinov, for instance, while accepting the analysis of the school of structural linguistics 'as analysis of a system of signs', beyond this insisted that language is 'a *socially produced* system of signs' (Williams 1983: 203), historically determined, prone to continual 'shift and change and initiation of meanings' (1983: 204) – a concept which Bakhtin then applied to literary analysis in his studies of Rabelais and Dostoevsky. And Murakowsky went even further: contending that 'aesthetic norms and aesthetic values are themselves always socially produced' (Williams 1983: 204).

Williams then proceeds to define the various structuralist positions, primarily in order to put himself at a distance from their more rigid concepts, but ultimately to set against them his own theoretical position – cultural materialism: 'the analysis of all forms of signification, including quite centrally writing, within the actual means and conditions of their production' (1983: 210). And this, by 1981 – though already set out in *Marxism and Literature* – had 'found new points of contact with certain work in more recent semiotics'; so that 'a fully historical semiotics would be very much the same thing as cultural materialism' (1983: 210). But, more important – and here he marks out the ground for a new and crucial emphasis – this specific form of cultural materialism (together with the Marxist position he had taken in *The Country and the City*) questions the orthodox paradigm 'as a governing definition of the object of knowledge'; insisting that the paradigm itself be exposed to analysis and reorganized in the light of 'serious and fundamental differences about the object of knowledge' (1983: 211).

On these grounds, in fact, the final emphasis of the lecture *Beyond Cambridge English* – an engagement with 'the central impulses of modernism' – is upon the necessity of moving beyond the cultural process of 'estrangement and exposure', of isolation, pessimism and despair, that characterizes the modernist movement even in the attempts of its artists to forge from language 'a possible aesthetic universality' (1983: 222–3). For in the long run

> what began in isolation and exposure ended, at many levels, in an establishment: as the decisive culture of an international capitalist world, which could trade both the original and the adapted forms (1983: 223).

Williams reacts delicately but with acute dissatisfaction to the theoretical systems produced out of the culture of modernism, looking at them with respect but at the same time 'with the eyes of a stranger'. 'I can feel the bracing cold of their inherent distances and impersonalities', he says drily, 'and yet have to go on saying that they are indeed ice-cold' (1983: 223). It is not that he does not accept that these systems 'have great explanatory power' (1983: 224). But he sees, too,

> the estranging consequences of the general assumption – as active in modernist literature as in theoretical linguistics and structuralist Marxism – that the systems of human signs are generated within the systems themselves and that to think otherwise is a humanist error (1983: 223).

And for him that is unacceptable, since it puts 'the form and the language of their explanations . . . at a quite exceptional distance from the lives and relationships they address' (1983: 224).

As for modernism itself, defined through the work of its great innovators (and Williams's list includes James, Conrad, Joyce, Eliot, Pound and Beckett), it 'was at root defensive: an intransigent response to a general failure, in which the unevenness – the willed and dominating unevenness – of literacy and learning was decisive'. And though at first it 'had no choice but distance', eventually 'the inherent contradictions of its own practice forced one or other general position, where we can see all the innovators divide'. In one direction there was a 'majority rejection of the orthodox social and cultural order in terms of an option for the past'. In the second, 'rejection went the other way: to ideas of absolute revolution, the new art and thought as revolutionary' (1983: 225). Williams's sympathies, of course, lie with the second. But because both are rooted in a profound disaffection from and pessimism about the world, they remain, in effect, insulated from those forces in society that would seek to break the impasse of capitalism.

At the same time, the culture of modernism has been stabilized and enshrined in the establishment institutions as part of the orthodox paradigm: a concept of art and culture as 'universal', 'ahistoric', 'inherently aristocratic'. Against this, Williams has always 'tried to be on the other side', working to overcome 'the unevenness within which modernism was formed'; conscious of the inequalities, the gaps between literacy and learning, which maintain too great a distance between the specialist concerns of academics and the deeper historical concerns of people using language (and literature) in the social practice of their lives. So he chooses to look beyond Cambridge English to those places where he believes new things are beginning to happen and

> to testing encounters with all those men and women who have only ever intermit-
> tently and incompletely been addressed: going to learn as well as to teach, within a
> now dangerous unevenness of literacy and learning which . . . is radically dislocating
> what had been assumed, in both literature and education, to be stable norms
> (1983: 225).

Thus, against dislocation and dispossession, language as activity, as practice, has to be made (I repeat) 'at once conscious and critical – subject to change as well as continuity – if the millions of people in whom it is active are to see it as active' (Williams 1976: 22). This, for Williams, is crucial. In a world in which 'further tendencies in monopoly capitalism have removed to an even greater distance the decisive individuals and functions and institutions by which most working-class life is formed' (1983: 237), he sees it as a priority of cultural theory and practice to encourage the active presence in people's lives of the wider forces of language and society as instruments of creative social change.

The issues at stake here, set against an economic world order which directly and physically affects us all at every point where determinations of need are being fought out, give the work of Raymond Williams a special kind of significance, a special cogency and urgency. He can be prolix – I suppose because he is so prolific. But in the course of the sustained investigation he has conducted on such diverse grounds, he strikes home so often that this does not matter. Committed as he is to the urgency of the quest for some kind of socialist transformation as a necessity of survival, he is always alert to the dangers that threaten our world at this crucial point in its history, and to the possibility – the unacceptable possibility – that all that remains unfulfilled could be brought to an end by the catastrophic forces of destruction accumulated since the end of the Second World War.

This involves us in what Raymond Williams calls 'the challenge to a necessary complexity' of response to the problems of living in the real world. Not the disgrace and deprivation of capitalism, or the monolithic bureaucracy of Stalinism (now perhaps in the process of being rooted out of Soviet society).

> It is only in very complex ways that we can truly understand where we are. It is only in very complex ways, and by moving confidently towards very complex societies, that we can defeat imperialism and capitalism and begin the construction of many socialisms which will liberate and draw upon our real and now threatened energies (Williams 1979: 437).

And right up till his death in 1988 he continued his search for arguments about literature and culture in terms of that complexity, because for him there was no other way to make sense of these activities.

12

E. P. Thompson versus Louis Althusser: whose side is Marx on?

The fundamental problems that lie behind this dispute between the Marxist historian and the Marxist philosopher – concerning the interrelation of philosophy and history, the linguistic orientation of thought and the material order of reality, history as scientific theory and historical discourse as determined by the changing conditions of material social activity – seem as irreconcilable as ever. Indeed, they take on a special kind of urgency in the context of the alarming polarization of attitudes that took place during the 1980s, with the Right everywhere seizing the initiative and going onto the offensive to extend and deepen its hegemonic control of society, and the Left in disarray, fragmented by the disruptive pressures of the system, robbed of its power to organize and concentrate against the forces of reaction. As Lenin's maxim has it: 'Action without theory is blind; theory without action is barren' (Mitchell 1970: 159). It is as if the Left had lost control of the *dynamic* of the interaction, the *sources* of its power, which Marx himself had taken such trouble to emphasize in defining again and again how the equation can be made to generate new forms of revolutionary activity across the barriers of divisiveness and dislocation.

No one on the Left needs to be reminded that for Marx it is the material environment that determines our ideas; that 'philosophy is in the service of history' (Marx 1975: 244), and not the other way round; that we are the *products* of history; and that our ideas, the 'legal, political, religious, artistic or philosophical' forms thrown up by social life, are determined by 'the contradictions of material life', the conflicts existing 'between the social forces of production and the relations of production' (Marx and Engels 1968: 182). So that even philosophy, though it may provide 'a recipe or schema . . . for neatly trimming the epochs of history', is no more 'an independent branch of knowledge' (Marx and Engels 1970: 48) than any other, since it is itself a product of history, and only appears to be otherwise as a consequence of the division of material and mental labour.

This is the assumption that is central to E. P. Thompson's argument in *The Poverty of Theory*, his 1978 polemical response to the structuralist philosophy of Louis Althusser. Thompson is concerned to define the categories and methods proper to the investigation of history, in order to defend these categories, and the relevance of historical materialism itself, against attack. For him, every 'disciplined historical discourse of the proof consists in a dialogue between concept and evidence, a dialogue conducted by successive hypotheses, on the one hand, and empirical research on the other' (Thompson 1978: 231). As he sees it,

> the investigation of history as process . . . entails notions of causation, of contradiction, of mediation, and of the systematic organisation (sometimes structuring) of social, political, economic and intellectual life. These elaborate notions 'belong' within historical theory, are refined within this theory's procedures, are thought within thought. But it is untrue that they belong *only* within theory. Each notion, or concept, arises out of empirical engagements, and however abstract the procedures of its self-interrogation, it must then be brought back to an engagement with the determinate properties of the evidence (1978: 235).

Thus, historical materialism itself – the theory formulated by Marx out of his rigorous analysis of Hegel and Feuerbach to demonstrate the logic of the movement of history – is a process that necessarily involves the closest interaction between theory and practice, in which direct social experience, 'human sensuous activity', the 'this-sidedness' of thinking (Marx and Engels 1968: 28), an empirical response to the problems of history (the struggles of classes), serves as a constant check to the tendency of theory to impose its own forms of closure and of stasis, of infallible doctrine, upon the unpredictable changing conditions of material reality. Furthermore, it is clear that this interactive process continued to develop in terms of the dialectical materialism which defines the cogency and significance of all Marx's writings, from the early works to the latest, from those (like *The Communist Manifesto* and *The Civil War in France*) which embody an immediate apprehension of history in action through the struggles of opposed classes, to *Capital*, his monumental analysis of the economic conditions characteristic of the capitalist mode of production.

In Thompson's (1978: 257–8) view, *Capital* is not, as Louis Althusser contends,

> an experience of a different order to that of mature bourgeois Political Economy, but a total confrontation *within* that order. As such, it is both the highest achievement of 'political economy', and it signals the need for its supersession by historical materialism. To say the former is not to diminish Marx's achievement, for it is only in the light of that achievement that we are able to make this judgement. But the achievement does not *produce* historical materialism, it provides the pre-conditions for its production,

containing a wealth of 'hypotheses, informed by consistent theoretical propositions . . . which historical materialism has been setting to work ever since' – not only to test and to verify, but also (wherever necessary) to revise and replace.

It is on these grounds that Thompson sets out to challenge and to refute the assumptions and arguments of Louis Althusser's structuralist theory of Marxism – his concept of 'theoretical practice', of the 'theory of theory and practice and their relationship' (Althusser 1979: 129), in terms of which 'the reality of theoretical formations in general (philosophical ideologies and science) can be considered' (Althusser 1970: 32); of the epistemological break said to have occurred between what he calls Marx's early 'ideological theoretical practice' and the 'scientific theoretical practice' of his maturity; of the ensuing distinction between historical materialism (the science of history) and dialectical materialism;

and thus of history as theory and history as practice, the order of thought and the order of reality, by which history is considered subservient to philosophy. In these terms, Althusser (1979: 119) identifies Marx's thinking as anti-humanist and anti-historicist in its theoretical consistency, its concern to set up scientific, objective standards of theory whose criteria are self-validating. And on this basis, *Capital* is conceived as a *totally different* order from that of mature bourgeois political economy, embodying the philosophy of dialectical materialism, the science of theoretical practice, which 'is indeed its own criterion' and 'has no need for verification from external practices to declare the knowledges [it] produces to be "true", i.e. to be knowledges' (1979: 59).

Thompson finds the circularity of this argument not only repugnant but alarming in its implications, both in the declared objectives (the philosophical abstractions) it sets up, and in what he considers its drift towards an anti-materialist and anti-historical transcendentalism. He has no hesitation therefore in declaring what he calls 'unrelenting intellectual war' (Thompson 1978: 381) on all such forms of 'theoretical practice', which he sees as offering only 'categories of stasis', an argument that takes place 'within the closed field of system or structure' (1978: 275), and ultimately – in the light of Althusser's explicit concept of history as 'a process without a subject' (1976: 51) – as reducing 'real' history (and historical materialism itself) to something unknowable and therefore inapplicable to the system.

For Thompson (1978: 276), 'in the last analysis, the logic of process can only be described in terms of historical analysis; . . . "history" may only be theorised in terms of its own properties'. Which is to say that historical materialism necessarily involves empirical methods of interrogation and response, since 'what requires interrogating and theorising is historical knowledge'. And because historical knowledge is never 'a finished theoretical "truth" (or theory)' but always 'a developing knowledge', it 'takes place both within theory and within practice', 'arises from a dialogue; and its discourse of the proof is conducted within terms of historical logic', which 'should be implicit in each empirical engagement, and explicit in the way in which the historian positions himself before the evidence and in the questions proposed' (1978: 242).

This argument is not, as Thompson (1978: 198) emphatically demonstrates, an argument for 'empiricism', the 'quite different ideological formation' which he accuses Althusser of confusing with the empirical. 'A historian in the Marxist tradition is entitled', as he points out, 'to remind a Marxist philosopher that historians also are concerned, every day, in their practice, with the formation of, and with the tensions within, social consciousness'. And the 'multiple evidences' that are there to be dealt with

in the medium of time . . . propose new problems, and above all . . . continually give rise to *experience* – a category which, however imperfect it may be, is indispensable to the historian, since it comprises the mental and emotional response, whether of an individual or a social group, to many inter-related events and many repetitions of the same kind of event (1978: 199).

In the Althusserian view, however, such practices are an irrelevance. As Barry Hindest and Paul Hirst conclude in their study *Pre-Capitalist Modes of Production*: 'Marxism, as a theoretical and a political practice gains nothing from its association with historical writing and historical research. The study of history is not only scientifically but also politically valueless' (Thompson 1978: 194).

The assertion is blunt enough; and no historian in the Marxist tradition would be likely to find it remotely acceptable. Thompson, at any rate, does not doubt that it denies the very basis on which Marx himself set out to challenge the bourgeois process and its ideological assumptions. 'What is being threatened – what is now actively rejected – is the entire tradition of substantive Marxist historical and political analysis, and its accumulating (if provisional) knowledge'. Thus, if this is actually the contention of the Althusserian critique, in Thompson's view the whole theory becomes suspect, and has to be challenged. For 'then what is at issue, within the Marxist tradition, is the defence of reason itself' (1978: 196).

Curiously enough, the initial effect of the vigour and penetration of Althusser's argument in many sections of *For Marx* makes one wonder whether Thompson's severity is not, after all, misplaced. For in its analysis of the stages which define the period of the break with Hegel and Feuerbach during which Marx was laying the foundations for his revolutionary concept of history, it even appears to obey Thompson's demand for empirical methods. It is a percipient fact of historical observation, for instance, that

> Marx did not choose to be born to the thought German history had concentrated in its university education, nor to think its ideological world. He grew up in this world, in it he learnt to live and move, with it he 'settled accounts', from it he liberated himself (Althusser 1970: 64).

And as Althusser (1970: 64) further observes:

> The art of historical criticism . . . consists of knowing how to lose time so that young authors can grow up. This lost time is simply the time we give them to live. We scan the necessity of their lives in our understanding of its nodal points, its reversals and mutations. In this area there is perhaps no greater joy than to be able to witness in an emerging life, once the Gods of Origins and Goals have been dethroned, the birth of necessity.

It is, however, the philosophical and theoretical conclusions that emerge from this revelatory observation of a creative mind at work that count – the absolutist theoreticism (what Thompson calls a 'theoreticist solipsism') which Althusser constructs upon the *results* of this process of birth. His claim is that once Marx, 'as a concrete individual and the actual history reflected in this individual development', has formulated what Althusser (1970: 63) designates as 'fully developed Marxism', then the theoretical principles take control as 'scientific principles', and these principles supersede the essentially unscientific (and unreliable) evidence of history. This was not Marx's conclusion of course, since he makes it quite clear that for him 'real history', as grounded on material practice, is 'an indispensable process', and that it

> does not end by being resolved into 'self-consciousness' as 'spirit of the spirit', but that in it at each stage there is found a material result: a sum of productive forces, an historically created relation of individuals to nature and to one another, which is handed down to each generation from its predecessor; a mass of productive forces, capital funds and conditions, which, on the one hand, is indeed modified by the new generation, but also on the other prescribes for it its conditions of life and gives it a

definite development, a special character. It shows that circumstances make men just
as much as men make circumstances (Marx and Engels 1970: 59).

But then Althusser is concerned with philosophy, not history; and philosophy
has to establish its scientific and irrefutable terms in order to proceed to its
conclusions. It therefore has to reject 'the necessary empirical dialogue' and 'the
practice of historical materialism' (Thompson 1978: 196), because these intro-
duce into the theoretical process the uncomfortable and disorientating phenomena of *change*, 'the thrusting-forth of the "real world", spontaneously and not
at all decorously, proposing hitherto unarticulated questions to philosophers'
(1978: 200).

And this is where Thompson's attack upon the theoretical absolutism of Louis
Althusser's system begins to strike back and to set up its own challenging defence
of historical materialism. For 'experience does not wait discreetly outside' the
offices of philosophers 'for the moment at which the discourse of the proof will
summon it into attendance. Experience walks in without knocking at the door,
and announces deaths, crises of subsistence, trench warfare, unemployment,
inflation, genocide', often in the name of philosophy! And 'people starve: their
survivors think in new ways about the market. People are imprisoned: in prison
they meditate in new ways about the law. In the face of such general experiences
old conceptual systems may crumble and new problematics insist upon their
presence'. And in Thompson's indictment of ahistorical theory, 'such imperative
presentation of knowledge effects is not allowed for in Althusser's epistem-
ology', which almost entirely 'overlooks . . . the *dialogue* between social being and
social consciousness' – that process by which consciousness, 'whether as
unselfconscious culture, or as myth, or as science, or law, or articulated ideology,
thrusts back into being in its turn: *as being is thought so thought also is lived*'
(Thompson 1978: 200–1).

While theory, in other words, assumes a static domination, purely *textual* and
linguistic in its consistency, practice is the active consequence of a dialogue
between being and consciousness, of the dialogic process that is continually at
work upon all *structures*. And the 'real' world – that pre-existent multiple context
which determines and modifies all structures, since these are products of that
context – cannot be ignored, since it is the ground for practice, the substance out
of which history is made and men and women make history. But for Althusser
(1979: 87), it seems, there is no dabbling with such raw material:

> Thought about the real, the conception of the real, and all the operations of thought
> by which the real is thought, or conceived, belong to the order of thought, the
> elements of thought, which must not be confused with the order of the real.

It is perhaps no accident that such an assertion, strikingly undialectic in its
separation of these 'orders', should have been received with such enthusiasm in
the 1970s. *Reading Capital* was first published in 1968, of course. But this
Althusser–Balibar delineation of 'an abstract theory of history', of historical
materialism as 'a true theoretical science, and therefore an abstract science'
(Althusser 1979: 202), had to wait till the effervescence of the 1960s had died
down to make its impact. The 1970s witnessed a seemingly unstoppable swing to
the Right, into a period of recession and disillusionment, a cold war aftermath of
the apparent (but foundationless) social advances of the 1960s. For by this time
promise and expectation had been blunted and sidetracked by what looked like

insuperable obstacles. History, that is, had intervened to deflate euphoria, and to show the Left that its triumphs were mere illusions; that it had failed to anticipate, and was powerless to combat, what was happening. The consequence was retreat and retrenchment, a return to the drawing-boards of the theorists. With the Left losing its nerve and its sense of direction, the intellectual debate turned inward, and the links between theory and practice weakened, thinned, became friable. If the intellectual activity of the 1960s was insurrectionary in its impact, the 1970s witnessed an alarming withdrawal, as Edward Said puts it, 'into the labyrinth of textuality', which increasingly became 'the exact antithesis and displacement of what might be called history'. For this was the climate of intellectual speculation in which the structuralist and post-structuralist emphasis upon 'a philosophy of pure textuality and critical noninterference . . . coincided with the ascendancy of Reaganism, . . . increased militarism and defence spending', a seizure of initiative by the Right which left the people exposed to ' "free" market forces, multinational corporations, the manipulations of consumer appetites' (Said 1984: 3–4). *Can* it be said to be an accident that the abstract intellectual discourse of an idealist metaphysics dominated by the new French *philosophes* made such spectacular gains at the very same time as the forces of reactionary power were everywhere in the West moving onto the offensive at the level of material practice? As Derrida (1976: 158–9) proclaims:

> There is nothing beyond the text . . . There never has been anything but supplements, substitutive significations, which could only come forth in a chain of differential references, the 'real' supervening and being added only while taking on meaning from a trace and from an invocation of the supplement, etc. And thus to infinity.

In other words, *there is no escape from language*: and language being ineradicably metaphysical, we cannot escape from *that* 'except by a flight into silence' (Callinicos 1982: 47).

'There is nothing beyond the text'; 'the order of the real' – the order of the Reagan deficit, of Thatcherite redistribution, of the nuclear arms race, of economic imperialism, of counter-insurrectionary tactics, and so on – 'cannot be *thought*'; 'thought about the real belongs to the order of thought'; thought is therefore always a process insulated from action; theory cannot ever interact (or make connection) with practice; the unity of theory and practice is a myth, except in theory; for the concepts of the thinker reality itself must always remain an abstract 'other world', essentially ungraspable; or, to put it at its crudest, the body in which the thinker thinks has no existence for the thinker, since it too belongs to another order. But if this were true ('there is nothing beyond the text'), then the textualist would not even have a body, and would not be able to produce the *words* of the text. For how could these words be produced if there were nothing to produce them from? Unless it is being suggested that the text produced itself, that it is not produced by the brain and hand, or that the brain and hand do not depend upon the body's nervous system, or that this in turn does not depend upon a pre-existent material process determined by the order of reality! Here, it seems, in Marx's comparison, 'philosophy and the study of the actual world have the same relation to one another as masturbation to sexual love' (1970: 103).

Whatever the answer to such questions, it is apparent that Althusser's argument for 'the theory of history as a science' (1979: 110) is pursued on the basis that theory precedes (or determines) practice – thus dismissing Marx's warning against the idea that you can ever get to an understanding of historical phenomena 'by using the *passe-partout* of some historical philosophical theory whose great virtue is to stand above history' (quoted in Carr 1978: 65); which is echoed by Carr's claim that 'the attempt to erect such a standard is unhistorical and contradicts the very essence of history', because it 'provides a dogmatic answer to questions which the historian is bound by his vocation incessantly to ask' (1978: 83). True, Althusser (1979: 109) accepts that the 'raw material' of theory is 'provided by real concrete history', and is 'realised in the "concrete analysis" of "concrete situations" '. But this theory is not to be 'worked out and developed' in the ways in which historians proceed, because (as he sees it) *all* historians confuse the issue by putting the concrete first. So that for them, it seems, 'history hardly exists other than . . . as the "application" of a theory', an application which somehow occurs 'behind the absent theory's back and [is] naturally mistaken for it'. From which Althusser (1979: 109–110) concludes that

> the theory of history, in the strong sense, does not exist, or hardly exists, so far as historians
> are concerned; that the concepts of existing history are therefore nearly always
> 'empirical' concepts, more or less in search of their theoretical basis – 'empirical', i.e.
> cross-bred with a powerful strain of an ideology concealed behind its 'obviousness'.

What he assumes here he assumes to be true even of the best historians. It seems that they, too, like the others, in spite of 'their concern for theory', confuse 'history as theory of history' with 'history as supposed "science of the concrete", history trapped in the empiricism of its object', history 'at the level of historical *methodology*' (1979: 110), where (as we have been told) theory hardly exists. In the hands of humanists and historicists, that is, 'Marxist philosophy loses the status of an autonomous discipline and is reduced . . . to a mere "historical methodology" ' (1979: 137). It loses 'its character as *scientific* knowledge' (1979: 132). There is a 'collapse of science into history' as 'the index of a theoretical collapse: a collapse that precipitates the theory of history into *real* history; reduces the (theoretical) object of the science of history to real history; and therefore confuses the object of knowledge with the real object' to become 'an empiricist ideology' (1979: 133–4). And this for him defines the drift even of thinkers like Gramsci, who makes the mistake of assuming – and here Althusser (1979: 137) lets Gramsci speak for himself – that 'the great conquest in the history of modern thought, represented by the philosophy of praxis, is precisely *the concrete historicisation* of philosophy and its identification with history'; which in Althusserian terms is itself a form of reductionism.

Thus – because for Althusser (1979: 119), 'theoretically speaking, Marxism is . . . an *anti-humanism and an anti-historicism*' – the praxis of Gramsci (as of Sartre, 'the philosopher of mediations') is seen to flatter 'scientific knowledge or philosophy, and at any rate Marxist theory, down to the unity of politico-economic practice, to the heart of "historical" practice, *to "real" history*' (1979: 136). This assumes the fact, as Thompson (1978: 214) concludes, that 'historical process is unknowable as a real object' – a consequence Thompson (1978: 194) rejects with contempt, because it suggests that the study of history *is* in fact 'not only scientifically but also politically valueless' (1978: 194). It is, that is to say, as ungraspable as the order of reality because it lies beyond the purely theoretical order of the text. And this applies as much to the study of Marx's *Capital* as to any other phenomenon of theoretical discourse. Apparently, 'history features in *Capital*' only 'as an object of theory, not as a real object; as an "abstract" (conceptual) object and not as a real-concrete object' (Althusser 1979: 117). In other words, its content, the substance on which Marx constructs his economic theory of the capitalist mode of production, does not *in itself* exist, except in terms of theory; for it is as a scientific theory, at once anti-humanist and anti-historicist, that it functions, against 'the humanist and historicist assault which, in some circles, has threatened Marxism continuously for the past forty years' (1979: 119). As Althusser (1971: 76) puts it in *Lenin and Philosophy*: 'Despite appearances, Marx does not analyse any "concrete society", not even England, which he mentions constantly in Volume One, but the Capitalist mode of production *and nothing else* . . .'. Or, to take the issue even further, as he stresses in *Reading Capital*:

> The transition from Volume One to Volume Three of *Capital* has nothing to do with the transition from the abstract-in-thought to the real-concrete, with the transition from the abstractions of thought necessary in order to know it to the empirical-concrete. We never leave abstraction on the way from Volume One to Volume Three, i.e., we never leave knowledge, the 'product of thinking and conceiving': *we never leave the concept*. We simply pass within the abstraction of knowledge from the concept of the structure and of its most general effects, to the concepts of the structure's particular effects – never for an instant do we set foot beyond the absolutely impassable frontier which separates the 'development' or specification of the concept from the development and particularity of things – and for a very good reason: *this frontier is impassable in principle because it cannot be a frontier, because there is no common homogeneous space (spirit or real) between the abstract of the concept of a thing and the empirical-concrete of this thing which could justify the use of the concept of a frontier* (Althusser 1979: 190).

This argument, except at the level of the autonomous abstract, not only makes no sense (in that it refutes the evidence of the senses); it is, in the insulated presentation of its terms, undialectical. The concept of an impassable frontier which is not impassable because there is no frontier to pass, or the concept of structure which admits of no limitations that could justify the concept of a frontier between the general and the particular, the abstract and the concrete, the theoretical and the practical, leaves us with an impassable gulf between theory and practice which depressingly confirms the incompatibility of 'the order of thought' and 'the order of the real'. In short, there is *no possible dialogue* between the two. The impassable frontier is no frontier because there is no connection, no contact, no communication, and hence no dialectic interaction, possible between them. They are different languages, different worlds. When *Capital* analyses capitalist modes of production, it does not analyse anything that is going on (or that has manifested itself) in the *real* world of concrete occurrences and events (the world of *real* history); it analyses something that is going on purely in the thinker's head and that acquires its consistency exclusively in terms of the conceptual structures of thought, irrespective of what is going on beyond its hypothetical frontiers, which do not exist because 'what is going on beyond them' does not exist. Indeed there *are* no frontiers 'within the abstractions of knowledge' because the order of thought has closed itself off from the order of reality – has *imposed* a closure, from inside which it can play upon its own conceptual abstractions without interference from the evidence of history. As Voloshinov (1986: 61) points out, commenting on the Saussurean view of history, such 'abstract objectivism' sharply opposes language as system (closed) and language as history (open), and in these terms (which are Althusser's) history is regarded 'as an irrational force which distorts the logical purity of the language system'. There is, one might echo, 'no common homogeneous space' between the system and the process – unless, that is, it can be conceded that 'history is a process without a subject' – or (to translate) a theory without a content; an abstract system sealed against the locations and discomforts of reality, which threaten *dis*location; a language proof against the modifications and bewildering transmutations of concrete acts of speech!

For Thompson, this closed system, what he calls a 'paradigm of structural stasis' (1978: 265), is antagonistic to the active changing conditions on which all knowledge (insisting on a dialogue between concept and evidence, the knowability of history) is based. It is a form of mystification – 'one more astonishing aberrant spectacle . . . [to be] added to the phantasmagoria of our time' (1978: 265) – and as such a symptom of the crisis we are involved in. As he sees it, this sort of mystification only seems to underline how *bad* a time it is 'for a rational mind in the Marxist tradition' to live through.

> For the real world also gesticulates at reason with its own inversions. Obscure contradictions manifest themselves, jest, and then vanish; the known and the unknown change places; even as we examine them, categories dissolve and change into their opposites. In the West a bourgeois soul yearns for a 'Marxism' to heal its own alienation; in the Communist world a proclaimed 'socialist basis' gives rise to a superstructure of orthodox Christian faith, corrupt materialism, Slav nationalism and Solzhenitsyn. In that world 'Marxism' performs the function of an 'Ideological State Apparatus,' and Marxists are alienated, not in their self-identity, but in their contempt for the people. An old and arduous rational tradition breaks down into two parts: an arid academic scholasticism and a brutal pragmatism of power . . .
> (Thompson 1978: 216–17).

And as Thompson (1978: 216–17) grimly observes: 'This is a time for reason to grit its teeth. As the world changes, we must learn to change our language and our terms. But we should never change these *without reason*.'

That was in 1978; and history has moved on since then, in directions which give reason even greater cause to grit its teeth. For everywhere in the West since then the ideologists of monopoly and finance capitalism have come out from behind the decorous façades of the institutionalized structures of the 'free' democracies to exploit the popular imagination at every level. Both the Reagan administration and the Thatcher regime were to set about putting into practice their own variants of 'the brutal pragmatism of power', while theorists of the Left continued to dispute arcane points of doctrine from a distance. These pragmatists of the 'New Right' have continued to thrust ahead, manipulating divisions at home and abroad and strengthening the powers of the hidden minorities that control the sources of wealth to force everyone and everything to submit to the operational demands of international capitalism. It is *their* claim, indeed, that even the so-called Gorbachev initiatives – the achievement of the 1987 INF Treaty and the radical changes now taking place in the Soviet bloc – are actually the consequence of NATO's 'negotiation from strength' (the cold war stance of the mid-1980s) and of irresistible pressure from the forces of the 'free' market economy.

Conditions conducive to the emergence of such overt regressiveness are already implicit in Thompson's critique of the social malaise of the 1970s. He does not delude himself into believing that the forces ranged against reason are to be dislodged without a struggle, either in the West or in the East. Indeed, it is his view that there can be no chance of fighting back except by confronting the crucial issues involved, both in theory and in practice – and certainly not so long as intellectuals in the West allow themselves to be seduced by the metaphysics of textuality, the arid logic of philosophical abstraction, the arrogance of a theoreticism which denies the existence of the order of reality or which relegates it to the sidelines of a debate which is itself insulated from any sort of active participation in the practice of history. So that 'what has, it seems, to be recited afresh is the arduous nature of the engagement between thought and its objective materials; the dialogue (whether as *praxis* or in more self-conscious intellectual disciplines) out of which all knowledge is won' (Thompson 1978: 229). For this engagement is an engagement between the complex changing conditions of historical process as 'knowable' and 'intelligible' in the order of reality, and the findings to be drawn from what these conditions can be made to signify as evidence for the interrogation of 'minds trained in a discipline of attentive disbelief' (1978: 221) – minds, one must add, like that of Marx, who, with his 'prodigious feeling for the concrete' (Althusser 1970: 71), considered it a primary task to refute the alienating disjunctions between history as theory and history as practice.

What Thompson insists on pulling the mind back to from the abyss of Althusserian theory is the necessity of its engagement with the process of history as a real object of investigation. For he knows how central a part the process of history has to play in determining, modifying and directing the pattern of reality. In 1979, asked to put into practice the principles on which his concept of Marxism was based at a time when the world was being plunged into a new stage of the cold war, he found himself called upon to speak for the silenced and acquiescent millions of Europe as part of the determined opposition set up by the peace movements of the West against the threat of an accelerating arms race between the superpowers. This was no diversion from more essential tasks, though Thompson has declared that he was reluctantly drawn into it, but a moment of historical necessity, the awakening of a movement of mass protest and of social consciousness, of history in action. For the campaign Thompson committed himself to was more than simply a campaign against nuclear weapons. It was at the same time a campaign against the power of what had come to be known as the 'military-industrial complex' which, generated by the invisible economic forces of international competition, was seen to constitute a devastating threat to the socially productive resources of the world and a source of intimidation, oppression and impoverishment, particularly to the smaller nations; and which therefore had to be confronted. Thompson and others saw the potentiality of this massed peace movement, mounted against the belligerent postures of the NATO powers from 1979 onwards, as a major force for social progress, mobilizing millions to act and to find the courage to act in resistance to the indoctrinatory fears instilled in them by the enemies of progress to keep them quiet. And so it could be said that Thompson's persistent call for the awakening of the people of Europe to the terminal threat that faces the world has helped to bring into being an active counterforce of social, communal and political resistance to the logic and validity of the powers that dominate world politics, since it demystifies the ideologies that justify these powers, exposes the invisible economic interests that lie behind them, and asserts the logic of an alternative based upon the social and economic rights of the oppressed, the recovery of their history, their past, and thus of the energies that can transform the world.

Thus for Thompson the experience of history is no mere abstract external 'order of reality' (or what Althusser (1979: 310) calls an 'absent cause') accessible only in the form of a text, but a process of immediate and contingent pressure which exposes theory to the severest tests of practice. This bears out his contention that

> in investigating history we are not flicking through a series of 'stills', each of which shows as a moment of social time transfixed into a single eternal pose; for each one of these 'stills' is not only a moment of being but also a moment of becoming; and even within each seemingly-static section there will be found contradictions and liaisons, dominant and subordinate elements, declining or ascending energies. Any historical moment is both a result of prior process and an index towards the direction of its future flow (Thompson 1978: 239).

Althusser will have none of this. For him it is a matter of absolute necessity to liberate

> the theory of history from any compromise with 'empirical' temporality, with the ideological concept of time which underlies and overlies it, or with the ideological idea that the theory of history, *as theory*, could be subject to the 'concrete' determinations of 'historical time' on the pretext that this 'historical time' might constitute its object (Althusser 1979: 105–6).

So what, in these terms, *is* the theory of history if it insists upon such detachment from the *practice* of history – that is, from the dialectic process which involves the interaction of theory and practice – but an empty supposition of structure: a structure 'unhinged from its content', autonomous, insulated against interference from historical time, and static?

Thompson (1978: 286) comes to the bluntest conclusions about Althusser's arguments. They represent, as philosophy,

> an inexorable structuralism, even though it is, in this or that respect, a different one from those derived from Saussure, Lévi-Strauss or Lacan. It shares fully in the ideological pre-disposition of that moment ('conjuncture') of the Cold War stasis, which Sartre has identified: a 'dominant tendency' towards 'the denial of history'. In this moment, structuralism 'gives the people what they needed ... An eclectic synthesis in which Robbe-Grillet, structuralism, linguistics, Lacan, and *Tel Quel* are systematically utilized to demonstrate the impossibility of historical reflection. Behind history, of course, it is Marxism which is attacked.

For it even seems to Althusser that Marx himself was actually putting forward a structuralism of similar consistency without being fully aware that he was doing so, and thus without coming to the logical conclusions which would have led him to a rejection of 'historicism'. Apparently 'Marx's methodological reflections in *Capital* did not give us a developed concept, nor even an *explicit* concept, of the *object of Marxist philosophy*' (Althusser 1979: 74). Or, 'if he did formulate the concept of his object without ambiguity, Marx did not always define with the same precision the concept of its *distinction*' from 'the object of classical economics' (1979: 75). That is, 'he did not think the *concept* of this distinction with all the sharpness that could be desired; he did not think theoretically, or in an adequate and advanced form, either the concept or the theoretical implications of the theoretically revolutionary step he had taken' (1979: 120–1).

But this is to assume that the sharpness of Marx's methodology was actually directed towards thinking the theoretical implications of revolution in purely theoretical terms, and that it was only because he did not think theoretically *enough* that this theory of a theory did not achieve a sufficiently advanced form. It is to ignore all the other aspects of Marx's thinking, his active organizational response to the challenge of the developing, changing process of the real history of his time, and the ways in which this response complemented and enacted the findings of *Capital*. It is to leave out of account the thrust of his thinking, as defined, for instance, in the *Address and Provisional Rules* for the First International and other writings produced by both Engels and himself in these crucial years, which indicate an imperative concern to create a theoretical framework for revolutionary *practice* – a dynamic, that is, by which *political* thinking could be transformed into *political* practice, with 'the economic emancipation of the working classes' as 'the great end to which every political movement ought to be subordinate as a means' (Marx 1974: 82). And to this end it could be said that even the monumental theoretical analysis of *Capital* was itself a means by which to articulate and to enact the historical tasks of the proletarian movement towards 'the abolition of classes' (1974: 281). In other words, history for Marx was always very much a process with a subject, since he always had in his mind's eye the developing consciousness of the European proletariat, together with the classes and forces it was in contention with in the 1860s and 1870s. As he puts it in *The Civil War in France*, in direct response to the defeat of the Commune, the working classes

> know that in order to work out their own emancipation, and along with it that higher form to which present society is irresistibly tending by its own economic agencies, they will have to pass through long struggles, through a series of historic processes, transforming circumstances and men (Marx and Engels 1968: 291);

and that this emancipation cannot be achieved without the experience of such struggles – participation in the active process of which (under the right conditions) will enable people to grasp the nature of the productive forces that determine their place in the system and thus transform that system. This is an active process, involving the interrelation of theory and practice, in terms of which men and women *themselves* become the makers of history.

Althusser appears to acknowledge this in his analysis in *For Marx* of the historical process which made revolution in Russia possible, confirming the unpredictable ways in which – suddenly, by chance combination – people and circumstances are drawn together and impelled by a momentum so intense and so potentially explosive as to be capable of producing the objective conditions for a revolution. Here the phenomenon of history seems to be accepted as an active process, driven by the movement in time of many different forces, with men and women as the concrete embodiment and the motivating energy of these forces, the experiencing subjects, the content of the process. Indeed, 'the whole Marxist revolutionary experience shows,' as he says,

> that if the general contradiction (it has already been specified: the contradiction between the forces of production and the relations of production, essentially embodied in the contradiction between two antagonistic classes) is sufficient to define the situation when revolution is 'the task of the day', it cannot of its own simple, direct power induce a 'revolutionary situation', nor *a fortiori* a situation of revolutionary rupture and the triumph of the revolution. . . . There must be an accumulation of 'circumstances' and 'currents' so that whatever their origin and sense (and many of them will *necessarily* be . . . foreign to the revolution in origin and sense, or even its 'direct opponents'), they '*fuse*' into a *ruptural unity*.

But *how* do they fuse? Not, one notes, as the product of a process without a subject, but as a result of

> the immense majority of the popular masses *grouped* in an assault on a regime which its ruling classes are *unable to defend*. [And] such a situation presupposes not only the 'fusion' of the two basic conditions into a 'single national crisis', but each condition considered (abstractly) by itself presupposes the 'fusion' of an 'accumulation' of contradictions. How else could the class-divided popular masses (proletarians, peasants, petty bourgeois) throw themselves (be thrown?) *together*, consciously or unconsciously, into a general assault on the existing regime? And how else could the ruling classes (aristocrats, big bourgeois, industrial bourgeois, financial bourgeois, etc.), who have learnt by long experience and sure instinct to seal between themselves, despite their class differences, a holy alliance against the exploited, find themselves reduced to impotence, divided at the decisive moment, with neither new political solutions nor new political leaders, deprived of foreign class support, disarmed in the very citadel of the State machine, and suddenly overwhelmed by the people they had so long kept in leash and respectful by exploitation, violence and deceit?' (Althusser 1970: 99–100).

How else, indeed, except by the interaction of men and women (the subjects of history) with the particular conditions conducive to such 'fusion'? And yet elsewhere Althusser (1976: 51) concludes that 'history is . . . a process *without a subject*'! So much, then, for classes and for the struggles of classes – for people as the agents of history, caught up in the processes of change (the accumulation of contradictions) urged upon them by the material conditions that make it possible for them (at the proper stage of development) to *become* the agents of history. So much, too, in Althusser's description of Gramsci's historicism, for Marx's 'direct appeal to "practice", to political action, to "changing the world", without which Marxism would be no more than the prey of bookworms and passive political functionaries' (1979: 129). Because for Althusser (1979: 128),

> the historicism of Marxism is no more than the consciousness of a task and a necessity: Marxism cannot claim to be the theory of history unless, *even in its theory*, it can think the conditions of this penetration into history, into all strata of society, even into men's everyday lives.

In other words, if it is to become *the* theory of history, Marxism must be accepted as scientific, as the only indubitable means of penetrating into and making sense of the *substance* of history, which is otherwise (in its concreteness and temporality) essentially unknowable. It would seem, in fact, that history – 'as an immense natural-human system in movement' (Althusser 1976: 51) – does not depend upon people at all, but can only be made sense of as theory, as 'the

Marxist theory of theory and practice and their relationship' (Althusser 1979: 129); an abstract structural 'process without a subject' which transforms practice itself into the theory of practice, and eliminates people altogether.

So what are we left with? A scientific theory of history which attempts to cross the boundaries between theory and practice? Or a set of concepts claiming scientific justification which separates theory *from* practice? According to Etienne Balibar, in his response to the Althusserian system, the essential principle is that *Capital* 'founds a new discipline: i.e. *opens up a new field* for scientific investigation'. And 'as opposed to the closure which constitutes the structure of an ideological domain, this *openness* is typical of a scientific field' (Althusser 1979: 308). But the problem is that the principle itself is grounded upon an ideological assumption about the nature of scientific investigation, which imposes its own closed forms upon the argument. Thus, for Thompson (1978: 359),

> Althusser's categories have already been de-socialised and de-historicised before we can start. They commence their life as *categories of stasis* . . . Moreover, we are offered an arbitrary selection of categories – as 'economics', 'politics', 'ideology' – and neither the principle of selection nor the categories themselves are examined.

Not only do we hear

> nothing about the State and almost nothing about classes. Other categories are absent throughout: we hear nothing about *power* – perhaps this is 'politics', although in 'real history' it may often also be 'economics' and 'law' and 'religion'. We hear nothing about *consciousness* (whether as *mentalité* or as culture or *habitus* or as class consciousness) and nothing about values or value-systems (unless in their dismissal along with 'moralism' and 'ideology') (1978: 287).

So that ultimately, in Thompson's view, Althusser's theoretical practice reduces 'the disciplines of knowledge to one kind of "basic" theory only', according to the conditions of which 'theory is forever collapsing back into ulterior theory'.

No doubt Althusser would answer this by insisting that the order of reality and the order of thought must be kept separate; that scientific knowledge can only be discovered in the theoretical field of thought; that this field (as defined by the criteria germane to it) is an open rather than a closed field; and that in its own proper terms, theory itself is a form of practice, a process of production. But the problem of the interaction between theory (operating within the order of thought) and practice (belonging to the order of reality) will not go away. Even though Althusser does his best to *explain* it away – by arguing, for instance, that Marx's 'most personally significant practical experiences . . . *intervened* in his theoretical practice, and in the upheaval which led him from ideological theoretical practice to scientific theoretical practice' – he has to concede that these experiences 'contributed . . . to the overthrow of the still ideological theoretical base on which he had lived (i.e. thought) till then' (Althusser 1979: 60).

So what are we to conclude from this – from the anti-humanist and anti-historicist direction of Althusser's thinking? That his structuralist concept of the process of knowledge operates as an open field for scientific inquiry? There is little doubt, as far as Thompson is concerned, that it does not; that it is a closed world of system and of structure; and that a gulf exists between this form of 'Marxism as closure' and the tradition Thompson builds upon, 'derivative from Marx, of open investigation and critique. The first is a tradition of theology. The second is a tradition of active reason. Both can derive some licence from Marx, although the second has immeasurably the better credentials as to its lineage' (Thompson 1978: 380). And the decisive point for Thompson (1978: 384) is that 'Marx is on our side; we are not on the side of Marx'.

This does not, of course, resolve the problems at issue here. And Althusser's question – 'by what mechanism does the production of the object of knowledge produce the cognitive appropriation of the *real object* which exists outside thought in the real world?' (1979: 61) – remains a tantalizing difficulty, which threatens to disrupt the relation between subject and object and the Marxian dialectic itself, even as it does the validity of Thompson's criteria for historical process. For it has to be admitted that, however we respond, we cannot escape from the abstract (and the abstractionist) nature of thinking. Language itself is a process of abstraction and of reduction. Words abstract from concrete situations, are selective summaries which gesture to an uncontainable reality.

And yet the *sense* of that reality, of all that goes to make up the concrete life of a historical period, say, can be registered sensuously, through the sensate properties of words, as the 'this-sidedness' of thinking, from the point of view of the senses becoming *'theoreticians* in their immediate praxis' (Marx 1975: 352). And the sense of history-in-the-making as an actual process going on around us and capable of being apprehended, recognized, made sense of in its essence and in the language that we employ (as rooted in its dialogic social usage) remains a *presence* – something other than the theory it may become. It animates the theory, influences and changes it, injects it with vitality, prevents it from seizing up, becoming rigid, degenerating into some form or other of *stasis*. And whenever theory may seem to have achieved a definitive structure – fixed at the centre of things, as the pre-Copernican believer held the earth to be – it must (if it is to have any active part to play in the world of human history) remain open to the forces of change, the energies of human action and reaction, the movement and the thrust of the historical process. The challenge of the present, in the emergence of unpredictable conjunctions of circumstance, confronts all pre-ordained systems with new conditions that demand appraisal. And in the struggle for any future which will resolve 'the antithesis between mental and physical labour' (Marx and Engels 1968: 320) and bring about a socialist transformation of society, this challenge is crucial because such a future will itself be unprecedented.

Thus, on these grounds, yes, Marx is with us, 'on our side', even if (under the conditions facing us in the late twentieth century) we have to modify his findings and move beyond him to make the kind of future that he spent his life working to bring into being.

Bibliography

Abbott White, George (1972). 'Ideology and Literature' in George Abbott White and Charles Newman (eds), *Literature and Revolution*. New York: Holt, Rinehart and Winston.

Althusser, Louis (1970). *For Marx*. Vintage Books.

Althusser, Louis (1971). *Lenin and Philosophy*. New Left Books.

Althusser, Louis (1976). *Essays*. New Left Books.

Althusser, Louis (1979). *Reading Capital*. Verso.

Anderson, Perry (1976). *Considerations of Western Marxism*. Verso.

Anderson, Perry (1983). *In the Steps of Historical Materialism*. Verso.

Arnold, Matthew (1932). *Culture and Anarchy*. Cambridge University Press.

Arnold, Matthew (1949). *The Essential Matthew Arnold*, ed. Lionel Trilling. Chatto and Windus.

Auden, W. H. (1941). *New Year Letter*. Faber and Faber.

Auden, W. H. (1950). *Collected Shorter Poems*. Faber and Faber.

Auerbach, Erich (1953). *Mimesis*. Princeton, NJ: Princeton University Press.

Bacon, Sir Francis (1914). 'Of Seditions and Troubles' in *Essays Civil and Moral*. Ward Lock.

Barthes, Roland (1972). *Mythologies*. Cape.

Barthes, Roland (1975). *S/Z*. Cape.

Barthes, Roland (1977). *Image-Music-Text*. Fontana/Collins.

Barthes, Roland (1982). *A Barthes Reader*, ed. Susan Sontag. Cape.

Baudrillard, Jean (1988). *Selected Writings*. Polity Press.

Berger, John (1973). *G*. Penguin.

Blake, William (1974). *Complete Writings*. Oxford University Press.

Bond, Edward (1978). *Plays Two*. Eyre Methuen.

Brecht, Bertolt (1975). 'The Popular and the Realistic' in David Craig (ed.), *Marxists on Literature*. Penguin.

Brecht, Bertolt (1976a). *Poems Part Two 1929–1938*. Eyre Methuen.

Brecht, Bertolt (1976b). *Poems Part Three 1938–1956*. Eyre Methuen.

Briggs, Asa (1965). *Victorian People*. Penguin.

Bronowski, J. (1972). *William Blake and the Age of Revolution*. Routledge and Kegan Paul.

Bullock, Alan (1952). *Hitler: A Study in Tyranny*. Odhams.

Burke, Edmund (1968). *Reflections on the Revolution in France*. Penguin.

Burke, Kenneth (1963). 'Commentary' in *Timon of Athens*, ed. Francis Fergusson. New York: Dell.

Callinicos, Alex (1982). *Is There a Future for Marxism?* Macmillan.

Carr, E. H. (1978). *What is History?* Penguin.

Chace, William (1972). *The Political Identities of Ezra Pound and T. S. Eliot*. Stanford, CA: Stanford University Press.

Churchill, Sir Winston (1964). *The Gathering Storm*, Volume One of *The Second World War*. Cassell.

Clare, John (1965). *Selected Poems and Prose*. ed. Robinson and Summerfield. Oxford University Press.

Clare, John (1966). *Selected Poems*, ed. J. W. Tibble and Anne Tibble. Dent Everyman.

Clark, Kenneth (1967). *Ruskin Today*. Penguin.

Cobbett, William (1967). *Rural Rides*. Penguin.

Colletti, Lucio (1975). 'Introduction' in Karl Marx, *Early Writings*. Penguin.

Collingwood, R. G. (1939). *An Autobiography*. Oxford University Press.

Cruttwell, Patrick (1970). *The Shakespearian Moment*. Chatto and Windus.

Derrida, Jacques (1976). *Of Grammatology*. Baltimore, MD: Johns Hopkins University Press.

Derrida, Jacques (1978). *Writing and Difference*. Routledge and Kegan Paul.

Derrida, Jacques (1981). *Positions*. Chicago University Press.

Dollimore, Jonathan (1984). *Radical Tragedy*. Harvester.

Dollimore, Jonathan (ed.) (1985). *Political Shakespeare*. Manchester University Press.

Eagleton, Terry (1976). *Criticism and Ideology*. Verso.

Eagleton, Terry (1983). *Literary Theory*. Blackwell.

Eliot, T. S. (1934). *After Strange Gods: A Primer of Modern Heresy*. Faber and Faber.

Eliot, T. S. (1951). *Selected Essays*. Faber and Faber.

Eliot, T. S. (1953). *Selected Prose*. Penguin.

Eliot, T. S. (1965). 'Ulysses, Order and Myth' (1923), reprinted as 'Myth and Literary Criticism' in Richard Ellmann and Charles Feidelson (eds), *The Modern Tradition: Background of Modern Literature*. New York: Oxford University Press.

Eliot, T. S. (1969). *The Complete Poems and Plays*. Faber and Faber.

Ewen, Frederic (1970). *Bertolt Brecht*. Calder and Boyars.

Fischer, Ernst (1963). *The Necessity of Art*. Penguin.

Foucault, Michel (1970). *The Order of Things*. Tavistock Publications.

Goode, John (1971). 'William Morris and the Dream of Revolution' in John Lucas, *Literature and Politics in the 19th Century*. Methuen.

Grassic Gibbon, Lewis (1973). *A Scots Quair*. Pan.

Hampton, Christopher (1980). *A Cornered Freedom*. Peterloo Poets.

Hampton, Christopher (1984). *A Radical Reader*. Penguin.

Harvey, A. D. (1980). *English Poetry in a Changing Society 1780–1825*. Alison and Busby.

Hauser, Arnold (1962). *The Social History of Art, Volume Two*. Routledge and Kegan Paul.

Hawkes, Terence (1986). *That Shakespeherian Rag*. Methuen.

Hazlitt, William (1969). *The Spirit of the Age*. Collins.

Heinemann, Margot (1985). 'How Brecht Read Shakespeare' in Jonathan Dollimore and Alan Sinfield (eds), *Political Shakespeare*. Manchester University Press.

Henderson, Philip (1967). *William Morris*. Penguin.

Herbert, Zbigniew (1979). *Poems for Shakespeare 7*. Globe.

Hill, Christopher (1979). *Milton and the English Revolution*. Faber and Faber.

Hobson, J. A. (1889). *John Ruskin, Social Reformer*. London.

Hynes, Samuel (1976). *The Auden Generation*. Faber and Faber.

Jameson, Fredric (1974). *Marxism and Form*. Princeton, NJ: Princeton University Press.

Jameson, Fredric (1981a). *The Political Unconscious*. Methuen.

Jameson, Fredric (1981b). 'Religion and Ideology' in Francis Barker *et al.* (eds) *Literature and Power in the 17th Century*. University of Essex.

Jens, Walter (1973). 'The Classical Tradition in Germany – Grandeur and Decay' in E. J. Feuchtwanger, *Upheaval and Continuity*. Oswald Wolff.

Jung, C. G. (1983). *Selected Writings*. Fontana/Collins.

Keats, John (1952). *The Letters of John Keats*. Oxford University Press.

Kiernan, Victor (1975). 'Wordsworth and the People' in *Marxists on Literature: An Anthology*. Penguin.

Knight, G. Wilson (1982). Contribution to C. Woolf and J. M. Wilson (eds), *Authors Take Sides on the Falklands*. Cecil Woolf.

Kolakowski, Leszek (1971). *Marxism and Beyond*. Paladin Books.

Labriola, Antonio (1966). *Essays on the Materialist Conception of History*. New York: Monthly Review Press.

Lacan, Jacques (1977). *Ecrits*. Tavistock Publications.

Lawrence, D. H. (1950). *Aaron's Rod*. Penguin.

Lawson, Nigel (1983). 'Chancellor with Shakespeare on his side', *Guardian* Interview, 5 September.

Leavis, F. R. (1978). *The Living Principle*. Chatto and Windus.

Leavis, F. R. (1984). *The Common Pursuit*. Chatto and Windus.

Lucas, John (1971). *Literature and Politics in the 19th Century*. Methuen.

Lukács, Georg (1963). *The Meaning of Contemporary Realism*. Merlin.

Lukács, Georg (1969). *The Historical Novel*. Penguin.

Lukács, Georg (1971). *History and Class Consciousness*. Merlin.

Macaulay, Lord (1862). *Essays*. Longmans Green.

MacDiarmid, Hugh (1970). *Selected Poems*. Penguin.

MacNeice, Louis (1966). *Collected Poems*. Faber and Faber.

Mann, Thomas (1942). *Order of the Day*. New York: Knopf.

Mann, Thomas (1975). *The Letters of Thomas Mann*. Penguin.

Marcuse, Herbert (1972a). *One-Dimensional Man*. Abacus.

Marcuse, Herbert (1972b). *Negations*. Penguin.

Marx, Karl (1972). *Capital, Volume One*. Dent Everyman.

Marx, Karl (1973a). *The Revolutions of 1848*, Political Writings, Volume One. Penguin.

Marx, Karl (1973b). *Surveys from Exile*. Political Writings, Volume Two. Penguin.

Marx, Karl (1973c). *Grundrisse*. Penguin.

Marx, Karl (1974). *The First International and After*, Political Writings, Volume Three. Penguin.

Marx, Karl (1975). *Early Writings*. Penguin.

Marx, Karl (1977). *Capital, Volume Three*. New York: International Publishers.

Marx, Karl and Engels, Friedrich (1968). *Marx/Engels: Selected Works in One Volume*. Lawrence and Wishart.

Marx, Karl and Engels, Friedrich (1970). *The German Ideology*, ed. C. J. Arthur, Students' edn. Lawrence and Wishart.

McGann, Jerome (1988). *The Clark Lectures*. Cambridge University.

Milton, John (1946). *The English Poems of John Milton*. Oxford University Press.

Milton, John (1958). *Prose Writings*. Dent Everyman.

Mitchell, David (1970). *Red Mirage*. Cape.

Moretti, Franco (1983). *Signs Taken For Wonders*. Verso.

Morris, William (1968). *Three Works by William Morris*. Lawrence and Wishart.

Morris, William (1973). *Political Writings*, ed. A. L. Morton. Lawrence and Wishart.

Namier, Sir Lewis (1962). *Vanished Supremacies*. Penguin.

O'Brien, Conor Cruise (1972). 'Passion and Cunning: the Politics of W. B. Yeats' in *Literature and Revolution*, New York: Holt, Rinehart and Winston.

Orwell, George (1961). *Collected Essays*. Mercury.

Orwell, George (1962). *The Road to Wigan Pier*. Penguin.

Owen, Wilfred (1931). *Poems*, ed. Edmund Blunden. Chatto and Windus.

Paine, Thomas (1969). *The Rights of Man*. Penguin.

Pound, Ezra (1954). *Literary Essays*. Faber and Faber.

Read, Herbert (1938a). *Poetry and Anarchism*. Faber and Faber.

Read, Herbert (1938b). *Wordsworth*. Faber and Faber.

Rickword, Edgell (1978). *Literature in Society*. Carcanet Press.

Rotman, Brian (1988). 'Who Is Jean Baudrillard?', *The Guardian*, 21 October, p. 27.

Said, Edward (1984). *The World, The Text, and the Critic*. Faber and Faber.

Sakharov, Andrei (1974). *Sakharov Speaks*. Collins/Harvill.
Sartre, Jean-Paul (1963). *The Reprieve*. Penguin.
Serge, Victor (1963). *Memoirs of a Revolutionary*. Oxford University Press.
Seton-Watson, R. W. (1939). *Munich and the Dictators*. Macmillan.
Shelley, P. B. (1934). *Poetical Works*. Oxford University Press.
Shelley, P. B. (1951). *Selected Poetry, Prose and Letters*, ed. A. S. B. Glover. London.
Sinfield, Alan (ed.) (1985). *Political Shakespeare*. Manchester University Press.
Skelton, Robin (ed.) (1964). *Poetry of the Thirties*. Penguin.
Sontag, Susan (1982). Introduction, *A Barthes Reader*. Cape.
Stow, John (1605). *The Annales of England*. London.
Stow, John (1631). *The Annales of England*, continued and augmented by E. Howes.
    London.
Stubbes, Philip (1583). *The Anatomy of Abuses*. British Library.
Tawney, R. H. (1964). *Equality*. Unwin.
Thompson, E. P. (1968). *The Making of the English Working Class*. Penguin.
Thompson, E. P. (1977). *William Morris: Romantic to Revolutionary*. Merlin.
Thompson, E. P. (1978). *The Poverty of Theory*. Merlin.
Timpanaro, Sebastiano (1980). *On Materialism*. Verso.
Voloshinov, V. N. (1986). *Marxism and the Philosophy of Language*. Harvard University
    Press.
West, Alick (1975). *Crisis and Criticism*. Lawrence and Wishart.
Willey, Basil (1962). *The Eighteenth Century Background*. Penguin.
Williams, Raymond (1954). *Preface to Film*. Film Drama.
Williams, Raymond (1963). *Culture and Society (1958)*. Penguin.
Williams, Raymond (1965). *The Long Revolution (1961)*. Penguin.
Williams, Raymond (1975). *The Country and the City (1973)*. Paladin.
Williams, Raymond (1976). *Keywords*. Fontana/Collins.
Williams, Raymond (1977). *Marxism and Literature*. Oxford University Press.
Williams, Raymond (1979). *Politics and Letters*. Verso.
Williams, Raymond (1980). *Problems of Materialism and Culture*. Verso.
Williams, Raymond (1983). *Writing in Society*. Verso.
Williams, Raymond (1985). *Towards 2000 (1983)*. Penguin.
Wilson, Edmund (1972). *To the Finland Station*. Fontana/Collins.
Woolf, Virginia (1986). *Three Guineas*. Hogarth.
Wordsworth, William (1969). *Lyrical Ballads*. Oxford University Press.
Wordsworth, William (1971). *The Prelude – A Parallel Text*. Penguin.
Yeats, W. B. (1950). *Collected Poems*. Macmillan.
Yeats, W. B. (1955). *Autobiographies*. Macmillan.
Zweig, Stefan (1943). *The World of Yesterday*. Cassell.

Index